IMMIGRATION AND THE AMERICAN FUTURE

IMMIGRATION AND THE AMERICAN FUTURE

Chronicles Press
Rockford, Illinois
2007

This book would not have been possible without the vision and leadership of David Hartman, the chairman of the board of directors of The Rockford Institute, and the generous financial assistance of the Hartman Foundation.

The cover photo is by Gregory McNamee. The cover design is by Melanie Anderson.

Library of Congress Cataloging-in-Publication Data

ISBN 978-0-9720616-6-7

CONTENTS

IMMIGRATION AND THE AMERICAN FUTURE

FOREWORD

by Chilton Williamson, Jr.

A nation-state is determined, defined, and described by its territorial borders, by the composition and size of its population, by its history and form of government, by its predominating culture and the degree of civilization attained by that culture, and by the level of economic well-being and of physical security enjoyed by its citizens.

Immigration to (as well as, of course, emigration from) a nation-state bears on each of these aspects of nationality directly—and massively, in those instances where immigration attains massive proportions. The United States of America today represents, as it has for the past forty years, the paramount example in modern times of a great nation in process of transformation by mass immigration unparalleled, perhaps, in all of human history. Consequently, the claim that mass immigration is the single greatest determining factor for the future of the United States cannot be called an exaggerated one.

The question is, Can immigration be expected to change America for better, or for worse? If we accept at face value President George W. Bush's claim that terrorism represents the gravest threat to America, as indeed it may, then we must ask ourselves whether terrorism, by itself, is capable either of obliterating the United States as—say—Rome eradicated Carthage from the map of North Africa, or of destroying it by effectively replacing the existing nation on what historically has been American soil with another and different nation. If the answer is "No," then we must agree that the terrorist threat is in fact a subset of the immigration one—and that mass immigration is a greater threat to the survival of our country than any terrorist campaign possibly could be. Which, it seems to me, is saying a very great deal about the dangers posed to the United States by mass immigration.

The contributors to the present volume consider the total effect of mass immigration to the United States in its various aspects, beginning with the highly topical one of national security and proceeding to evaluations of immigration's expectable and even probable impact on America's economic, political, social, and cultural institutions, as well as upon our natural resources and the environment of the central North American Continent as a whole. The book concludes with a comparative treatment of Western Europe's attempts (or lack thereof) to come to grips with the threat of mass immigration, mostly from the Near East, Asia, and Africa, and also a consideration of mass immigration in its moral, theological, and humanitarian dimensions, as formulated dramatically more than 30 years ago by the French writer Jean Raspail, when he stated in his prophetic novel *The Camp of the Saints* that, for the West to refuse the Third World hordes yearning to set sail for Europe would be to destroy them, but that to accept them would be to destroy us.

In Chapter 1, "Homeland Security: Our Nonexistent Borders," Wayne Allensworth argues that George W. Bush has so far failed, despite assertions to the contrary, to take homeland security seriously. In proof of this allegation, Mr. Allensworth points to the Bush administration's immigration policy, which is essentially one of open borders. Homeland security and immigration restriction are inextricably linked. "[T]he White House's wrong-headed 'War on Terror,'" Allensworth contends, "is a distraction from the real threat to the United States, which stands at our very borders and in our hometowns, not in Baghdad or Tehran . . . [A]s long as Washington remains wedded to globalization and multiculturalism," he concludes, "America will not be secure." Mr. Allensworth's argument is both complemented and ratified by The Honorable James Bissett in his essay, "The Northern Border: A Threat to National Security?" (Chapter 2), where he insists that "One of the most serious drawbacks in the war against terror has been the failure of politicians to acknowledge the direct linkage between immigration and the terrorist threat," owing in part to mass migration to North America and Western Europe from the Third World. "There can be no excuse," Mr. Bissett writes, "for the United States and Canada to continue the politically correct pretense that it is not Islam itself that presents the real challenge, but only a tiny minority of extremist fanatics. The reality is that millions of Muslims around the world sympathize with and openly support the goals of the extremists." For this reason, "One of the key elements in [the War on Terror] will be to ensure that North America does not follow the European model by failing carefully to regulate and control the numbers and quality of Muslim immigrants wishing to settle in the United States and Canada."

In "The Economics of Illegal Immigration to the United States" (Chapter 3), David A. Hartman, after presenting a broad treatment of his subject, refutes the popular notion that illegal immigration benefits the U.S. economy and, indeed, all Americans. To the contrary, he writes, "we may conclude that the principal economic beneficiaries of illegal immigration to the United States fall into three categories: the immigrants themselves; their employers, particularly in the service sectors of the economy; and those consumers with higher incomes who desire more and cheaper personal services. The principal losers are the native workers whose incomes have been depressed by the excessive supply of immigrant ones," as well as the three fifths of all Americans who are compelled to subsidize, by their personal income-tax payments, immigrant and native-born welfare recipients alike. Mr. Hartman's conclusions are examined in detail in "An Interview with George Borjas on the Costs of Immigration" by Peter Brimelow (Chapter 4), in which the two economists contemplate the paradox that, as Mr. Brimelow puts it, "Everyone knows, or concedes, that immigration is good for the economy—except the economists"—despite the fact that, since the 1990s, labor economists have widely agreed that mass immigration is of no particular economic benefit to native-born Americans considered as a whole. In Chapter 5 ("Big Business and Immigration: Inside the Mind of the Corporate Elite"), Brimelow considers the self-interestedness of the corporate mind, but also its long-term flexibility that allows him to predict that "if offered a carrot like a true guest-worker program—that is, not an amnesty for illegal aliens already here and coupled with reform of the Fourteenth Amendment's 'citizen-child' clause . . . the business elite would almost certainly ditch the rest of its 'opinion-former' allies without a qualm." Following Mr. Brimelow's essay, Chapter 6—"Immigrants in American: A Statistical Overview," by Edwin S. Rubenstein—argues that no economic rationale exists for a federal policy that has "steered the U.S. into the greatest immigration storm in its history." (As to whether there is a plausible political or moral rationale for mass immigration, Mr. Rubenstein leaves his readers to decide for themselves.) The final word regarding the economic argument against immigration goes to James A. Bernsen, who (with William Lutz and Christine DeLoma), in "The Costs of Illegal Immigration to Texas" (Chapter 7), applies the critical thinking and research methods employed by previous contributors to the case of one of the several states most heavily impacted by immigration.

"National Sovereignty Goes Local" (Chapter 8) by Roger McGrath takes up the subject of the recent push by government at the state and local levels to take responsibility for immigration control that the federal government has largely refused, despite being entrusted with such responsibility by the U.S. Constitution. In "Greetings From Ground Zero" (Chapter 9), Steven Greenhut describes the "cultural tsunami" that has struck California, the enormous strain mass immigration has placed upon the public sector in terms of service costs, and the "political earthquake" that the demographic transformation of California represents, including the socialization of the state through ever-bigger government. Thomas Fleming's essay, "Up Mexico Way: The Cultural Transformation of America" (Chapter 10), argues that, in respect of immigration, we need to think realistically in terms not of assimilation but of amalgamation. "The first step toward addressing and resolving the cultural problems presented by mass immigration is to quit denying their existence. The second is to give up the glib and futile language of assimilation and recognize the fact that immigrants will affect us as much as we affect them. The third is to recognize that the larger part of the problem is of our own devising: American mass culture, including the schools that purvey mass education, are breeding grounds for anti-American resentment and American self-hatred." And in "Immigration, the Border, and the Fate of the Land: Notes on a Crisis" (Chapter 11), Gregory McNamee offers an environmental perspective on the subject of immigration, insisting that *who* comes across the border—whether Mexicans, Irishmen, or Eskimos—is not the point. "In an overcrowded lifeboat, it does not necessarily matter who is drawing the rations. If we agree that there is no room at the inn, immigration must halt or at least be radically curtailed from everywhere. And, quite apart from deciding whether our immigration laws will be made fair and rational, it is in the national interest to reduce pressures to emigrate, no matter from where, and particularly by those who have no skills."

In the book's final section, Alberto Carosa, in "From Invasion to Conquest: Illegal Immigration Into Europe and the United States" (Chapter 12), compares the European crisis with the American one and suggests lessons the United States stands to learn from Western Europe's struggle to manage and control illegal immigration; while Guido Vignelli's "False Rights, Real Duties, Prudent Rules: A Christian View of Immigration" (Chapter 13) assesses the moral justification for the frequently heard claim, often from religious circles, that an absolute right to immigration is among the basic human rights. (Mr. Vignelli concludes that "Christian doctrine does not require that a civil people, in exercise of the virtue of social charity, must deny its cultural tradition and religious ethics, submit to invasion by foreigners, or to political, legal, and economic ruin," nor does it teach that "a society [should] succumb to chaos, or commit suicide, in the illusory hope of saving an ill-fated people.") Lastly, my own contribution, "Dystopia Unlimited: Or, the Flowers of Regress (and Catastrophe)," in part sums up arguments made in the foregoing essays, while developing the further point that "everything that makes our country agreeable to us Americans, and attractive to foreigners who wish to come here, stands to be wrecked by mass immigration to the United States, making the place nearly uninhabitable for the native-born and a serious disappointment to the lately arrived foreign-born, their children, and their descendants."

Taken together, these essays provide a comprehensive and, we believe, irrefutable case against continued mass immigration to the United States, a phenomenon the authors have long believed represents a dire threat to our nation's future. The Rockford Institute has been engaged with the issues of immigration reduction and control (principally in the pages of *Chronicles: A Magazine of American Culture*, published by the Institute since the magazine's founding in 1977) in the face of considerable opposition from a mainstream political culture that has failed, until comparatively recently, to grasp the enormous significance mass immigration has for the well-being—even the survival—of the historical American nation. In this respect especially, The Rockford Institute owes a debt of gratitude for the support of its Board of Directors, past and present, to its current Board Chairman, Mr. David A. Hartman, and to The Hartman Foundation, a generous grant from which alone made possible both this book and an earlier one, *Peace in the Promised Land: A Realist Scenario* (Chronicles Press, 2006), a book of essays that attempts to assimilate and present, in a clear and accessible fashion, the facts pertaining to the cultural struggle in the Middle East that has lasted for nearly 14 centuries now, and thus to encourage the making of responsible judgments regarding that struggle as it persists in contemporary form.

1

HOMELAND INSECURITY: OUR NONEXISTENT BORDERS

by Wayne Allensworth

In November 2005, President Bush emphasized the importance of securing the United States borders—a topic he had previously avoided—in Arizona, a state that had become Ground Zero for the illegal immigration invasion. Speaking at Davis-Monthan Air Force Base, Bush asserted that "securing our border is essential to securing our homeland." The president also took the occasion to praise the Border Patrol, an institution that had also not figured prominently in his previous addresses on "homeland security." "America is grateful to those on the front lines of enforcing the border," he averred.[1]

In Arizona, the president enumerated steps he claimed his administration was taking to enforce border security and protect the American homeland. Mr. Bush stated that funding for border security had risen by 60 percent during his presidency, and that more illegal aliens were being apprehended and deported than previously. The president further outlined a three-part plan to deal with illegal immigration that included plans for detaining illegal aliens, deporting them more quickly, and beefing up law enforcement efforts along U.S. borders. "We want to make it clear," the president said, that illegal aliens are "going to be sent home and they are going to stay home."[2]

Bush aimed especially at the notorious practice known as "catch-and-release"—releasing detained illegal aliens for whom there was simply not enough space to hold in detention—and played up plans for an "expedited removal" process that would deport illegal aliens in less than 32 days. The expedited removal process would also end current legal requirements, forcing immigration officers to release illegal aliens if their home countries failed to take them back within a specified period of time, a requirement that had formerly allowed violent criminal aliens to remain in the United States.[3] As these measures would require additional manpower, the president promised that the Homeland Security budget would increase funding to raise the number of border security officers to 12,500 by the end of 2005.[4]

It is noteworthy that Mr. Bush focused his remarks regarding expedited removal on the potential threat from non-Mexican illegal immigrants: The president clearly addressed the question of border security and the terrorist threat.[5] Nevertheless, Mr. Bush's veiled references to terrorists at the border seemed only a pretext for coming to the real point of his border security rhetoric: the necessity for an amnesty of illegal aliens under the guise of a "guest worker" program, though the president was loath to call it that. Mr. Bush's remarks did not concede the extent to which his obsession with guest worker proposals had encouraged illegal immigration and overwhelmed our southern border in particular.[6] In fact, illegal immigration has surged during the Bush presidency, likely swelling the numbers of illegal aliens in the United States to a figure even larger than official estimates, which range as high as more than 20 million people.[7]

The United States is currently experiencing the largest tidal wave of mass immigration in the country's history, raising serious questions about how even the comparatively beefed-up border security measures Mr. Bush spoke of in Arizona could possibly cope with a mass of humanity, including both illegal and legal immigrants.[8] Given the Bush White House's lax attitude in the past toward illegal immigration and border security issues, it is fair to wonder whether the president was simply manipulating public anxiety about these matters to build a rhetorical Trojan Horse for his "guest worker" amnesty plan.[9] It is one thing to talk up border security measures and quite another to see them through, a reality immigration reformers have encountered in the past.[10]

In any case, with a presidential election looming in 2008 and immigration reform still a burning issue with Republican voters in the wake of the mid-term elections, the Bush White House may well be feeling the pressure from worried House Republicans demanding that the White House do something to satisfy their constituents. Representative John Culberson (R-Texas) apparently voiced the concerns of many Congressional Republicans and of his own Houston constituents when he stated, "Our constituents are berserk with fury over the unprotected borders. . . . The borders have been entirely unprotected for far too long. . . . But until we get the borders under control." Culberson added, "We'll never win the war on terror and it's pointless to discuss the guest-worker program."[11]

Indeed, Kara Hopkins has noted that the September 11 terrorist attacks have recast immigration reform in "security terms," connecting it with the "war on terror."[12] Bryan Preston, writing on an immigration reform Web log, opined that "the un-enforced border remains our national security Achilles heel." Mr. Preston speculated on what might eventually force the Bush White House to take border security seriously: "If terrorists do strike us on our soil again, and that attack has any connection to border insecurity, it won't be just a wartime attack and a tragic loss of life — it's the end of the Bush presidency and GOP credibility on national security, period. If that happens after Bush's watch, he'll still get the blame. And he'll deserve it, unless his administration gets serious about border security in a hurry."[13] And in the wake of the sound and fury emanating from the Bush White House on border security, Osama bin Laden, as if on cue, resurfaced to remind us what is at stake. In an audiotape released in January 2006 bin Ladin warned that his operatives were making preparations to again attack the United States. U.S. experts subsequently reported that they believed the tape to be authentic.[14]

"Special Interest Aliens" and Border Security

American officialdom calls them "Special Interest Aliens," as much because they might have a special interest in us as we in them. These are people from countries that are considered potential sources of terrorist attacks on the American homeland. And their numbers are reportedly growing. "People are coming here with bad intentions," an anonymous Border Patrol agent stated in an interview with NBC 4 TV in Los Angeles in November 2004. "We know for a fact that people coming from the Middle East are now coming into Mexico and spending a year, even two years . . . to learn how to speak Spanish," he added. These Special Interest Aliens (SIAs) intend to pass themselves off as Mexicans, presumably to increase their chances of following the millions of illegal Mexican immigrants who have entered the United States.[15] Even as the president was working to sell his guest worker program by seeming to address the issue of border security, Homeland Security Secretary Michael Chertoff told MSNBC that the increasing numbers of SIAs caught at the border made one thing clear: "If you don't control your borders . . . you don't have security against terrorists."[16] Clearly, the Special Interest Alien problem had been growing at a rapid rate in recent years: According to the Homeland Security Department's own figures, between October 1, 2002, and June 30, 2003, 4,226 SIAs were caught entering the United States along the borders of Mexico and Canada. By June 30, 2004, that number had grown by 42.5 percent to 6,022 SIAs from what Homeland Security officials call "countries of interest" — that is, states classified by the U.S. State Department as terrorism sponsors (Cuba, Iran, Libya, North Korea, Sudan, Syria) and those known to be home territory for militant Islamic groups in Egypt, Afghanistan, Indonesia, Iraq, Jordan, Kazakhstan, Kuwait, Lebanon, Pakistan, Saudi Arabia, Somalia, and Yemen. Data from 2004 indicated that seven Saudis, ten Syrians, 18 Lebanese, 19 Iranians, 25 Egyptians, 28 Jordanians, and 164 Pakistanis, among others, had been captured while illegally entering the United States. If the numbers seem relatively small, consider, as one observer had noted, how much damage 19 terrorists armed with box cutters did on September 11,

2001.[17] And the vast majority of those apprehended were let go—catch-and-release—to present themselves later for a deportation hearing, something that seldom happens, according to the natural course of things.[18]

Referring to the official figures on SIAs, Congressman Tom Tancredo (R-Colorado) has noted that even the most conservative estimates of those who elude the Border Patrol and enter the United States amount to two to three times the number of aliens caught. If that is, in fact, the case, then at least 18,000 SIAs entered the United States in the first nine months of 2004 alone.[19] And this is apart from those who, having obtained visas, overstayed them by remaining in the United States.

Apart from the SIA figures themselves, there is evidence that Osama bin Laden's Al Qaeda does, indeed, see America's porous borders as the Achilles heel of U.S. security. According to a host of news reports, the southern border of Mexico has attracted the attention of Islamic terrorists. In March 2005, *Time* magazine, citing U.S. intelligence officials, reported that Abu Mousab al-Zarqawi, a ringleader of attacks on U.S. personnel in Iraq who was killed in June 2006, considered hitting "soft targets" in the United States, including movie theaters, restaurants, and schools. According to the *Time* report, Al-Zarqawi had reportedly been in contact with Osama bin Ladin, who urged him to plan attacks on the United States.[20] A bulletin circulating in security circles, at the time, stated that al-Zarqawi believed: "If an individual has enough money, he can bribe his way into the U.S." Al-Zarqawi saw the path opened by first obtaining a visa to Honduras then passing through Mexico and crossing the U.S. border.

Increasingly, those intending to enter the United States illegally are first going to Mexico, then crossing the border by foot. "I absolutely believe that the next [terrorist] attack we have will come from somebody who has come across the border illegally," said Eugene Davis, a retired Border Patrol sector chief. Davis told the Associated Press: "We have no more border security now than we had prior to September 11. Anybody who believes we're safer, they're living in Neverland." In the Texas Rio Grande Valley, over 90 percent of the "Other than Mexicans" apprehended by the Border Patrol have been freed because of the lack of holding space in border detention centers: Catch-and-release all over again.[21]

Media reports on the steadily growing number of SIAs among the "Other than Mexicans" being apprehended at the southern border jumped dramatically beginning in 2004. In a November 2004 Los Angeles TV report, Congressman Dana Rohrabacher (R-California) stated that he and other members of Congress had sent a letter to the Department of Homeland Security demanding answers to important questions, such as "How many people have been stopped at our southern border who . . . [are] coming from hostile countries?" Rohrabacher guessed

"It could be in the hundreds, it could be in the thousands." Douglas, Arizona resident Larry Vance showed TV reporters a Middle Eastern prayer rug left behind by one of a host of illegal aliens who used his property as a transit point to heartland America: "I think it would be incredibly naïve, to the point of stupidity, to not believe there are terrorists coming through here," Vance said.[22]

A Tucson, Arizona, NBC TV affiliate station subsequently carried a similar report: A former Border Patrol supervisor claimed that aliens from states considered potential sources of terrorism were crossing the border at will; a diary written in Arabic was left behind by one illegal alien; and a Border Patrol agent told reporters of an incident involving an alien from Pakistan apprehended along the Arizona-Mexico border who was identified as an associate of an Islamic terrorist group. The Border Patrol veteran told reporters: "We were told specifically that these people had terrorist pasts and they were coming here . . . to carry out a terrorist attack."[23]

The Los Angeles and Tucson television investigations followed on the heels of numerous reports of terrorists having possibly entered the United States over the summer of 2004. In July of that year, for instance, Farida Goolam Mohamed Ahmed was detained at the McAllen, Texas, airport, on her way to New York. She carried a South African passport and travel itineraries showing a flight from Johannesburg to London on July 8. From there she flew to Mexico City before illegally crossing the Rio Grande near McAllen. Ahmed was on a terrorism watch list and has allegedly entered the United States as many as 250 times! Border Patrol agents reportedly ran across dozens of Middle Eastern men trying to enter the United States illegally that summer. In June 2004, 77 Middle Eastern men were reported to have been apprehended in Arizona alone.[24]

In November 2005 Texas Representative Culberson sounded the alarm once more about the possibility of would-be terrorists crossing our borders. In testimony to the House Subcommittee on Immigration, Border Security, and Claims, Culberson, a member of the Congressional Immigration Reform Caucus, headed by Colorado Republican Rep. Tom Tancredo, stated that he was "particularly concerned that aliens from countries such as Iraq, Iran, Syria, Indonesia, and the Sudan [were] entering our country illegally." Culberson claimed that Texas law enforcement officials were reporting Al Qaeda-related arrests and activity, adding that lack of border enforcement was making it easier for suspected terrorists to infiltrate the United States. Culberson further testified that such Special Interest Aliens were trying to dupe authorities by scrapping their Arabic surnames and adopting Hispanic ones, aiding them to blend with the flow of Mexicans illegally entering the country. Concurrently, Culberson spokesmen told news media that the Congressman's office had information concerning the arrest by Mexican authorities at the border of an Al Qaeda suspect, who was subsequently taken into custody by American officials. This claim was made even as U.S. media reported that drug traffickers had established para-military training camps near the border. A Texas law enforcement official said he had been informed that Special Interest Aliens had been observed in the camps.[25] It is not implausible that the same terrorist networks reportedly seeking to exploit channels by which illegal aliens can enter the United States might establish a relationship with drug traffickers as well.

U.S. Border Patrol Overwhelmed, Ill-Equipped

Whether or not Mr. Bush's promises on border security are fulfilled, it is worth considering whether the shear numbers of immigrants, legal and illegal, and the vast network of support systems for illegal aliens in the United States could still overwhelm the Border Patrol and other security bodies, who have historically been undermanned and ill-equipped despite numerous promises to reverse the situation. In 2005, the United States had around 150,000 "boots on the ground" in Iraq, yet the job the United States faces in protecting our borders is every bit as big and the security question more immediate for the American citizenry. And the same administration that had previously insisted that securing our own border is a virtually impossible task took steps to do just that in Iraq in 2005, tightening security along that country's borders with Syria and pledging to Saudi Arabia to keep those borders secure to prevent jihadists from passing through to the oil-rich desert kingdom.[26] T. J. Bonner, president of the union representing Border Patrol agents, has frankly criticized the United States government for the lack of seriousness it has shown in defending our borders. "There's been a greater amount of lip service, but there hasn't been a greater amount of atten-tion to border security," said Bonner. "It's a shell game, and the American public is the loser in this game."[27] The union itself sharply criticized the Bush administration's 2006 budget, which would have provided for hiring an addi-tional 210 Border Patrol agents. Although the intelligence-reorganization bill that President Bush signed in 2004 called for hiring 10,000 more agents over five years, in 2005, according to Bonner, fewer than 11,000 agents patrolled more than 6,000 miles of the country's perimeter on an around-the-clock basis.[28]

Millions of aliens attempt to cross the U.S. border illegally each year, the vast majority of whom are not apprehended by our understaffed, overworked Border Patrol. *Time* magazine's Donald Bartlett and James Steele told the shocking story in an investigation of the illegal immigration problem in a 2005 article: According to *Time*, an estimated three million illegal aliens entered the United States in 2004 alone! Packs of illegal aliens, sometimes numbering in the hundreds, cross into U.S. territory along thinly guarded, or unguarded, stretches of the southern border. Cars, trucks, and planes deliver tons of illegal narcotics, and if smugglers can deliver such contraband, they can also deliver nuclear, biological, or chemical materials to terrorists already in the United States. "Interior enforcement," meaning rounding up and deporting illegal aliens within the United States, was virtually halted in the 1990s, which spurred on the human tidal wave—a huge influx that provides cover for would-be terrorists, lost in the massive invasion of alien illegals. Aliens know that, once they could get beyond the border zone, they are home free.[29]

The Border Patrol is woefully ill-equipped to do its job. As an anonymous Border Patrol agent told a Tucson reporter in 2004, "over 50 percent" of the vehicles at his station were out of service at one time, cameras and infrared lenses for night patrol did not function, and agents lacked proper training. According to this source, the Border Patrol was under enormous pressure to rush people through checkpoints and to keep the border traffic moving; agents could not take the necessary time to check out suspicious border crossers. There are simply too many of them and far too few Border Patrol agents.[30] With would-be terrorists reportedly attempting to blend into the flow of Mexicans crossing the border, how many have already slipped past the Border Patrol or have been returned to Mexico where they are free to cross again, as the Mexicans are mostly able to do?

Illegal Immigration and America's Terrorist Support System

With millions of illegal aliens residing in the United States, channels for obtaining fraudulent documents can be of great use to terrorist networks. Moreover, the illegal alien problem is not confined to the Mexican border. The U.S. government, for instance, does not attempt to ascertain the identity or background of millions of foreigners to whom it grants visas, many of whom overstay those visas and remain in the United States. According to the *Time* immigration story cited previously, as many as 190,000 aliens from countries other than Mexico, including Middle Eastern states, had melted into the American population by the fall of 2004.[31]

Policies that have allowed millions to migrate to the United States have created, along with the ongoing social, cultural, and demographic transformation of America, an Islamic network composed of mosques, schools, and social organizations across the United States with the potential to provide cover for terrorist activities. The Bush White House remains oblivious to current realities, making war on Islamic states while simultaneously allowing an influx of Moslems into the country in defiance of Islam's history of anti-Christian violence and of our long-standing Middle Eastern policy, which has antagonized the Moslem world for decades. Estimates of how many Moslems reside in the United States vary (from 1.5 to seven million), but the numbers are striking, no matter which estimate is accurate.[32]

Paul Sperry, in his book *Infiltration*, gave readers a hint as to the possible depth of Islamist penetration of the United States. In the months after September 11, Sperry claims that the FBI undertook the difficult task of ascertaining just how many Al Qaeda terrorists and fellow travelers might be present in the country. "Question is," writes Sperry, "exactly how many [terrorist] cells are there? What is Al Qaeda's strength inside America? The months before 9/11, the FBI was conducting 57 full-field investigations throughout the U.S. that were related to Al Qaeda. The individuals under surveillance were either suspected operatives or sympathizers who could graduate to become operatives. . . . But that is just a small sample of Al Qaeda's presence inside America. U.S. intelligence says the organization has trained up to 120,000 terrorists around the world, and *as many as five thousand of them*[33] may be inside the U.S."[34]

According to Sperry, U.S. security officials list major cities across the country as "areas of concern." Al Qaeda is suspected of having a presence in Dallas, Denver, San Diego, Los Angeles, Seattle, Detroit, Chicago, Kansas City, Philadelphia, Boston, New York City, Washington, DC, and in several cities in Florida, among other areas not here listed.[35] The places deemed most likely to harbor Al Qaeda foot soldiers are, not surprisingly, those with the highest concentrations of Arabs and Muslims, representing the "largest and closest-knit Arab communities in America." Falls Church, Virginia, for example, is a Washington, DC, suburb "where one in every ten residents is Arab." Falls Church also "provided refuge to the [September 11] hijackers who attacked the Pentagon." It seems obvious that Islamist terrorists can use Arab and Muslim communities "as cover to blend in and live low-profile lives, undetected by authorities" until they are activated by their leaders. Sperry adds that "these ethnic communities are also places to raise cash and recruit sympathizers and facilitators like those who assisted the [September 11] hijackers in a number of different ways."[36]

Sperry cites the FBI's own reports on the September 11 attacks to back up his claims, including one made by the Bureau's Investigative Services Division:

> In addition to frequent and sustained interaction between and among the hijackers. . . . the group maintained a web of contacts both in the United States and abroad. These associates, ranging in degrees of closeness, include friends and associates from universities and flight schools, former roommates, people they knew through mosques

Wayne Allensworth: Homeland Insecurity

and religious activities, and employment contacts. Other contacts provided legal, logistical, or financial assistance, facilitated U.S. entry and flight school enrollment, or were known from [bin-Ladin]-related activities or training.[37]

Islam's holy book, the Koran, underscores the importance of what Sperry is saying. Those who aid and support the jihadists will also have their reward: "Those who fight for the Faith in the cause of Allah—as well as those who give them asylum and aid—these are all in very truth the Believers. For them is the forgiveness of sins and a provision most generous."[38]

Islamic Recruitment of Americans

In reviewing Sperry's book, I noted a sinister trend: "Muslims often seek native-born Americans not of Middle Eastern origin to do their dirty work, so as to dodge any future profiling. An alarming number of converts to Islam come from among American blacks."[39] Indeed, Sperry's account of Islam's recruitment of prisoners (most are apparently black, but others are Latino and even Asian-American) points to a deep-seated problem in America and, indeed, in Western societies. As I wrote in my review, "The social, spiritual, and structural problems inherent in modern societies have disrupted the socialization of our people, producing generations of Americans and Europeans alienated from their traditional cultures and civilization. How can we even hope to assimilate and socialize waves of immigrants from vastly different cultures and civilizations (a very dicey proposition in any case) when it is our own children who are in need of assimilation and socialization? If Al Qaeda can recruit John Walker Lindh, then how many Third Worlders will sympathize with, if not join in, the jihad?"[40]

The problems, then, that mass immigration from the developing world entails include not only the often hostile attitudes of the immigrants themselves but also their sheer numbers, facilitating both the building of Islamic networks and the recruitment by radical Islamists of segments of the native-born population.

In an article in the July/August 2005 edition of *Foreign Affairs* ("Europe's Angry Muslims"), Robert Leiken looks at the growth of militant Islam in Europe. Leiken points out that Muslim citizens of Germany, France, the United Kingdom, or the Netherlands, born and raised in those countries, do not necessarily produce citizens loyal to them in the second and third generations. Rather, many second- and third-generation Muslims are susceptible, through "adversarial assimilation" to jihadist indoctrination. In this context, Paul Sperry underscores another alarming phenomenon at work: In part, the Muslims are becoming the alienated us; but also we are becoming the alienated them. Adversarial immigrants are converting us to their own hostile ideology, even as America and the West are being colonized by the bearers of that ideology.

Muslims in the West and the Terrorist Threat

Srdja Trifkovic, author of *Sword of the Prophet* and foreign-affairs editor for *Chronicles*, has recommended that Islamic ties should be viewed as political, rather than purely religious, activity. "The sharia, to a Muslim, is not an addition to the 'secular' legal code with which it coexists; it is the only true code, the only basis of obligation. To be legitimate, all political power therefore must rest exclusively with those who enjoy Allah's authority on the basis of his revealed will. Politics is not 'part of Islam,' as this would imply that, in origin, it is a distinctly separate sphere of existence that is then eventually amalgamated with Islam. Politics is the intrinsic core of the Islamic imperative of Allah's sovereignty."[41] Citing terrorist cases involving American citizens, Trifkovic told the story of an Arab-American student who was convicted of joining Al Qaeda and plotting to assassinate President Bush and hijack airplanes. The student, 24-year-old Ahmed Omar Abu Ali, "is an American citizen who grew up in northern Virginia."[42] And regarding attitudes of Muslims to the United States and the West, Trifkovic writes that "[It is] our considered opinion that the application of political criteria in determining the eligibility of prospective visitors or immigrants to the U.S. should become an essential ingredient of a long-term anti-terrorist strategy." Thus, "Islamic affiliations should be treated as political, rather than religious activity."

Trifkovic has argued that Islam's comprehensive world view, one that does not recognize any division between religious life and the state, is a telling indicator of Islam's incompatibility with Western political systems. He has further pointed to the alienation that Muslim immigrants and their progeny have indicated in polls taken after the July 7, 2005 terrorist bombings in London: "According to a detailed survey of the attitudes of British Muslims prepared for the *Daily Telegraph* in the immediate aftermath of the London bombings . . . one in four sympathizes with the motives of the bombers, and six percent insist that the bombings were 'fully justified.' In absolute numbers this means that there are over 100,000 Muslims in Great Britain who are either prepared to carry out terrorist acts or are ready to support those who do. And a substantial majority—56 percent—say that whether or not they sympathize with the bombers, they can at least understand why they behave in this way. The sheer scale of Muslim alienation from British society that the survey reveals is remarkable: nearly a third of them, 32 percent, believe that

'Western society is decadent and immoral and that Muslims should seek to bring it to an end.'"[43]

Muslim attitudes to the United States as revealed in other surveys cited by Trifkovic are even worse—more negative than views of Great Britain or any other European country. Eighty-one percent, or over four-fifths of Pakistanis, for example, "dislike" America. In Lebanon, 73 percent believe that suicide bombings are justified. This amounts to what Trifkovic describes as the "baggage" Muslims immigrants bring with them to America and transmit to their children who are born here. "The sense of hostile detachment from any recognizably American identity and values that breeds terrorist intent is not confined to any single group of Muslims. It transcends class and affects students, Ivy-League-educated doctors, and criminals alike. The problem is not limited to those Muslims who came to the United States as adults: In December 2003 five U.S.-born Muslim youths from upstate New York were convicted of aiding Al Qaeda and plotting attacks on Americans."[44]

Immigration Reform, the Terrorist Threat, and Border Security

As of this writing in late 2006, there is some cause for guarded optimism. Immigration reform and border security issues are now going mainstream, and, though no one knows what will emerge from the expected bargaining involving the newly elected Democratic House and Senate and the Bush White House over pending border security and immigration legislation, the "cat is out of the bag."[45] Border security and immigration reform issues will not go away; indeed, they have emerged as a central point of contention in American politics.

I hope I have made evident in this chapter that real homeland security depends upon a comprehensive approach involving enhanced border security and interior enforcement (including, in part, the deportation of illegal and otherwise dangerous aliens), immigration reform (the enactment of standards for regulating immigration both numerically and in terms of national security), and redirections in American foreign policy.

It is evident that the Bush administration has thus far not taken homeland security seriously. What is more, the White House's wrong-headed "War on Terror" is a distraction from the real threat to the United States, which stands at our borders and in our hometowns, not in Baghdad or Tehran. It should be clear to all who have paid attention to the international situation and have put loyalty to country ahead of loyalty to party that the Bush administration's misadventure in Iraq is unjustified, has produced a quagmire for the U.S. Armed Forces, and is actively promoting efforts by terrorists. Patriots who opposed this war did so precisely because we regarded the invasion of a country that had not attacked us and did not represent a threat to the United States, as morally indefensible and contrary to American interests. Many of us were appalled that the administration was a chock-full of officials whose primary allegiance was apparently to a foreign power (Israel) and that these officials had helped push America into an unnecessary war to defend someone else's country. We were angered that the administration did next to nothing to defend our homeland from attack, as the readily available information pertaining to the border-security crisis made plain.

The Bush administration's "War on Terror" has drained resources that could have been used not only to pursue and to punish those responsible for the September 11, 2001, terrorist attacks but also to defend our country where it really mattered—on our own soil. To do so effectively requires revising our immigration and border-security policies; reevaluating our relations with our neighbors, Mexico and Canada,[46] which would entail demanding that they do their share to help the United States counter the terrorist threat and police our common borders; and reviewing a foreign policy that unquestioningly supports Israel without any regard for cost, antagonizes the Islamic world, and undermines the standing and reputation of the United States around the globe.

Finally, as long as Washington remains wedded to globalization and multiculturalism (President Bush himself has assured us, despite all contrary evidence, that Islam is "a religion of peace"), America will not be secure. There is no reason for the United States to make war on the entire Islamic world—but neither is there any reason to allow a substantial portion of that world into the American homeland, gaining a foothold that constitutes a serious threat now and a greater one in the future. Patriots should not be distracted by the administration's slay-dragons-across-the-sea policies, the same that have allowed the Islamic threat to penetrate our country. Real homeland security demands an uncompromising love for that homeland, a devotion to her people, and a willingness to act. If the United States can deploy 150,000 troops to Iraq, America can defend her own borders. If Americans are willing to fight and die in distant lands, then surely we must be willing to move decisively to defend our own homes and neighborhoods.

Endnotes

[1] http://www.foxnews.com/story/0,2933,176879,00.html.

[2] http://www.foxnews.com/story/0,2933,176879,00.html.

[3] This part of Bush's border security plan would require Congressional action. The president called on Congress to "end these senseless rules" (http://www.foxnews.com/story/0,2933,176879,00.html).

[4] http://www.foxnews.com/story/0,2933,176879,00.html.

[5] http://www.vdare.com/mann/051129_bush.htm.

[6] See Juan Mann's vdare.com article on why a "guest worker" program would not relieve pressure on the border (http://www.vdare.com/mann/051130_bush.htm) and his estimation of how many exceptions there may be to Mr. Bush's policy of swift deportation of illegal aliens (http://www. vdare.com/mann/051129_bush.htm).

[7] http://usliberals.about.com/od/immigration/a/IllegalImmi.htm; http://www.vdare.com/rubenstein/ 051128_nd.htm.

[8] Researcher Fred Elbel has estimated that the U.S. illegal alien population is growing by at least 2.2 million annually. Even at estimates of half that number, Edwin Rubenstein, of ESR Research Economic Consultants, calculates that 21 million illegal aliens have been added to the U.S. population since the 1986 illegal alien amnesty (http://www.vdare.com/rubenstein/051128_nd.htm). For more on illegal immigration under the Bush presidency, see http://usliberals.about.com/od/immigration/a/IllegalImmi.htm. Furthermore, the number of immigrants entering the United States since 2000 makes the half decade since then the period in which immigration rates were the highest in American history, according to a study by the Center for Immigration Studies. According to this study, a total of 7.9 million immigrants have come to the United States since 2000 (http://www. usatoday.com/news/nation/2005–12–12-immigration_x.htm).

[9] Kara Hopkins, writing in the January 16, 2006, issue of *The American Conservative*, certainly thought so: "Now, odds are Bush hasn't undergone some epiphany in the last two months. Yet he can promise enhanced enforcement in good conscience because, on his theory, border control will become increasingly unnecessary. While the immigration-reform movement is busy congratulating itself on winning a 60 percent increase in border spending, he plans to make it irrelevant by inviting the former illegals inside. 'Bush decided to give these guys their rhetorical pound of flesh,' a Republican official close to the White House told *Time* magazine. 'In return, he wants a comprehensive bill, which is what he has always wanted. He's just going to lead with a lot of noise about border security.'"

[10] W. James Antle III, writing in *The American Conservative*: "Guest-workers proponents are likewise unrealistic about the immigration status quo. The repeated assertions that we have tried enforcement but failed are based on the amount of money spent on border-patrol agents and bureaucratic budgets without looking at whether Washington actually did anything with the money. Interior enforcement has been lax and employer sanctions underutilized. Workplace arrests of illegal aliens actually declined between 1999 and 2003 and employment-verification programs are in their infancy. As long as illegal aliens can find employment and work without realistic fear of deportation, new border-security initiatives will do little to keep them from flouting immigration laws" (http://www. amconmag.com/2005/2005_11_07/article1.html).

[11] http://www.mercurynews.com/mld/mercurynews/news/13403981.htm.

[12] http://www.amconmag.com/2006/2006_01_16/article2.html.

[13] http://michellemalkin.com/immigration/2005/08/24/02:29.pm.

[14] http://www.freemarketnews.com/WorldNews.asp?nid=5797.

[15] See Wayne Allensworth, "War on the Home Front: Real Homeland Security," *Chronicles*, February 2005 (http://chroniclesmagazine.org/Chronicles/2005/February2005/0205Allensworth.html).

[16] http://www.msnbc.msn.com/id/10242059/.

[17] http://michellemalkin.com/immigration/2005/08/24/02:29.pm.

[18] U.S. security officials' Congressional testimony cited in my article "Losing the 'War on Terror' at the Border," *Chronicles*, October 2005.

[19] http://michellemalkin.com/immigration/2005/08/24/02:29.pm.

[20] "Losing the 'War on Terror' at the Border," *Chronicles*, October 2005.

[21] "Losing the 'War on Terror' at the Border."

[22] "Losing the 'War on Terror' at the Border."

[23] "Losing the 'War on Terror' at the Border."

[24] "Losing the 'War on Terror' at the Border."

[25] http://www.wnd.com/news/article.asp?ARTICLE_ID=47401.

[26] "Losing the 'War on Terror' at the Border," *Chronicles*, October 2005.

[27] "Losing the 'War on Terror' at the Border."

[28] "Losing the 'War on Terror' at the Border."

[29] Bartlett and Steele, "Who Left the Door Open?" *Time*, September 20, 2004. You can read the article here: http://www.kfi640.com/time_dooropen.html.

[30] "Losing the 'War on Terror' at the Border."

[31] Bartlett and Steele, "Who Left the Door Open?" *Time*, September 20, 2004.

[32] For a review of the penetration of the United States—and the U.S. government and security apparatus—by Islamist groups, see Paul Sperry's *Infiltration: How Muslim Spies and Subversives Have Penetrated Washington* (Nashville, Tennessee, 2005). The estimate of the number of Muslim residents in America is cited in "War on the Home Front: Real Homeland Security," *Chronicles*, February 2005 (http://chroniclesmagzine.org/Chronicles/2005/February2005/0205Allensworth. html). For an account of Islam's violent past, see Srdja Trifkovic's *The Sword and the Prophet: History, Theology, Impact on the World* (Boston, Regina Orthodox Press, 2002).

[33] My emphasis.

[34] Paul Sperry, *Infiltration: How Muslim Spies and Subversives Have Penetrated Washington.* Nashville, TN, 2005, p. 61.

[35] Sperry, *Infiltration*, p. 64.

[36] Sperry, *Infiltration*, pp. 65–66.

[37] Sperry, *Infiltration*, p. 68.

[38] The Koran, Surah 8:74. Cited by Sperry, *Infiltration*, p. 67.

[39] Wayne Allensworth, "An Adversarial Culture," *Chronicles*, February 2006.

[40] Allensworth, "An Adversarial Culture."

[41] http://www.chroniclesmagazine.org/cgi-bin/newsviews.cgi/Islam/Insecure_Homeland.printer.

[42] http://www.chroniclesmagazine.org/cgi-bin/newsviews.cgi/Islam/Insecure_Homeland.printer.

[43] http://www.chroniclesmagazine.org/cgi-bin/newsviews.cgi/Islam/Insecure_Homeland.printer.

[44] http://www.chroniclesmagazine.org/cgi-bin/newsviews.cgi/Islam/Insecure_Homeland.printer.

[45] For an early review of the bill and what might follow, see http://www.vdare.com/mann/051219_hr4437.htm.

[46] "The virtually undefended 4,000-mile border with Canada may be just as much a potential entry-way for terrorists as the 2,000-mile border with Mexico. Canadian security officials have admitted that as many as 50 terrorist groups are operating in their territory. Because Canada's immigration and asy-lum polices are more lax than even our own, can we simply ignore the threat?" Wayne Allensworth, "War on the Home Front: Real Homeland Security," *Chronicles*, February 2005 (http://chronicles-magazine.org/Chronicles/2005/February2005/0205Allensworth.html).

2

THE NORTHERN BORDER: A THREAT TO AMERICAN SECURITY?

by The Honorable James Bissett

For decades, Canadian and U.S. politicians boasted that the border separating the two countries along the 49th parallel was the longest undefended border in the world. There was good reason for mutual congratulation. There had not been trouble along the border between the United States and Canada since the Fenian raids into Canada in the years immediately following the Civil War. For generations, the undefended border stood as an example to other nations of how countries might get along with each other. The northern border of the United States had become a remarkable symbol of peace and good will, illustrating that good neighbors need not be separated by fences and barbed wire.

All of this changed after the terrorist strikes of September 2001. Fearing further attacks, the United States rushed National Guardsmen to strengthen and reinforce the northern border. Since then, the number of Border Patrol agents along the 4,000-mile boundary have tripled in numbers, from the 300 officers assigned before September 11 to 1,000 today. Other measures have also been taken to guard against the possible entry of terrorists into the United States from Canada.

In December 2005, the Homeland Security Department announced that every port of entry into the United States had been equipped with a system to fingerprint and digitally photograph foreigners entering the country. In the same month, the House of Representatives passed a Defense appropriation to carry out a feasibility study for the construction of a fence along the Canada-U.S. border. In January 2007, all Canadians and Americans were required to possess valid passports to enter the United States if traveling by air. In June 2009, this require-ment will also apply to those traveling by land or sea.

The northern border is no longer undefended, and the United States now looks upon it as a more serious threat to national security than the southern bor-der with Mexico. There are a number of reasons, some valid and some not, for this change in perception. Nevertheless, at the heart of the problem is the assess-ment that Canada has not taken the terrorist threat seriously, and that Canada's immigration and refugee policies present a real and present danger to the safety and security of Americans.

The Situation Before September 11

Canada and the United States are major receiving countries for immigration. Both have a long tradition of welcoming newcomers and both consider immigration an essential part of their national heritage. Immigration is interwoven into their romantic myths of nation building, and ethnic politics play an important part in the political life of both countries. Political parties in Canada and the United States support expansive immigration programs. Until September 11, the enforcement of immigration laws and the control of aliens already present were not taken seriously by either country.

For years the United States has tolerated large-scale illegal immigration from Mexico. Only token efforts have been made to stem the flow of illegal Mexicans who stream across the porous southern border, with the result that 11 to 20 million—or even more—Mexicans live and work illegally in the country. They are in little danger of being apprehended; while, if they are caught and sent home, they will soon return again, encouraged by employers who rely on them as a source of cheap labor. Despite the scale of the problem—a problem that presents a very real threat to the sovereignty of the United States—there does not seem to be the political will to resolve it. Before September 11, every attempt to get serious about immigration reform was thwarted by politicians influenced by lobbyists and the growing electoral power of Mexican-American voters.

At the time of the September terrorist attacks, there were 314,000 illegal aliens in the United States who had been ordered deported but remained at large. More seriously, 78,000 of these were people who had come from terrorist-producing countries. In New York, Chicago, Los Angeles, and other major urban centers, city fathers prohibited local law enforcement agencies from reporting to federal authorities illegal aliens who had been apprehended unless there was evidence that those apprehended had committed a criminal offense. In the United States, as in Canada, people who entered as students or visitors were not required to inform the authorities of their whereabouts. There were no exit controls and no system for tracking aliens. Illegal aliens were easily able to obtain a driver's license, social security card, or to open a bank account. In both countries, the inland immigration resources were underfunded and inadequately staffed. In terms of government priorities, immigration enforcement activities received little attention.

Abroad, visas to enter the United States were frequently issued by locally engaged employees. Often, visas were issued by mail without the individual having been seen or interviewed by Consular officers: Emphasis was placed on the rapid approval of people wishing to enter the country and facilitation of their entry. All of the terrorists involved in the September 11 attack entered the United States with legally issued temporary visas. Some had received their visas without being seen by any American official.

Unlike Europeans, Canadians and Americans were unaccustomed to requirements that they possess and carry identity cards, or to check their travel documents when registering in hotels. They could travel between their two countries without passports, and normally a driver's license was all that was needed for identity purposes, while routine police checks to confirm identity were not a common occurrence in either Canada or the United States. This relaxed attitude toward internal security was the natural result of the domestic peace and tranquility that had existed in and between the two democracies for over 140 years. A large scale terrorist attack was not only considered impossible, but also it was not considered at all.

Yet there had been clear warning signs that the United States (if not Canada) was a target of Islamist extremists. An unsuccessful attack against the World Trade Center in 1993 left six people dead. Five years later, in 1998, the bombings of the U.S. embassies in Tanzania and Kenya resulted in the death of 224 people. In 1999, an Algerian refugee entering the United States from Canada was apprehended with a car load of explosives, planning to blow up the Los Angeles airport. In 2000, the USS *Cole* was the target of a successful suicide bomb attack in Yemen that killed 17 American sailors. These incidents should have served as grim harbingers of what was yet to come.

After the East Africa bombings, U.S. intelligence learned that Osama bin Laden and Al-Qaeda had planned and carried out these attacks. Bin Laden was placed on the FBI's ten most wanted list, yet his explicit threats did not result in any concrete steps to strengthen immigration control systems or to tighten up on the issuance of visas from countries known to be tolerant of Islamist extremists. The reluctance to foresee or recognize the connection between immigration and a potential terrorist attack by Islamist terrorists within the United States was acknowledged only after the catastrophe of September 11.

Post September 11—The American Experience

The shock of the completely unexpected suicide strikes against the World Trade Center and the Pentagon made Americans realize they were vulnerable to attack from within. For the first time in generations, war had reached the shores of the United States itself. Moreover, future attacks might be even more devastating if the terrorists used weapons of mass destruction. A new reality had thus emerged that threatened the safety and security of the United States. It was a frightening reality. It was also a reality that demanded an immediate political response in the form of retaliatory measures.

The government reacted swiftly and decisively. President Bush immediately declared war against terrorism and assumed extraordinary powers normally used only in time of war. Military action against Osama bin Laden and the Taliban in Afghanistan followed quickly. At home, security became the number one priority as the people demanded assurances that measures were being taken to prevent further attacks. Security and intelligence agencies were accused of failing to forewarn or to prevent the attacks. Immigration and Consular services were also accused of laxity in the screening of people entering the United States.

One of the first steps taken in response to the attacks was to tighten security along the border with Canada and at all airports and sea ports. A new department of Homeland Security was created out of the Customs Service, the Coast Guard, the Border Patrol, the Emergency Management Agency, and the Immigration and Naturalization Service. The new organization was allotted a budget of $38 billion and a staff of 170,000 employees. The aim of this consolidation was to improve interagency cooperation and intelligence sharing within the government, although some critics feared that the sheer size of the new department would inhibit rather than improve communication.

Congress rapidly passed the Patriot Act that gave law enforcement agencies broad and extraordinary powers of surveillance and investigation, as well as expanded authority to carry out activities designed to identify and apprehend terrorists and to inhibit their financial and logistical support. An enhanced Border Security and Visa Reform Act was passed, subjecting everyone entering or leaving the United States to strict controls. A tracking system for foreigners was introduced requiring that they be fingerprinted and photographed upon entry. The seriousness of this commitment was underlined when the deadline set for the completion of this elaborate system by 2005 was conscientiously met.

The measures taken by the Bush administration in the weeks following the September attacks received the full support of Congress and the American public. Initially, at least, the security of United States citizens was not a politically divisive issue. Later, when the initial shock and fear began to wear off and no further attacks occurred, critics of the administration's policies raised concerns about human rights violations, foreign policy, and the conduct of the Iraqi invasion.

In the days following September 11, rumors circulated that the hijackers had entered the United States from Canada. Senator Hillary Clinton (D-New

York), who was one of those who asserted this rumor as fact, later withdrew her accusation when it was established that all of the 19 terrorists involved in the September 11 attacks had entered the country legally in possession of visas issued by U.S. Consular officers abroad. Some of the terrorists had in fact received their visas without having been seen by an American official. Nevertheless, the rumor persists and continues to be repeated—most recently in December 2005 by Montana Senator Conrad Burns on the Fox News Channel. Canadian politicians, of course, are made unhappy by this false charge, and the Canadian Ambassador in Washington has done his best to assure Americans the suicide bombers did not enter from Canada.

Nevertheless, Canada's track record in dealing with the terrorist threat is not without fault. The government on the one hand has taken a number of actions that to some extent parallel the measures adopted by the United States. On the other hand, Canada has shown a definite reluctance to take the war on terror seriously.

Post September 11—The Canadian Experience

The first mixed signal sent to the United States after the destruction of the World trade Center came from the Canadian Prime Minister Jean Chrétien, when, in expressing regret for the incident, he concluded that the motivation for the attack was caused by economic disparity existing between the various regions of the world. This statement quite properly was interpreted by Americans (and many Canadians) as unsympathetic and misguided. Moreover, it set the stage for what later appeared to be reluctance and hesitancy on the part of Canada fully to appreciate that North America was vulnerable to further terrorist attacks and that Canada, if not a prime target herself, could serve as an ideal haven for terrorists planning strikes against the main enemy, the United States.

Despite the Prime Minister's insensitive remarks, actions taken by Canada in the weeks following September 11 were impressive. Canada quickly dispatched troops to Afghanistan to help overthrow the Taliban regime; Canadian troops remain there and are taking casualties. An omnibus anti-terrorist Act, similar to the U.S. Patriot Act, was rushed through the Canadian Parliament; many in Canada regarded Bill 36, as it was called, as draconian in giving police and intelligence agencies extraordinary powers not normally exercised in time of peace. Nevertheless, the bill passed through parliament without opposition.

The government created a new Department of Public Safety and Emergency Preparedness, bringing together a number of agencies involved in security activities. The new department, a close replica of the Department of Homeland

Security, had a similar purpose, that is, to achieve the closer coordination of security agencies and improve information sharing between them. The government also produced a National Security Plan and a Threat Assessment Center, and established four Integrated National Security Enforcement Teams whose purpose was to disrupt terrorist activities. And, in December 2001, Canada signed a Smart Border Declaration with the United States that contained 30 points aimed at making the border more secure for people and goods, while facilitating cross border traffic.

These measures would seem to indicate that Canada, far from being "soft" on terrorism, was following the American lead and pursuing the war on terrorism with alacrity and determination. Unfortunately, the introduction of new legislation and the rearranging of bureaucratic structures do not tell the full story. A closer examination of what has actually been done in concrete terms to fight terrorism reveals a reluctance and hesitancy on the part of the government to take the threat seriously.

The controversial Bill 36 provided for the prosecution of people identified as active terrorists and provided for the listing of organizations the government identified as "terrorist." However, unexplainable and lengthy delays occurred before the government decided to identify as terrorist such obviously listable organizations such as Hamas, Hezbollah, the Al Aqsa Martyrs' Brigade, and the Armed Islamic Front. Only after pressure from the Canadian media and Jewish organizations were these organizations finally placed on the list.

The failure to identify terrorist organizations was particularly puzzling given that, as early as 1998, the Canadian Intelligence Service had reported 50 terrorist groups to be active in Canada. Although the report did not name these groups, it did issue a clear warning that a terrorist strike somewhere in North America was only a matter of time.

One of the organizations among the unnamed 50 referred to by the Intelligence Service was Babar Khalsa, the Sikh terrorist organization held responsible for the death of 329 Canadians in the bombing of an Air India jet off the coast of Ireland in 1985 in retaliation for the storming of the Sikh Golden Temple at Amritsar by Indian troops. Yet Babar Khalsa was not listed by the government until June 2003, almost 20 years after the worst terrorist attack in Canadian history, for fear of offending the large Sikh population in Canada. The decision to add Babar Khalsa to the list came only after the Canadian Security Service publicly identified it as one of the aforesaid terrorist groups operating in Canada.

Canada also has one of the largest concentrations of Tamils in the world, outside of Sri Lanka: An estimated 300,000 Tamils reside in and around Toronto. Many thousands of them arrived in Canada as asylum seekers and now have acquired citizenship and voting rights. It was because of Tamil voting support that the government refused to include the Liberation Tigers of Tamil Eelam on Canada's terrorist list. (Shortly after assuming power, the new Conservative Government added the Tamil Tigers to the terrorist list.)

It would almost seem the government passed Bill 36 with no intention of alienating ethnic supporters by going as far as actually to implement the bill's provisions. Further reluctance was caused because passage of the bill was greeted by cries of outrage from human rights groups, lawyers, and the media, all of whom demanded the law be retracted. This overreaction to a law designed to provide security authorities with the means required to combat an intelligent and fanatical enemy is worrisome: It shows that significant sectors of the Canadian populace believe a mild security bill to be a more serious threat than is the possibility of a catastrophic bomb blast by Al-Qaeda agents. Such an attitude is symptomatic of a disconcerting ignorance regarding the objectives of Islamist terror and reveals a dangerous complacency not uncommonly to be found in prosperous democratic societies.

In April 2005, the Auditor General reported a number of serious security gaps in Canada's effort to combat terrorism, including the ease with which Canadian passports could be obtained by potential terrorists and the failure to adequately train personnel responsible for responding to a terrorist attack. A Senate Committee on Security in the same month revealed 62 border posts not linked to the major watch-list computer system and pointed out that there remained 225 unguarded cross–border roads into the United States. A more recent internal audit obtained by the media in January 2006 revealed that the government's national customs strategy and border security program were behind schedule, underfunded, over budget, and ineffective in key areas. Further, the audit found that the newly formed Canadian Border Services Agency had not received the funding it had been promised to enable it to participate in full-time anti-terrorist operations. The agency's enforcement activities had shown little improvement since 2000, owing primarily to timely intelligence and a lack of tools. (In August 2006, the Conservative Government announced new funding for the hiring of 400 new border guards and that for the first time in history they would be armed.) Of these, one of the most important used by the border agency—the logging and tracking of airline passenger data—was over-budgeted and handicapped by poor quality information submitted by airlines. The audit found also that expensive vehicle and cargo inspection equipment went frequently unused owing to an insufficiency of trained staff to operate the equipment. Eleven mobile units costing 2.5 million dollars each were underutilized and positioned in locations where their presence could be easily spotted by approaching vehicles.

Thus, the Canadian response to the war on terrorism has left much to be desired. After getting off to a reasonably good start, it soon lost momentum. The responsibility for this failure to follow through rests entirely with the political leadership of a country that is affluent, self-satisfied, and self-absorbed. The possibility of a terrorist attack has not been taken seriously by Canadian political leaders, by the media, or by the people. Nothing illustrates this complacency more than Canada's present system for dealing with people who arrive wishing to make a claim for political asylum.

Canada's Refugee System

Two months after September 11, the government passed a new Immigration and Refugee Act that made it easier for people to claim refugee status in Canada and even more difficult to remove those who were found not to qualify as refugees. The new legislation expanded the definition of refugee beyond the definition set out in the United Nations Refugee Convention and allowed anyone to make an asylum application who claimed persecution in his own country. The new Act also added several levels of appeal and review before unsuccessful claimants could be removed. While the refugee bill was being considered by the Canadian Senate, a group of former Canadian ambassadors and senior public servants plead strongly that it be returned to the House of Commons for reconsideration in the light of the events of September 11, but their representations were totally ignored and the bill was passed.

Canada already had the most generous refugee system in the world, as well as a reputation as the easiest country in which to qualify for asylum. In the past 20 years, more than 600,000 refugee claimants have entered Canada. Many of these were smuggled into Canada by international criminal gangs and arrived either with forged documents or without any documentation. Many of the claimants have come from terrorist-producing countries, including large numbers from North Africa and Pakistan. Yet, even after September 11, few of these undocumented arrivals have been detained. Instead, they continue to be released and asked to attend their refugee hearing, often not scheduled for months. Since there is no tracking system, the immigration authorities have no idea whether the claimant will show up or not. In fact, many do not appear for their hearing. In 2003, the Auditor General reported to parliament that there were 36,000 warrants outstanding for the arrest of people whose refugee claims had been refused but whose whereabouts were unknown. It is estimated that figure would now be closer to 50,000. Despite this alarming revelation, nothing has been done about the problem.

In December 2004, as part of the Smart Border Declaration, Canada and the United States put into effect a "safe third country agreement," which prevents some asylum claimants in the United States who appear at the land border from entering Canada to submit a refugee claim. The agreement also applies to the same categories of people in Canada who wish to cross into the United States to claim asylum there. Those affected by the agreement must now make their asylum claim in the country where they reside.

After signing the agreement, the Canadian government, fearing that it could prevent individuals in the United States who had been charged or convicted of an offense that might entail the death penalty from finding refuge in Canada, passed regulations exempting those individuals from the terms of the agreement. Consequently, any person in the United States who is charged with, or already convicted of, murder, or who is a known terrorist bomber is to be allowed entry into Canada if he seeks entry at the border. This is tantamount to laying out a welcome mat for murderers. It is difficult to argue that the government that passed this kind of regulation, after September 11 and the bombings in Madrid, can be said to have taken the war on terrorism seriously.

Almost all of the known terrorists who have been apprehended in Canada entered the country as refugee claimants. There are three terrorists now in custody in Canada, all of whom entered as claimants. Because the Canadian Charter of Rights Freedoms protects anyone in Canada—not just Canadian citizens—and because Canada is a signatory to the United Nations Convention against Torture, it is unlikely they can be removed to their homelands. Since they cannot be detained indefinitely, it is possible that, in time, they will be released

Every month thousands of people arrive in Canada seeking asylum. None has undergone even the most basic screening for ill health or criminality, or as a security threat. That the system is exploited by criminal groups involved in human trafficking is well known. That it is vulnerable to the terrorist threat is self-evident. The system is out of step with every other Western democratic country's method of dealing with asylum seekers, yet even the Conservative Government has shown no inclination to change the system. If the Canadian government's refusal to reform the refugee system stemmed from a perverted sense of wishing to do good, then at least it might be understood, if not forgiven. Sadly, this is not the case. The decision to make the refugee system even more generous than it was before September 11, and to open the border to criminals fleeing a possible death penalty, was motivated by a desire to placate and meet the demands of special interest groups. A powerful refugee lobby exists in Canada consisting of lawyers, immigration consultants, religious denominations, and nongovernmental organizations. The "refugee business" is a multimillion dollar industry, whose pressure groups are highly organized and influential. These are described by government spokesmen not as lobbyists but as "stakeholders," and they are always the first to be invited to present their views on refugee issues before Parliamentary Committees.

Canada's wide-open asylum system presents a grave threat to North American security, undermining everything the United States and Canada have done to make their citizens more secure. When a nation gives up its right to decide who can or cannot enter its borders and compounds this folly by forfeiting its right to remove undesirables from its territory, it has in effect abandoned its sovereignty. Canada's asylum system stands as a symbol of a country oblivious to the possibility of a catastrophic strike by Islamist terrorists. It also stands as a serious threat to Canada's southern neighbor.

Immigration Policy

In contrast to its asylum policy, Canada's system for the selection of immigrants does not present a direct threat to the security of the United States. All immigrants to Canada require visas before being allowed entry, and all are required to be in good health and have a clean criminal record. Security screening is carried out for those who fit a security profile but checking of the elderly and children is normally waived. (Essentially, the value of security screening is deterrence. Few potential terrorists are caught by screening since most are unknown and have no previous record of criminal or terrorist activities.) Indeed, before September 11, the Canadian immigration system was more selective and careful in its screening of immigrants and tourists than was the United States. With few exceptions, the only people who were allowed to enter Canada without a visitor visa issued by Canadian posts abroad were countries belonging to the European Union and the United States. Visitors requiring visas were normally interviewed by Canadian immigration officers posted to Canadian embassies abroad. The waiving of interviews was the exception rather than the rule.

Paradoxically, as a major effort to prevent people from arriving in Canada who might apply for asylum there, Canadian enforcement officers are stationed at key airports overseas to prescreen passengers destined for Canada. Those suspected of not being bona fide visitors, or those found to be in possession of fraudulent documents, are not be allowed to board the aircraft. These immigration control officers also train foreign airline staff and liaise with local law enforcement officers to cooperate in combating trafficking and people smuggling.

It is important to make a distinction between Canada's immigration system and its asylum system. Canada takes care to ensure that immigrants are selected carefully and meet all requirements before they are issued visas to enter the country. This care is cast aside when it comes to people arriving who claim persecution. As described previously, the system for dealing with asylum seekers is the weakest aspect of Canada's effort to prevent terrorists from entering the country. Another aspect of the immigration system that stands in need of improvement is the enforcement of the immigration laws. Laxity in this respect is a definite weakness that Canada shares with the United States, and many other democratic countries. But the days when Canada or any other Western democracy can continue to look upon immigration irregularities as no more than minor misdemeanors is over. Effective management of immigration and strict control of those permitted to enter the country is an essential factor in the ongoing war against the terrorist threat.

The first line of defense against foreign terrorists takes place outside the country, upon the issuance of visas. The second line is at the point of entry. Although Canada and the United States have taken a number of steps since September 11 to strengthen these defenses, much more needs to be done, as skepticism in both countries prevails against an understanding that immigration laws need to be taken seriously and a willingness to accept the reality that the world is entering into an era of immigration control and border security.

As the London bombings have shown, there will always be the threat of terrorist attack from native-born terrorists, and it is possible this may present the major threat. (In June 2006, 17 Canadian-born Muslims were arrested and charged under the new terrorist legislation for planning bomb attacks against targets in Toronto.) Nevertheless, it is likely that the main threat to North America will continue to be from terrorists entering from outside the continent. In order to carry out terrorist activities abroad, Islamist terrorists must be able to cross international boundaries. Consequently, border security is a critical factor in the ability of any country to protect its citizens. The dream of a "borderless world" that not so many years ago seemed within reach was shattered with the emergence of radical Islam and the suicide bomber.

A North American Perimeter Shield

There is a strong case to be made that, despite all efforts to defend the Northern border, there is little likelihood that these steps alone will be effective. That border, over 4,000 miles long, passes through terrain as varied as North America itself. Hundreds of areas are almost impossible to keep under surveillance—notwithstanding modern electronic equipment, border patrols on the ground, and helicopter scrutiny overhead. The sheer volume of traffic across it presents an awesome challenge. Over 500,000 people and 50,000 trucks cross the border every day. Approximately 3.5 million containers arriving at Canadian sea ports are destined for cities in the United States, and only about three percent of those are checked by customs agents using gamma ray scanners. The margin for error is high, and the costs are burdensome.

Furthermore, the costs in terms of constructing a physical barrier, of long line-ups at border crossings, and the inconvenience caused by the need to examine all vehicles and passenger traffic cannot be measured in terms of additional border guards and sophisticated equipment only. When the Ambassador Bridge connecting Detroit and Windsor was temporarily closed down in the hours immediately following the September 11 attacks, it caused a line 35 kilometers long. Several U.S. automobile plants were forced to shut down because supplies from Canada were caught up in 18-hour border delays. The congestion and blockage caused alarm among both Canadian and American business interests. A tough border policy between the two countries has an adverse impact on the two billion dollars a day exchange in trade that operates across the border.

Americans who are preoccupied with security concerns tend to overlook the importance of trade between the two countries. Canada is the United States' largest trading partner. In 2004, it accounted for 17.41 percent of total U.S. exports, compared, for example, with Britain (3.16 percent), Germany (5.26 percent), and Mexico (10.60 percent). Only China, accounting for 13.38 percent of U.S. exports, came close to matching Canada. Canada is the biggest export market for 37 of the 50 states. Equally important, Canada is the number one supplier of oil to the United States, ranking ahead of Saudi Arabia, Mexico, Nigeria, and Venezuela. It also ranks first in supplying its neighbor with natural gas. The economies of the two countries are inextricably linked to each other.

Canada's economy is almost totally dependent on its ability to export its goods and services to the United States. Almost 90 percent of Canada's exports are to the United States; any curtailment of that trade directly threatens the Canadian economy and the standard of living of every Canadian. President Bush's announcement that security trumps trade did not go unnoticed by Canadian business interests. Their concern gave new life to the idea of a customs union between the two countries. This is a concept that has been discussed for a number of years as a logical evolutionary step, following the activation of the North America Free Trade Agreement (NAFTA) in January 1994.

Even before September 11, the former United States Ambassador to Canada, Gordon Giffen, went further by proposing, in October 2000, a North American security perimeter as a sensible and logical move to coordinate and make more effective the security of the continent. This idea has been supported by the Canadian Council of Chief Executives representing 150 of Canada's largest corporations, and recommended by the Foreign Affairs and International Trade Committee of the Canadian House of Commons. However, the proposal for a common security perimeter has not been embraced by the governments of either Canada or the United States. The former Canadian Deputy Prime Minister John Manley rejected the idea, which he interpreted as a "dismantling" of the border and a threat to Canadian sovereignty. He also suggested there was no interest at the "highest levels" of the U.S. government for a commonly managed border.

Nevertheless, the rejection by the Deputy Prime Minister did not prevent Canada from signing the 30-point Smart Border Declaration with the United States. Moreover, this agreement, notwithstanding Mr. Manley's remarks, in effect provides the structure and broad outline for a security perimeter and a common security shield aimed at protecting the citizens of both countries from terrorist penetration. The Smart Border Declaration entails cooperation in a number of areas such as the removal of people ordered deported from either country; the designation of terrorist organizations; the sharing of intelligence and advance information regarding travel passengers; freezing the assets of organizations suspected of financing terrorist groups; and joint training exercises between officers of both countries. A common security shield does not, as Mr. Manley suggested, imply a dismantling of the border, but more properly should be seen as an enhancement of existing border security by both Canada and the United States. As for a threat to Canadian sovereignty, this is nonsense. United States Customs and Border agents are already situated in Canada to conduct prescreening of people traveling to destinations in the United States and to assist in the inspection of sea-going containers. Furthermore, Canada is already an active partner in the North America Aerospace Defense Command (NORAD). Established in 1958, NORAD was designed to safeguard the air sovereignty of both countries and is, in effect, a defense perimeter shield of itself. Indeed, the establishment of a security shield appears to be entirely consistent with the spirit and purpose of NORAD.

It is interesting to note that the European community is gradually doing away with internal borders and allowing the free movement of citizens between member states. The EU has been able to do this by the creation of an external perimeter of immigration control for all member countries and by stepping up internal security and anti-terrorist operations. (However, it remains to be seen if the outer defenses will be effective in inhibiting the activities of Islamist terrorists, since the threat in Europe seems more likely to come from among the millions of Muslims now living in member countries.) The creation of a North American security shield seems a logical and sensible arrangement for the added protection of the citizens of both countries. Such an arrangement need not involve major policy changes on the part of either government. It could simply take the form of amending or broadening the current Smart Border Declaration, which is already providing the essential elements of a security shield, whether or not it is acknowledged as such by our political leaders.

Additional measures to supplement the current agreement might entail further agreement on a common policy for designating countries as visa-exempt for tourists and business people. Another would be to develop common guidelines concerning the type of questions to be asked of applicants for visas, together with agreement about reasons for refusal. On the Canadian side, it would be essential to reform the dysfunctional asylum policy now in effect by restricting access to the system to those arriving directly from countries not considered "safe" by the United Nations High Commissioner for Refugees. Canada would also have to bolster its capacity to detain people arriving with false documents, or without documents, until their identity was established, and vastly improve its ability to remove immigration violators.

Unfortunately, in spite of the obvious advantages to be gained, there was little likelihood of the two countries reaching formal agreement on the establishment of a security perimeter under the previous Liberal government. Contrary to what might have been expected, the September 11 attacks did not bring the two neighboring countries closer together. Indeed, in the months following the terrorist attack, Canada-U.S. relations had not been at so low a point since the end of the Civil War. Part of the explanation for this deterioration in bilateral relations is to be found in the very real concerns held by Americans about Canada's indecisive reaction to the war on terror. Other irritants adversely have been Canada's last-minute refusal to participate in the invasion of Iraq and Prime Minister Paul Martin's sudden about-face in deciding not to sign on to the Missile Defense System after initially agreeing to do so. Tactless comments about President George Bush made by some Liberal Party members of the Canadian Parliament only exacerbated an already worsening relationship. On the Canadian side, the decision by the United States to deport a Canadian citizen of Syrian origin to Syria where he claimed to have been tortured outraged many Canadians. The softwood lumber dispute and the banning of Canadian beef by U.S. authorities have also become major aggravates in the relationship.

Clearly, until relations between the two countries improve, it is unlikely that any progress can be made toward the creation of a comprehensive North American security perimeter. On a more optimistic note, the victory of the Conservative Party under the leadership of Prime Minister Stephen Harper has witnessed a decided improvement in the bilateral relationship. During the election campaign, the new Prime Minister promised to restore good relations with the United States of America. It is likely that his determination to rebuild the Canadian military, to revisit the question of the Missile Defense System, his "get tough on crime" legislation, and his more serious and forceful approach to security may indicate that a common security shield is not a dead issue. Of course, a North American security perimeter would, by logic and definition, have to include Mexico and the southern border. The possibility of this happening is even more remote than a security arrangement between Canada and the United States, as the issue with Mexico has less to do with September 11 than it has with the long-standing problem of the millions of illegal Mexicans who for years now have been crossing into the United States to find work and a higher standard of living.

Nothing illustrates the ambivalence of the United States' approach to the enforcement of its immigration laws as does the refusal of successive Aministrations to resolve the increasing problem of illegal migration from Mexico. Every attempt to do so has, in the final analysis, failed owing to a lack of political will to act in the national interest. Furthermore, as Mexico is not on Osama bin Laden's hit list, there is little incentive for Mexico City to take measures to secure the borders of the Republic of Mexico. The northern border is a different case entirely, since both countries have been identified as targets of Islamist terror and both are engaged in military action against Islamist forces. It is therefore not in the interest of the United States or Canada to go their separate ways in preparing to meet the possibility of an Islamist terrorist strike. The construction of a 4,000-mile fence is not a guarantee for preventing terrorist infiltration, and it is not a cost-effective method of deterrence. The two countries share too much in common and have been good neighbors for too long, to permit a temporary lapse in friendly relations to overrule common sense. The formation of a common security perimeter to act as an effective shield should be a first priority of both Ottawa and Washington, DC.

On the Canadian side, further consideration of a security perimeter will depend on whether the present Conservative Government under Prime Minister Stephen Harper can win a majority in the next general election. As it stands now, the opposition parties led by the Liberal Party have made it clear that they do not take the terrorist threat seriously. In the closing weeks of February 2007, the opposition parties were able to nullify two critical clauses of the Anti-terrorist legislation by outvoting a Conservative Party's attempt to have these clauses extended for a further three years. Equally disturbing was a ruling in the same month by the Supreme Court of Canada that the use of security certificates used by the Immigration Service to detain and remove foreign terrorist suspects was unconstitutional. These two setbacks have made Canada more vulnerable to terrorist activity and, at the same time, have underlined in a striking fashion that the northern border does indeed constitute a threat to the United States.

Conclusions

The tragic and preventable events of September 11 should have taught Canadians, as well as Americans, a number of basic truths about the real threat to North American security. Curiously, it is not clear that, even today, the political leaders of either country have completely grasped the real nature of that threat. As the history of the 20th century aptly demonstrated, democracies are slow to acknowledge threats to their existence, even when the enemy is at the gate.

One of the most serious drawbacks in the war against terror has been the failure of politicians to acknowledge the direct linkage between immigration and the terrorist threat. During the past 30 years, the demographic landscape of North America and Western Europe has been profoundly altered by massive immigration flows from the developing countries.

The impact has been greater in Western Europe, for which there are a number of reasons. One is that the European countries, not expecting the migrants to remain permanently, established few programs to help the newcomers integrate with the host societies. The immigrants tended to be poorly educated and unskilled. Additionally, they were concentrated in the suburbs of major urban centers. Many of them lived in public housing, on welfare, and did not learn the language of their hosts. By 2001, over 21 million foreign nationals were estimated to be living in Western Europe. As most of these immigrants were Muslim, they found it difficult to accept the values of a secular society. This was a recipe for trouble. It remains to be seen if countries like France, England, and the Netherlands will be able to successfully combat extremist Muslim terrorist activities. The large concentration of Muslims in their urban centers and the growing political power of Muslim voters make these countries particularly vulnerable to the threat of terrorism. Even if all further immigration of Muslims into Europe were to be halted, the demographic trend favoring the growth of Islam would not be.

The success of the Muslim jihadists in driving the Soviet armies from Afghanistan was an inspiring event for Muslims around the world. The victory signaled a resurgence of Islamic pride and provided hope that Islam might once again emerge as a dominant force throughout the world. It is no accident that the Islamic triumph in Afghanistan was soon followed by increased vandalism, violence, and delinquency in the Muslim enclaves in European cities. The wars in Chechnya, Bosnia, and Kosovo gave further opportunity for the spread of

Islamic radicalism—radicalism that has, ironically, been encouraged and supported by United States policies.

Incredible as it may seem, it was not until four years after September 11 that the President of the United States finally identified the war on terror as really a war against Islamic radicalism. In a speech in Washington, in October 2005, to the National Endowment for Democracy, the President for the first time defined the enemy as "radical Islam." One hopes that this speech marked a turning point in the war against Islamic fundamentalism, and that it will be followed by more realistic and focused policies designed to ensure the safety and security of North America.

The United States and Canada can have no excuse to continue the politically correct pretense that it is not Islam itself that presents the real challenge but only a tiny minority of extremist fanatics. The reality is that millions of Muslims around the world sympathize with and openly support the goals of the extremists. Of course, not all Muslims are extremists, but all the extremists are Muslims, and, like it or not, it is the rise of an aggressive and militant Islam itself that must be taken into account if the war against terror is to be won.

One of the key elements in this struggle will be to ensure that North America does not follow the European model by failing to regulate carefully and control the numbers and types of Muslim immigrants wishing to settle in the United States and Canada. All prospective immigrants from Muslim countries should be carefully examined to ensure that they are able to live comfortably in a secular society that sanctions, among other things, equality of women, gay rights, separation of church and state, religious tolerance, freedom of expression, and other values that might conflict with those held by some Muslims.

Immigration has played a primary role in the history of North America. It has been a driving force in the prosperity and affluence of both the United States and Canada, and it has enriched and broadened the cultural life of both countries. Yet uncontrolled and unrestricted immigration can do great harm to a nation. The political leaders of the United States and Canada must recognize that immigration control and the effective management of immigration programs are critical factors in ensuring the security of their citizens and the future of North America.

3

THE ECONOMICS OF ILLEGAL IMMIGRATION TO THE UNITED STATES

by David A. Hartman

Mass immigration is changing the fundamental character of America—our culture, institutions, standards, and objectives. Until recently, our society was the envy of the world, so why are these changes even necessary? In addition to the ruling class's commitment to globalism and multiculturalism, the chief reason that is given in support of open borders is the economic benefit to both the United States and the world as a whole. The burdens, however, are outweighing the alleged benefits.

The following questions will be addressed as central to those economic issues raised by immigration and its consequences:

1. Do current demographics relating to foreign-born residents in the United States foretell a net positive economic contribution to the general welfare, or a net burden of dependency?
2. What is the effect of immigration upon native employment and compensation, and upon American competitiveness in international trade?
3. What would be the economic consequences of another amnesty for illegal aliens, and the effect on the retirement of the Baby Boomers?
4. What are the economic effects of immigration regarding public equity, efficiency, and security?
5. On the basis of the answers to these questions, who are the beneficiaries, and who are the benefactors of current immigration law and its enforcement?
6. What improvements to American immigration and related public policy are evident and commendable according to the findings of this study?

It will be shown as these questions are addressed that the economic effects of immigration to the United States are generally misunderstood, resulting in the misinformation of U.S. citizens and costly public policies.

Demographics of Immigrants to the United States

To get a sense of the size of the burden, we have to look at the demographics of the current immigrant population and compare them with those of native-born U.S. citizens. A recent study by the Congressional Budget Office (CBO), released in November 2004,[1] succinctly summarizes the statistical nature of the foreign-born residents compared to the native born U.S. population. Since less than 12 percent arrived before 1965, foreign-born residents in the United States at present are representative of the immigrants that arrived since 1965. Tables 1–8 which follow were, in part, condensed from the CBO study, with augmentation of data from the U.S. Census Bureau.

Table 1: The Foreign-Born Population,
by Region of Origin and Period of Arrival, 2003

	Total	% of U.S. Pop.	Period of Arrival				
			Before 1970	1970-1979	1980-1989	1990-1999	2000 or later
Total Foreign-Born Population	33,472	11.7%	4,066	4,600	8,035	12,235	4,536
Naturalized U.S. Citizens	12,837	4.5%	3,290	3,202	3,884	2,206	255
Not U.S. Citizens	20,635	7.2%	776	1,398	4,151	10,029	4,281
Region of Origin							
Europe	4,593	1.6%	1,576	559	656	1,361	440
Asia	8,372	2.9%	502	1,439	2,285	2,981	1,164
Latin America	17,840	6.2%	1,538	2,292	4,536	6,910	2,563
Other Areas	2,667	0.9%	449	309	558	983	368
Total U.S. Population	285,933	n.a.	n.a.	n.a.	n.a.	n.a.	n.a.

Note: All figures are in thousands unless noted.

Sources: Congressional Budget Office using data from Department of Commerce, Bureau of the Census, Current Population Survey: Annual Social and Economic Supplement (March 2003).

As of 2003, foreign-born residents who arrived before 1970 made up less than two percent of the total U.S. population, and, of these, 81 percent were naturalized U.S. citizens. Total foreign-born residents, however, were 12 percent of the population, and 62 percent of them were not U.S. citizens. Those who had arrived before 1970 were primarily Europeans and Latin Americans — 39 and 38 percent of the total, respectively. As of 2003, however, 53 percent of foreign-born residents were Latin Americans, 25 percent were Asians, and only 14 percent were Europeans.

Table 2: Native and Foreign-Born Populations, by Region and Age, 2003

Age	Native Pop.	Foreign-Born Pop.	Region of Origin of Foreign-Born Population			
			Europe	Asia	Latin America	Other Areas
Under 18	27.9	8.9	6.0	7.8	10.3	8.0
18 to 34	22.0	33.2	18.5	30.3	38.4	33.1
35 to 54	28.4	37.3	32.6	40.8	36.8	38.2
55 and Older	21.7	20.5	42.9	21.1	14.5	20.5
Total	100.0	100.0	100.0	100.0	100.0	100.0
Median Age (Years)	35.1	38.4	50.4	40.0	35.5	38.7

Notes: All figures are percentages.

Sources: Congressional Budget Office using data from Department of Commerce, Bureau of the Census, Current Population Survey: Annual Social and Economic Supplement (March 2003).

The age distributions for immigrants by country of origin as shown in Table 2 do not differ significantly in total from those for native Americans, except that they appear to have a lower proportion of children under 18 years of age. This reflects the fact that most immigrants come to the United States as adults, while their children born in the United States are classified as natives. When these distributions are corrected for children, the differences are significantly reduced. The immigrants, in general, have moderately higher fertility rates than do natives. On average, immigrants will retire with a slightly greater substitution of offspring as workers to support their retirement.

Fertility provides a back door for immigration, as any baby born here is automatically a U.S. citizen. This, in turn, makes it easier for his parents to be eligible for naturalization. It is all too common for pregnant Mexicans, in order to secure citizenship for their children, to cross the border and present themselves at American hospitals that cannot legally refuse them care.

Table 3: Employment Status of the Native and Foreign-Born Working-Age Populations, by Region of Origin, March 2003

Employment Status	Native Pop.	Foreign-Born Pop.	Region of Origin of Foreign-Born Population		
			Europe	Asia	Latin America
Total Population					
Civilian Working-Age Population	143,999	26,012	2,860	6,800	14,245
Labor Force	114,104	19,775	2,166	5,062	10,922
Labor Force Participation Rate (%)	79.2	76.0	75.7	74.4	76.7
Unemployment Rate (%)	5.6	7.2	4.6	6.3	8.3
Men					
Civilian Working-Age Population	70,064	13,242	1,373	3,182	7,564
Labor Force	59,470	11,732	1,162	2,742	6,858
Labor Force Participation Rate (%)	84.9	88.6	84.6	86.2	90.7
Unemployment Rate (%)	6.2	6.8	6.0	5.2	7.8
Women					
Civilian Working-Age Population	73,935	12,770	1,487	3,618	6,681
Labor Force	54,634	8,044	1,004	2,320	4,063
Labor Force Participation Rate (%)	73.9	63.0	67.5	64.1	60.8
Unemployment Rate (%)	5.0	7.7	3.0	7.4	9.2

Notes: All figures are in thousands unless noted. The data cover people ages 20 to 64.

Sources: Congressional Budget Office using data from Department of Commerce, Bureau of the Census, Current Population Survey: Annual Social and Economic Supplement (March 2003).

The workforce-participation rates of foreign-born citizens differ little among ethnic groups, but they are moderately lower than native rates, primarily because fewer foreign-born women work. The unemployment rates of Asians and Latin Americans are higher than those of native workers, with significantly higher unemployment rates for women—whereas men make up the majority in the unemployment line among native workers.

Table 4: Occupations of the Native and Foreign-Born Populations, by Region of Origin, 2003

Occupation	Native Pop.	Foreign-Born Pop.	Region of Origin of Foreign-Born Population			
			Europe	Asia	Latin America	Other Areas
Management, Professional, and Related	36.2	26.9	41.3	47.0	12.7	37.6
Sales and Office Occupations	27.4	18.0	21.8	22.0	15.1	19.4
Service Occupations	14.9	23.3	15.4	15.0	29.3	20.4
Production, Transportation, and Material Moving	12.1	18.4	11.8	12.0	23.5	14.7
Construction, Extraction, and Maintenance	9.0	11.8	9.4	3.5	16.9	7.1
Farming, Fishing, and Forestry	0.5	1.6	0.3	0.4	2.5	0.7
Total	100.0	100.0	100.0	100.0	100.0	100.0

Notes: All figures are percentages.

Sources: Congressional Budget Office using data from Department of Commerce, Bureau of the Census, Current Population Survey: Annual Social and Economic Supplement (March 2003).

Comparison of foreign-born versus native workers by occupation shows comparable distribution, except for Latin Americans who differ very significantly, with 72 percent employed in blue-collar jobs compared to 36 percent for native workers.

Table 5: Distribution of Earnings, Native & Foreign-Born Workers, 2003

Earnings in 2003	Total Pop.	Native Pop.	Foreign-Born Population		
			Naturalized Citizen	Not U.S. Citizen	Year of Entry 2000 to March 2004
Persons 15 years old and over with earnings	100.0	100.0	100.0	100.0	100.0
Under $15,000	8.9	7.8	8.3	19.6	24.5
$15,000 to $24,999	19.5	17.8	21.0	34.2	33.0
$25,000 to $34,999	19.9	20.3	19.0	17.0	13.6
$35,000 to $49,999	21.4	22.3	20.1	12.9	13.7
$50,000 to $74,999	17.3	18.2	16.8	9.0	8.3
$75,000 and over	13.1	13.6	14.9	7.2	6.9
Median earnings	$35,795	$36,784	$35,813	$23,140	$21,762

Notes: All figures are percentages unless noted.

Sources: Statistical Abstract of the U.S., 2006, U.S. Census Bureau. Table 45, p. 46.

The earnings distribution for individual workers shown in Table 5 should be viewed in context of the median 2003 earnings—$35,795—for all workers. It will be seen that naturalized workers have a very comparable distribution by earning brackets compared to native Americans. "Not U.S. citizens" have substantially lower incomes on average compared to either native or natural-ized citizens, with 71 percent below median total. However, Latin American immigrants are even more heavily distributed in lower-paid income brackets, with 74 percent of men and 81 percent of women below U.S. median worker earnings as of 2003.[2] Noncitizen workers have a comparably low distribution of earnings, primarily because Latin Americans comprise the majority of illegal workers.

Table 6: Distribution of Family Earnings,
Native & Foreign-Born Workers, 2003

Income in 2003	Native Pop.	Foreign-Born Population			
		Naturalized Citizen	Not U.S. Citizen	Latin American	Year of Entry 2000 to March 2004
Persons 15 years old and over with earnings	100.0	100.0	100.0	100.0	100.0
Under $15,000	8.3	8.3	15.2	14.7	19.8
$15,000 to $24,999	10.1	11.6	17.8	19.1	17.7
$25,000 to $34,999	10.8	10.8	15.7	17.6	16.8
$35,000 to $49,999	15.1	15.2	16.7	17.5	15.7
$50,000 to $74,999	21.0	20.0	16.1	16.3	14.7
$75,000 and over	34.6	34.1	18.5	14.8	15.2
Median earnings	$55,914	$54,520	$35,804	$33,963	$31,930

Notes: All figures are percentages unless noted.

Sources: Statistical Abstract of the U.S., 2006, U.S. Census Bureau. Tables 43 & 45, pp. 45-46.

Distribution of family incomes are shown in Table 6, comparing natives, naturalized, and noncitizen populations. The distribution of incomes of naturalized citizens compared to natives is much the same for both families and individual workers. This is not the case for non-U.S. citizens and Latin Americans, who are again skewed toward the lower income brackets for families. Furthermore, an additional distribution for entrants from 2000 to March 2004 shows that six million migrants had an even lower median income. This represents an increase of over 1.4 million per year in the immigrant population, as reported by the U.S. Census Bureau for the 4¼ year period 2000 thru March 2004.

Table 7 shows that educational attainment is reasonably comparable between the native population and the immigrants of origins other than Latin American; half of the latter are not high school graduates, and a quarter hold

Table 7: Educational Attainment of the Population Age 25 or Older,
by Region of Origin and Sex, 2003

	Native Pop.	Foreign-Born Pop.	Region of Origin of Foreign-Born Population				
			Europe	Asia	Latin America	Central America	Other Areas
Less than High School Diploma	12.5	32.8	15.1	12.6	50.9	61.2	16.5
High School Graduate	33.3	24.5	30.9	20.7	24.5	23.0	24.6
Some College or Associate's Degree	27.0	15.5	18.6	16.7	13.0	9.8	21.7
Bachelor's Degree	18.1	17.2	19.9	30.9	8.3	4.7	24.2
Advanced Degree	9.1	10.0	15.5	19.1	3.3	1.4	13.0

Notes: All figures are percentages. Data are by years of school completed, not attended.

Sources: Department of Commerce, Bureau of the Census, Current Population Survey: Annual Social and Economic Supplement (March 2003).

only high school diplomas. Central Americans (principally Mexicans) account for two-thirds of the Latin American population with even fewer educational skills. Comparison of Table 7 to Table 5 shows that distribution of education skills predicts earnings distributions, particularly as an explanation of earnings below the median, as reported previously by George J. Borjas.[3]

Given the obvious correlation of earnings with skills, it comes as no surprise that the distribution of poverty level by age of naturalized citizens is comparable across age groups to that of native Americans, as shown in Table 8. Immigrants who are not citizens have twice the proportion of poverty of natives across the range of children, workers, and retirees.

The educational employment, earnings, and poverty distributions for non-Latin Americans closely mirror those for native Americans, whereas those for all foreign workers do not. From the fact that the inferior distribution of earnings for "Latin American foreign born" mirrors that of "non-U.S. citizens" and the clear inference

Table 8: Percentage of the Native and Foreign-Born Populations at or Below the Poverty Level, by Age

	Native Pop.	Foreign-Born Pop.	Foreign-Born Population	
			Naturalized U.S. Citizen	Not U.S. Citizen
All Ages	11.5	16.6	10.0	20.7
Under 18	16.2	28.5	16.4	31.0
18 to 64	9.7	15.6	9.2	19.2
65 and Older	9.9	14.7	11.9	21.0

Notes: All figures are percentages.

Sources: Department of Commerce, Bureau of the Census, Current Population Survey: Annual Social and Economic Supplement (March 2003).

of other demographics as well, it is evident that the illegal immigrant population (led by those from Mexico) comprises primarily Latin American immigrants.

As will subsequently be shown, illegal immigrants depress U.S. wages and salaries, increase the burden of welfare, and add to the costs of insecurity.

Effect of Illegal Immigration on U.S. Employment, Compensation, and Growth

Starting around 1972, the average real compensation per unit of output of all U.S. private-sector employees, both salaried and hourly, began to plummet—a trend that has continued to the present. "Real compensation" comprises earnings plus fringe benefits and payroll taxes, CPI adjusted for inflation, and "all private employees" include hourly and salaried personnel. This general decline of nearly one-quarter was far exceeded by the U.S. manufacturing sector, which declined by nearly one-half as shown in Table 9.

Basically, during this period, all private business-sector employees were receiving a decreasing share of real Gross Domestic Product (the measure of

Table 9: Trends of U.S. Employee Productivity & Compensation, 1955-2005

Year	Business Sector			Manufacturing Sector		
	Output per hour	Real Hourly Compensation	Compensation per Unit of Output	Output per Hour	Real Hourly Compensation	Compensation per Unit of Output
%Chg. 05/65	132.1%	76.4%	(24.0%)	252.9%	79.5%	(49.1%)
2005	136.55	121.84	89.23	171.15	128.53	75.10
%Chg. 05/95	34.5%	23.5%	(8.2%)	55.6%	28.4%	(17.5%)
1995	101.50	98.68	97.22	109.96	100.08	91.01
%Chg. 95/85	16.5%	7.3%	(7.9%)	33.6%	5.0%	(21.4%)
1985	87.13	91.96	105.54	82.30	95.30	115.8
%Chg. 85/75	16.5%	9.3%	(6.2%)	28.0%	11.6%	(12.8%)
1975	74.79	84.12	112.47	64.30	85.40	132.81
%Chg. 75/65	27.2%	21.8%	(4.2%)	32.6%	19.3%	(10.0%)
1965	58.82	69.08	117.44	48.50	71.60	147.63
%Chg. 65/55	34.8%	32.3%	(1.9%)	25.0%	27.0%	1.6%
1955	43.62	52.21	119.69	38.80	56.40	145.36

Notes: Bureau of Labor Statistics indices, 1992=100

Sources: U.S. Department of Labor, Bureau of Labor Statistics, Major Sector Productivity and Costs Index

output). Moreover, the earnings of all production workers (those paid by the hour) per unit of output declined by more than half, and, in manufacturing, by nearly 70 percent. These exhibits are based upon Bureau of Labor Statistics data, as presented in Table 10.

Curiously, unemployment rates first rose and then fell over this period. Labor had little pricing power, but the reduction in the cost of labor created new service-sector jobs, which filled the gap.

Many changing economic forces affecting supply and demand for goods and services, and for employees, must be considered to determine which were primarily causal. Without question, the augmentation of the workforce by the Baby Boomers following on the limited supply of Depression Babies was the largest

Table 10: Trends of U.S. Production Workers' Productivity & Earnings, 1955-2005

Year	Business Sector			Manufacturing Sector		
	Output per hour	Real Hourly Earnings in 2005$	Earnings per Unit of Output	Output per Hour	Real Hourly Earnings in 2005$	Earnings per Unit of Output
%Chg. 05/65	132.1%	1.7%	(56.4%)	252.9%	7.2%	(69.7%)
2005	136.55	$15.96	79.00	171.15	$16.56	61.00
%Chg. 05/95	34.5%	8.5%	(19.4%)	55.6%	4.7%	(33.0%)
1995	101.50	$14.71	98.00	109.96	$15.81	91.00
%Chg. 95/85	16.5%	(4.8%)	(18.3%)	33.6%	(7.3%)	(30.5%)
1985	87.13	$15.45	120.00	82.30	$17.06	131.00
%Chg. 85/75	16.5%	(6.6%)	(20.0%)	28.0%	(0.1%)	(21.6%)
1975	74.79	$16.54	150.00	64.3	$17.07	167.00
%Chg. 75/65	27.2%	5.4%	(17.1%)	32.6%	10.5%	(16.9%)
1965	58.82	$15.69	181.00	48.5	$15.45	201.00
%Chg. 65/55	34.8%			25.0%		
1955	43.62			38.80		

Notes: Bureau of Labor Statistics indices, 1992=100

Sources: U.S. Department of Labor, Bureau of Labor Statistics, Major Sector Productivity and Costs Index

single force affecting the supply of workers. But at the same time, the Boomers added an offsetting source of demand for goods and services. The transition to the Information Age is supposed to have created demand for more skilled workers, but, over the past two decades, this was not apparent in the United States from the constant ratio of hourly to salaried workers in the private-business sector. Despite the rate of increase of productivity in manufacturing—twice that of the private-business sector as a whole—a rising flood of imports cut the U.S. workforce's share of manufacturing workers by 60 percent, driving them to seek employment in other sectors. Workers with greater skills sustained their incomes by adjusting to the new technologies, but the surplus of unskilled workers found employment in highly price-sensitive services sectors and faced stagnant hourly rates and fewer available hours to work, which meant a severe cut in pay.

Even an increase in fringe benefits could not prevent the share of personal income for private-sector employees from declining. (Of course, along with more fringe benefits came higher FICA taxes, whose gleanings were redistributed from workers to retirees, as well as an inflation of health-insurance costs that provided lesser coverage and only favored healthcare providers.) The increase of women in the workplace, particularly married mothers whose families could not make ends meet, was as much an effect as a cause of the extra supply of labor and the depression of income among unskilled workers overall.

To this indigenous list of augmentations of supply to the U.S. workforce were added two exogenous factors, which have also played a major role in the depression of U.S. workers' incomes. They were the gratuitous gifts of the U.S. federal government to the world at large: nonreciprocal free trade and porous borders for immigration.

The United States has led the world in reducing tariffs with the goal of global free trade without the impediment of tariffs. But the rest of the world has replaced tariffs with border-adjusted taxes—value-added taxes or retail sales taxes—which serve the same role as tariffs. Mostly VATs, these border adjusted taxes are rebated on their exports (to the United States) with the average effect of 18 percent tax subsidies, while they are levied on average as an 18-percent double taxation on U.S. exports, since U.S. manufacturers receive no comparable rebate of U.S. taxes. The effect is reciprocal for all the foreign countries with border-adjusted taxation, but not for the United States, with the consequence of a U.S. trade deficit on goods with virtually every trade partner. Foreign VATs have had a devastating effect on the manufacturing sector, which now produces goods equal to only two-thirds of the goods the United States consumes, with consequent loss of better-paying jobs equal to more than ten percent of the U.S. workforce. Business services are facing a comparable problem due to outsourcing to foreign workers; *Business Week* estimates that 14 million business service jobs may be at risk.[4] Since foreign border-adjusted taxation does not double-tax capital, it encourages saving for investment, compared to U.S. income taxation that does double-tax investment and encourages consumption over saving (witness the downtrend in U.S. personal saving, now at negative net personal saving).

Some make the case that immigration serves a useful purpose for the United States by providing skilled workers who are currently in short supply—for example, doctors from India who help to fill vacancies and contain runaway health care costs. (Why the world's largest producer cannot provide its own skilled workers in such fields is a separate question.) Even if the argument were valid, a similar case could not be made for the unskilled workers who currently account for two-thirds of the U.S. foreign-born population and three-quarters of Latin American immigrants.

One cannot exactly determine the relative extent to which open-border immigration of unskilled workers versus nonreciprocal free trade has depressed U.S. hourly workers' earnings. However, comparison of earnings in current dollars as of 1972 compared to 2005, subsequent to the Immigration Act of 1965, in Table 11 for the economic sectors that hire the bulk of unskilled immigrants shows what excessive labor supply has done to earnings. Reductions of weekly wages over this period, ranging from four percent to 40 percent, averaging nine percent for all hourly workers in the U.S. private sector, clearly reflect both the effects of the unskilled immigrant invasion and the reemployment of the exodus of workers from manufacturing to services at lower hourly earnings.

Table 11: Production Workers Weekly Earnings for Selected
& All Private Industries 1972 vs. 2005, 2005$

Industry	1972			2005			% Change
	Hourly Earnings	Weekly Hours	Weekly Earnings	Hourly Earnings	Weekly Hours	Weekly Earnings	
Construction	$25.89	36.90	$955	$19.45	38.48	$748	(21.6%)
Manufacturing	$17.28	40.50	$700	$16.56	40.60	$672	(4.0%)
Retailing	$16.46	35.10	$578	$12.36	30.60	$378	(34.5%)
Transport & Warehousing	$25.31	40.80	$1032	$16.71	37.00	$618	(40.1%)
Leisure & Hospitality	$9.49	29.70	$282	$9.14	25.70	$235	(16.7%)
All Private Production Workers	$16.08	36.90	$593	$15.96	33.80	$539	(9.1%)

Sources: U.S. Department of Labor, Bureau of Labor Statistics, Employment, Hours, and Earnings from the Current Employment Statistics Survey (National)

As any economist can tell you, there is no such thing as "the unemployed" but rather workers at the margin of productivity unwilling to work for the prevailing marginal wage. The question is, what marginal wage—that of the applicable wage prevailing in Latin America, in Africa, or in Asia? It seems only fair that American workers, as citizens, should be entitled, at minimum, to a living family wage, without artificial depression of wages as the result of allowing a limitless number of unskilled workers, whether legal or not, to enter the United States; and that workers should not be subjected to the depressing effects on U.S. prices and outputs of goods and services that are primarily born by labor's wages as the consequence of bogus nonreciprocal free trade benefiting foreign producers and runaway U.S. producers exporting to the U.S. from abroad.

The coming increase in the ratio of retirees to workers to be caused by the aging of the Baby Boomers has prompted fears that the Social Security and Medicare trusts will soon be insolvent. Immigration will help solve this problem, but only if it is targeted at skilled workers; "next of kin" immigrants, as well as refugees and those seeking asylum, will push the unskilled labor markets to the limits, depressing wages, and adding to public burdens for retirement welfare benefits. Amnesty for illegal immigrant workers would cost in unearned retirement entitlements an additional burden being overlooked by those who regard immigrants as a source for contributions to an aging America.

The Public Welfare Burden of Amnesty

Before 1965, the requirement of sponsors and the denial of public welfare to immigrants were principal assurances that immigration to the United States would be in the economic public interest. Since that year, owing to the liberal zeal to redistribute income under the welfare programs of the Great Society, immigrants of lower income classifications became eligible for a wide range of welfare programs. Since then, the Personal Responsibility and Work Opportunity Reconciliation Act of 1996 passed by Congress included in its broad reform of welfare entitlements stricter limitations for eligibility of immigrants than were generally in effect.

As this act was further augmented by the Balanced Budget Act of 1997, and the Deficit Reduction Act of 2005, the general public mistakenly perceived welfare for immigrants to be effectively terminated, and no longer an issue. However, naturalized citizens have not been denied access to welfare entitlements in general, but are only required to wait for five years from date of naturalization. Refugees and asylum aliens may receive welfare for seven years after entering the United States, under present law, which also allows other need-based aid, at the discretion of the states, to most legal immigrants who have lived in the United States for five years.

While this legislation does clearly address ending entitlements for illegal immigrants, other legal rights granted by U.S. Supreme Court decisions supersede much of its purported intent. Regardless of an end to Medicaid eligibility for illegal aliens, no hospital can legally deny "emergency" treatment, which includes much of what Medicaid would cover (at twice the cost). Similarly, the other most costly welfare entitlement, public education, cannot be denied by a school district for a resident child, legal or not. Even harder to explain is why Mexican children are allowed to attend U.S. schools along the border without qualifications of residency, citizenship, or tuition payment.

Table 12: Texas Costs of Illegal Immigration

Item	Costs	
Public Education	$3.746 billion	
Higher Education	$34.5 million	
Education	$3.781 billion	
Health and Human Services	**State**	**Federal**
Health Care	$572.5 million	$385.5 million
Criminal Justice	$119 million	
Cost of Illegal Immigration	$4.47 billion	
Tax Receipts (Sales 60%, Property 40%)	$965 million	
Net Cost of Illegal Immigration	$3.51 billion	

Sources: Bernsen, James, "The Cost of Illegal Immigration to Texas," The Lone Star Foundation, Austin, TX, 2006, p.2.

According to James Bernsen of the Lone Star Foundation, the cost of providing public education to immigrants significantly exceeds the costs borne by the state of Texas for health care, human services, and criminal justice for immigrants. In total, Texas is spending a net $3.5 billion per year on immigrants ($4.5 billion per year minus $1 billion in estimated taxes collected). Bernsen considered various estimates and concluded that the best guess of the number of illegal immigrants currently in Texas is 1.5 million. Extrapolation of CBO estimates as of the year 2000, together with recent U.S. Census Bureau updates that reveal 444,000 more estimated annual entrants than legally admitted since 2000, yields an estimate of 13 billion illegal immigrants in the United States as of 2006. Since Texas is relatively frugal in dispensing welfare, a conservative national estimate of the annual cost of welfare at the state and local levels for 13 million illegal aliens would be $30 billion.

The cost of immigration in terms of welfare benefits in the event of a sweeping amnesty granted to illegal immigrants is the most underestimated of all. This is due to cost of retirement entitlements, owing to the lower skills distribution of this group and its consequent lower earnings distribution. It can be shown that personal income tax payments made by families of lower-income workers, as well as FICA taxes (often negated by Earned Income Credit), do not come close to funding the composite cost of their Social Security and Medicare retirement benefits.

Estimates, prepared by Bernsen, of the net lifetime cost of Social Security and Medicare benefits incurred by a representative demographic range of low-income "amnesty naturalized" U.S. citizens are shown in Table 13, the methodology for which requires explanation. The range of representative cases were selected to examine costs for married and single households, with and without children, at two household income levels representing income brackets, so as to include the lower income range of family earnings for three retirement ages and two sets of life expectancies.

The public welfare burden of retirement was determined as the sum of personal FIT (adjusted for EIC) plus personal and employer-paid FICA taxes, less Social Security income per the entitlement schedule, and Medicare average benefits from date of retirement through life expectancy. The results were shocking: Net retirement cost to the public ranges from $435,000 to $20,000 per family for 42 of the 48 representative family cases evaluated, with only six public benefit outcomes ranging from $6,000 to $90,000 per family.

In order to estimate the total cost of amnesty, the number of excess lower-income noncitizen families was determined by comparison with the income distribution of native-born citizen families. Used together, the married vs. single, with and without children, demographics were applied to median net costs. The estimated consequent cost of the public retirement burden caused by amnesty of the present illegal alien population is $350 billion, for an average of $157,000 per family naturalized by amnesty. It should be noted that these costs are stated at present, not future, value; Social Security and Medicare premiums and benefits are inflated annually based upon increases in average employee compensation, which substitutes for adjustment of future retirement benefits for the time value of money. Since the illegal aliens costs did not all arrive in a single year, the potential $350 billion liability figure was accumulated over a period of years.

Table 13: Estimated Net Lifetime Cost of Social Security and
Medicare Benefits for Low-Income Naturalized Immigrants

Household Earnings: $26,000 per year

	Retire at 62 (B)	Retire at 62 (A)	Retire at 65 (B)	Retire at 65 (A)	Retire at 67 (B)	Retire at 67 (A)
Married, kids	(241,510)	(448,365)	(116,337)	(324,452)	(40,878)	(256,073)
Married, no kids	(188,342)	(395,197)	(63,169)	(271,284)	13,253	(201,942)
Single, kids	(254,372)	(461,227)	(129,118)	(337,233)	(52,642)	(267,837)
Single, no kids	(181,920)	(388,775)	.	(56,240)	(264,355)	20,520	(194,675)

Household Earnings: $34,700 per year

	Retire at 62 (B)	Retire at 62 (A)	Retire at 65 (B)	Retire at 65 (A)	Retire at 67 (B)	Retire at 67 (A)
Married, kids	(172,038)	(378,893)	(49,220)	(262,591)	30,826	(190,345)
Married, no kids	(148,214)	(355,069)	(23,377)	(236,748)	56,669	(164,502)
Single, kids	(223,772)	(430,627)	(98,650)	(312,021)	(18,414)	(239,585)
Single, no kids	(144,604)	(351,459)	(19,482)	(232,853)	60,754	(160,417)

Notes: All figures are in dollars.
*A = life expectancy of all races, which is 75 for men and 80 for women.
*B = life expectancy for African-Americans, which is 69 for men and 75 for women. Although specific numbers for immigrants (mostly Hispanics) are not available, available research indicates it lies between these two numbers.

Sources: Bernsen, James, "The Cost of Illegal Immigration to Texas," The Lone Star Foundation, Austin, TX, 2006, p.4.

But it does tell us that an additional 444,000 illegal aliens per year, at current estimate, could carry a future actuarial amnesty bill of $44 billion per year as the cost of retirement of future amnestied aliens.

And there is an additional cost of amnesty, often forgotten. As soon as an illegal alien is amnestied and naturalized, his spouse, brothers and sisters, grandparents and children, and perhaps their families as well—all of them likely to be low-skilled—are entitled to citizenship as well. Because the Census Bureau reports, as of 2004, show that 82 percent of immigrants admitted to the United States belonged to the categories "family sponsored" and "immediate relative," the price of amnesty including relatives will clearly be far higher than estimates for the immediately amnestied illegal aliens alone suggest.

Another overlooked, though major, cost of immigration relates to required capital investment for infrastructure and employment. The nondefense infrastructure that government provides for transportation, education, water supply, sanitation, and other public services require investment cost of $8.4 trillion dollars at current value, in terms of public investment since 1960.[5] This amounts to $58,700 per worker, to which each immigrant would be entitled by naturalization or an amnesty. The 40 percent of families who pay no family income taxes—the same earning brackets in which the majority of illegal alien families fall—will require investment in these services at other Americans' expense. At the same time, the average worker requires $96,600 in private investment per worker employed, based upon $13.3 trillion in tangible assets as estimated by the IRS at cost.[6] The lower income families, on average, are not creating personal savings (other than remissions forwarded to the "old country") that would help create the investment required for their employment. A total of $158,000 investment allocated to each illegal alien naturalized as a citizen on good faith argues for sound economic selection criteria before citizenship is considered.

Effect of Illegal Immigration on Public Efficiency and Security

According to the U.S. Census Bureau, in 2003, English was not the language spoken at home in 42.2 million U.S. households, which translates into 18 percent of the country and 35 percent of the households in the southern border states (Texas, New Mexico, Arizona, and California). Of the 25 largest American cities, the highest proportion of households speaking a language other than English was found in El Paso (76.5 percent) and Los Angeles (59.9 percent). This balkanization of America is similar to that caused by the great wave of immigration that began in the 1880s, which led to the public outcry of the 1920s, culminating in the Immigration Act of 1924.

A study by the Dallas Federal Reserve Bank found that students in public schools on the American side of the border had higher illiteracy rates than those on the Mexican side, which is partly the result of the insistence of U.S. schools on bilingual education. The poor communication skills of these immigrants contribute to high levels of welfare dependency and crime; Latin American immigrants are twice as likely as native-born Americans to have incomes at or below the poverty level.

Ethnic areas in which immigrants are not assimilated are hotbeds for gang activity and organized crime, particularly the narcotics trade. It has been estimated that 70 percent of criminal behavior is related to narcotics distribution or addiction. The basic security of Americans is being threatened by immigrant gangs, as drugs imported by aliens are sold openly on the streets. Reasonable criteria for the admission of immigrants include the possession of adequate useful employment skills, and, for naturalization, proficiency in the English language. The United States, until now the world's most successful and envied nation, is conducting a dangerous experiment in creating a borderless multicultural society. The Research Director of the Center for Immigration Studies, Steven Camarota,[7] has conducted an eye-opening inquiry as to how 48 terrorists came to this country to implement five lethal attacks successfully, starting in 1993 and culminating with the second attack on the World Trade Center on September 11, 2001. Camarota relates that 45 of the 48 terrorists had official contact at ports of entry; 41 were approved for entry visas by U.S. consulates; five were naturalized citizens; and 13 had overstayed visas. Virtually all had reasonable grounds for refusal of admission to the United States, if anyone had checked them out properly. So much for the purported benefits of open borders. The consequent costs are the repugnant regimentation of native Americans, the terrorist incidents themselves, and "homeland security" that cannot be a reality absent secure borders.

The United States is being invaded—literally—by Central Americans pouring across our southern border. The disinclination of these illegal immigrants to speak English and assimilate, their welfare requirements, their depression of U.S. workers' incomes, and their sheer numbers are intolerable. Washington must demand that the Mexican government stop this illegal invasion of our borders. With Mexican cooperation—militarily, if necessary—a regulated temporary-worker program can be possible. Without such cooperation, the erection of a physical barrier, reenforced by the U.S. military, will be necessary, along with the complete cessation of all employment assistance to their excess workers. The United States simply can no longer ignore the effects of excessive illegal immigration—and the eventual Mexican annexation of the border states, which is the inevitable consequence of our current policy.

The United States must adopt an effective temporary-worker program, much like the one Canada uses. Transportation and its costs are borne by employers.

Wages are the prevailing level for Canadian workers. A large proportion of the earnings are withheld until the workers return home. The workers are employed on a yearly basis and must return home annually. Living quarters and working conditions must meet state standards. An agent of the Mexican government is available to police the workers and resolve problems. The Mexican government chooses the workers who participate in the program. The workers get the jobs they need, the effect on prevailing wages is regulated, employers get the workers they seek, and immigration of unwanted citizens is reduced.

The Beneficiaries and Benefactors of Illegal Immigration to the United States

The principal economic beneficiaries of illegal immigration to this country fall into three categories: the immigrants themselves, their employers, and consumers. Typically, the immigrants and their families improve their incomes and standard of living substantially. Employers benefit from depressed wages and salaries, along with an increase in sales, particularly as a result of poorly paid hourly workers employed in highly priced elastic services markets, conducive to higher profits and higher returns of capital. Consumers, in general, also benefit from the depression of wage compensation resulting in lower prices, in particular for personal services enjoyed principally by upper-income Americans. Lower prices of goods also have been due to competition by foreign producers and U.S. manufacturers who have moved production overseas (owing to Washington's failure to adopt reciprocal border adjusted consumption taxation), but an excess supply of low-skilled immigrants has had an effect on domestic production prices as well.

The principal victims of the Immigration Act of 1965 and subsequent immigration legislation have been the native-born workers who have seen their earnings stagnate or decline due to the added supply of migrant labor—most particularly, hourly labor. Other benefactors are the three-fifths of all Americans who pay personal income taxes to subsidize below-poverty-level hourly wages with welfare entitlements (in reality subsidies to their employers).

Overall, the investors, professionals, managers, and government workers who shared the benefits of the growing import of goods and services have prospered at the expense of less skilled or unskilled workers, as witnessed by the growing gap between upper- and lower-income distributions in the private sector.

Summary Observations and Recommendations

The findings of this inquiry provide clear-cut answers to the questions posed at its outset.

The demographics of immigration since 1965 show two distinct roads taken by immigrants to the United States: legal admission leading to naturalization and citizenship and illegal entry in search of amnesty. Since the demographics of naturalized citizens are reasonably comparable to those of native Americans with respect to age, education, and income distributions, the admission of these people is probably justifiable in economic terms. By contrast, illegal entrants, mostly Latin American, have substantially lower incomes and less educational attainment on average than the native-born. Despite legislation passed in 1996 and subsequently, those illegal immigrants still qualify for an estimated $30 billion per year in welfare benefits—principally public education and health care mandated by the U.S. Supreme Court—in addition to unemployment benefits.

Since the early 1970s, increased immigration has shown a depressing effect on the incomes of workers in the private business sector, particularly the less-skilled hourly workers. This resulted in the rapid growth of highly price-sensitive, low-wage personal service sectors as opposed to the manufacturing sector, which has been severely depressed by foreign border-adjusted value-added taxation starting in the late 1960s that, in effect, tax-subsidizes exports to the United States and double-taxes U.S. exports to foreign markets.

Amnestying illegal aliens would not be beneficial overall in alleviating the burden of retired Baby Boomers and retirees thereafter. While providing additional workers in the near term, they would comprise an excessive proportion of low-income families paying little or no income taxes, thus accumulating a net public future burden of $350 billion, at present value, in Social Security and Medicare expenses upon retirement as naturalized citizens. This figure probably represents a small fraction of the cost of the expected total retirement burden, given the flood of "family sponsored" and "immediate" relatives, which would be consequent to the amnesty tidal wave.

The cost of public investment in infrastructure amounting to $58,700 per worker, and the employment of private investment at $99,600 per worker, means discretionary immigration should be limited to skilled workers capable of paying, through taxes, for their share of infrastructure investment while enabling saving for private investment purposes. An excess of low-income workers who arrive in the United States as illegal aliens find ways to secure legal residency, together with their subsequently admitted relatives, in addition to asylum and refugee entrants. Admission of workers employable in sectors characterized by depressed wages and salaries, or excessive unemployment rates, should be limited.

There is persuasive evidence that the foreign-born population is more unassimilated than is desirable in the interest of functional social cohesion, as is demonstrated by the reliance on foreign languages within communities of the foreign-born. Such groups lack the proficiency in the English language necessary to optimum schooling and constructive civic participation, and are principle sources of organized crime in the United States. Both the drug trade that is related to 70 percent of criminality in the United States, and the terrorism that threatens homeland security, come to the United States through porous borders that must be secured, and reside in ghettos that should be dispersed.

All things considered, we may conclude that the principal economic beneficiaries of immigration to the United States fall into three categories: the immigrants themselves; their employers, particularly in the service sectors of the economy; and those consumers with higher incomes who desire more and cheaper personal services. The principal losers are the native workers whose incomes have been depressed by the excessive supply of illegal aliens. The three-fifths of Americans who pay income taxes that subsidize the below-poverty-level wages paid to lower-income native and immigrant workers alike with public welfare lose out as well.

What then, are the rational steps necessary to best serve the interests of the United States and its citizens for reform of U.S. immigration?

1. *Limitation of Amendment XIV, Section 1, of the U.S. Constitution*
   The XIV Amendment, Section 1, was adopted in 1868 with the intention of protecting citizenship for emancipated slaves and their offspring. The right to citizenship for children of aliens born in the United States by chance or intent (with resultant preferential status to secure naturalization for their parents and next of kin) is uncommon in other nations, and unjustifiable. The Fourteenth Amendment should be amended for Section 1 to read: "All persons born to U.S. citizens or naturalized . . ." to remedy this unintended source of immigration.

2. *Amend the Constitution for English as the Official Language for the U.S. Government*
   Ironically, English has become the worldwide language but is no longer the official language of the United States. Adoption of this amendment would end inefficient bilingual schools (replaced where necessary by English immersion), accelerate absorption of immigrants and their offspring, and help eliminate illegal voting and welfare.

3. *Establish Formal Programs for Temporary Alien Workers*
   End illegal immigrant employment (and thereby eliminate the major reason for illegal immigrations) by federal government regulated temporary worker programs. The guidelines should use the principles used by Canada for its temporary worker program. Transportation and its

costs are borne by the employer. Wages are set at the prevailing level for Canadian workers. A sizable portion of the earnings are withheld until the workers return home. The workers are employed on an annual basis, and must return home annually. Living quarters and working conditions must meet state standards. The Mexican government screens and monitors the workers who participate in the program. The workers get needed jobs; the effect on prevailing wages is regulated; employers get the workers they need; and permanent immigration of unwanted citizens is avoided.

4. *Defend U.S. Borders*

   The borders of the United States, both North and South, must monitor diligently the entry and presence of noncitizens at immigration checkpoints after due diligence by a screening process—not only to provide the procedures and database necessary to arrest illegal immigration in general—but also security from prospective terrorists and drug dealers, in particular.

   Acceptance for naturalization should be selective, primarily based on skills and character, and limited to next of kin, with valid asylums and refugees offered temporary visas. Naturalization would require testing civics for U.S. citizens, plus English reading and writing proficiency at a functional level.

5. *Limited Amnesty for Illegal Immigrants*

   Illegal immigrants should be deported but given the opportunity to register and to apply for temporary worker programs if free of criminal records or illegal receipt of welfare. They would face neither preference nor prejudice for temporary workers' jobs but would be required to return to their native land to receive their assignment. They would be allowed to apply for naturalization after a return to their homeland with a punitive period of layoff, subsequent to satisfactory temporary employment and meeting civics and English requirements.

   U.S. employers of illegal immigrants would be given an amnesty up to a certain date that would also enable them to apply for temporary workers. After that, stiff fines would be levied upon employers of illegals, with incarceration for willful repeat offenders.

6. *Require Mexico's Cooperation in Sealing the Borders*

   Mexico should be held responsible for stopping rather than encouraging the million aliens per year invading across the Mexican-U.S. border, by use of their Army if necessary. In the event that Mexico fails to cooperate in ending this illegal invasion, the United States will have no alternative other than to build a continuous border barrier, militarily enforced, plus curtail the employment of Mexican citizens, and reciprocal trade.

7. *Appropriate U.S. policy and enforcement should clearly focus on proper selection of naturalized citizens versus rejection of illegal immigrants*

The mutual benefits of individual opportunity for "would-be-Americans," and the contributions to America of accepted immigrants who bring skills, initiative, and responsibility comparable to native Americans, result in positive contributions of output and incomes from the average naturalized immigrant. This most certainly includes Hispanics, just as well as any other source of new legal citizens. The same cannot be said for illegal immigrants, including those naturalized by amnesty. Whereas naturalized citizens on average have comparable demographic distribution of educational attainment and earnings to native Americans, the illegal immigrants differ substantially.

The real compensation of white- and blue-collar workers, including fringe benefits, declined 24 percent per unit of output over the period 1965–2005. The real earnings of hourly workers declined 56 percent per unit of output over the same period. This period covers the opening of immigration policy, the amnesty of 1996, and the subsequent deluge of additional illegal immigration. Although the blame must be shared with the failure of the U.S. federal tax code to provide border-adjusted taxation to match foreign value added taxes' effect on import and export prices, excess illegal immigration has clearly played a major role in depressing both white-collar and blue-collar earnings and benefits.

The United States of America has no special moral obligation to become an amalgam of every group of people that desires to relocate here. Immigration to the United States should be in the best interests of all Americans. Furthermore, our government has no right to depress native-born workers' incomes by opening our borders to excessive immigration or nonreciprocal free trade to enrich employers here or abroad, and it cannot justly continue to allow the fabric of our nation to be unraveled by immigrants who spurn our language and culture. If America does have a unique obligation, it is to preserve her heritage as an example of how individual freedom, private property, and limited government can thrive and prosper when based on individual, family, and community responsibility and sacred ethics. Immigrants should be carefully selected as prospective guardians of that heritage, as were our immigrant forefathers.

Endnotes

[1] "A Description of the Immigrant Population," Congressional Budget Office, WDC, November 2004, 24 pages.

[2] Ibid 2, Table 16, p. 22.

[3] George J. Borjas, *Heaven's Door*, Princeton University Press, 1999, Chapter 2.

[4] Ashok Deo Bardhan, and Cynthia Kroll, The New Wave of Outsourcing, Research Report, U C Berkeley, Fall 2003. Available at http://www.haas.berkeley.edu/news/Research_Report_Fall_2003.pdf.

[5] Table 3.9.6, NIPA Accounts, 1958–2005, BEA, U.S. Census Bureau (data adjusted to 2005$ by NIPA government deflator).

[6] Net Book Value of Fixed Assets, "C" & "S" Corporations, Partnerships & Proprietorships, Tax Returns 2001, IRS, WDC, 2006.

[7] Steven A. Camarota, "How the Terrorists Get In," *The Public Interest*. New York, Fall 2002, pp. 65–78.

4

AN INTERVIEW WITH GEORGE BORJAS ON THE COSTS OF IMMIGRATION

by Peter Brimelow

Everyone knows, or concedes (except economists), that immigration is good for the economy. Amazingly, since the early 1990s, a consensus has existed among labor economists that the current unprecedented influx into America is of no particular economic benefit to native-born Americans in aggregate. I reported this consensus in my 1995 immigration book *Alien Nation: Common Sense About America's Immigration Disaster*, and it was confirmed by the National Research Council's 1997 study *The New Americans: Economic, Demographic, and Fiscal Effects of Immigration*,[1] the survey of the technical literature on the economics of immigration done at the behest of the Jordan Immigration Commission. Equally amazingly, this consensus has been totally ignored in the public discourse on immigration — one of the most startling failures of democratic debate of which I am aware.

No one has more to do with the new consensus about the economics of immigration than George J. Borjas, professor of Economics and Public Policy at Harvard University's John F. Kennedy School of Government and a research associate at the National Bureau of Economic Research. Borjas first began to depart from the optimistic orthodoxy with his 1990 book *Friends or Strangers: The Impact of Immigrants on the U.S. Economy*. His most recent full-length treatment of the subject is his 1999 book *Heaven's Door: Immigration Policy and the American Economy*. Borjas, a Cuban immigrant himself, has every emotional reason to favor immigration. That he does not is entirely a function of the data — and his scrupulous scholarship. I spoke to him in his Cambridge office and began by asking him to summarize the findings of the NRC's *The New Americans*.

Borjas: Basically, the "immigration surplus" — the net gain to people already living in the United States — was very small: one-tenth of one percent GDP, or at that time around ten billion dollars in a five to six trillion dollar economy. It's trivial.

Brimelow: That's not net of transfer payments like welfare and education, right?

Borjas: That's correct. There's another chapter where the authors estimate that, on net, native-born households in the United States paid about $200 a year more in taxes because of immigration. That would add up to something like $10 to $20 billion a year. So net, it's basically a wash. Whatever the "immigration surplus," it's eaten away by the cost of providing services to immigrants.

Brimelow: But the redistribution impact within the native-born community is very large.

Borjas: Yes. Let me make that very clear. At the time I wrote that initial paper,[2] I was basically taking a relationship out of the labor demand literature—an X *percent* increase in labor would lower wages by Y *percent*.

That meant current immigration had lowered the total wage of natives by about two percent. And all that goes straight to the employers, to the capitalists. In the long, long run, some of that would filter down to the consumers also. But I didn't do that in my paper. Nobody knows what the breakdown is between consumers and employers.

So the way we freeze the argument is that immigration redistributes wealth from people who compete with immigrants—namely, workers who have the same jobs as immigrants—to people who use immigrants. For example, a California family—gardener, the maid, all that stuff.

Brimelow: Why do you think the National Research Council findings had absolutely no effect on public debate?

Borjas: I don't know. Certain parts seem to be cited over and over. For example, *The Wall Street Journal*—they often cite that there is no wage impact based on the National Research Council. They'll also cite another chapter, that if you were to follow immigrants and their children for 300 years, and assume a tax increase, then immigrants could be a huge benefit to the United States, even though a 300-year projection is complete nonsense. They choose and pick what they want.

Brimelow: But the fundamental conclusion, that there are no substantial aggregate benefits for the native-born from current immigration, was completely buried?

Borjas: Completely.

Brimelow: And, for example, the microstudy showing that immigration means a $1,100 fiscal transfer from every native-born family in California was completely buried too. Why?

Borjas: [*Laughs, throws up hands*] I don't really know the answer. I think part of it has to do with a sort of an implicit bias in the media. Not just in terms of the

National Research Council study, but in terms of the general immigration debate. At least, until recently, the mainstream press, when it covered immigration, would begin with a very sentimental kind of story about a particular immigrant. And then they would proceed to describe how good immigration is. That was more true for some papers than for others, but it generally describes the typical immigration story for a long time. It is only more recently that people have begun to discuss whether, in fact, there could be a negative impact on wages, on social programs, and so on.

Maybe it's because of the way they frame the problem. But I'm not a journalist—I really don't know, okay?

Brimelow: It was interesting to see Paul Krugman cite you recently in the *New York Times.*[3]

Borjas: That's right, Paul Krugman cited the paper[4] on immigration's wage impact I did with Larry Katz. It's only about a year old, but the paper it was based on was published in 2003.[5] Nobody talked about that in the media when it was published.

Brimelow: Do you find that the Krugman column made a difference?

Borjas: Huge. It was amazingly influential. The minute it came out, the e-mails started flowing in.

Brimelow: So what's happened in academe since 1997?

Borjas: In 1997, at the time of the NRC report, it was generally thought that immigrants had a minimal impact on wages for the following reasons: studies tended to focus on comparing how natives do in cities that have large immigrant populations like San Diego or Los Angeles, with cities that have few immigrants, like Pittsburgh or Oklahoma City. When you do that, you tend to find a very weak impact.

People were aware of two potential problems. One was that immigrants gravitate to cities that pay higher wages. That could build a positive correlation between high wages and immigration, which could easily swamp anything in the real market.

Reason number two was that if immigrants are going to a city like San Diego, both native workers and native capital will respond. Native workers will move out. Native capital will move in, where wages are low. These equalizing flows would tend to take away negative impacts.

So now there is a consensus that cross-city correlations don't really matter. To gauge the wage impact of immigration, you have to move to the national level. And that's eventually what I ended up doing in the paper that was published in 2003, that I wrote with Richard Freeman and Larry Katz.[6]

The key insight there was, look, immigrants have come in over the last 30–40 years at different education levels. But the age structure of immigration varies a lot over time. So what I ended up doing was using data from 1960–2000 and looking at the wage from each group defined by education and age to see how the evolution of the wage of a given education group over 40 years responded to immigration.

The minute you do that, the negative wage impact of immigration becomes very apparent. And remarkably enough, it was about what we estimated before. The ten percent increase in supply reduced wages by three percent. It confirmed what we thought we knew about labor demand in the context of immigration.

This was not a paper that was picked up in the newspapers. *The Wall Street Journal* didn't grab it, the *New York Times* didn't run an op-ed about it. I mean, it was just terrible. Economists recognized that it was important, but the media did not.

I suspect very strongly that had I come out with a different answer, it would have been picked up.

Actually, I'll give you the best piece of evidence for why wages must drop with immigration. There have been a ton of hearings in Washington regarding the guest worker program. Who exactly is lobbying for guest workers? Is it you and me? No, it's employers, right? Why would employers tend to go to Washington and expend their resources lobbying for something that doesn't benefit them?

Brimelow: It can all be explained in rather crass Marxist terms, can't it? The class analysis works.

Borjas: Of course! Of course! The Marxist analysis works.

Brimelow: The thing that is interesting is that neither the labor unions nor the leaders of the minority groups are opposed to it.

Borjas: But I have a feeling that will change soon. You're beginning to see a breakdown in the model of political correctness.

Brimelow: What else is happening in the field?

Borjas: You heard about the Ottaviano-Peri paper[7] that was cited in *The Economist*[8] right? What my 2003 paper assumed is that the low-skilled-group immigrants and natives are what we call perfect substitutes. They tried to relax that. And they ended up with a result that basically says that in the long run, the average native wage goes up, not down, by one or two percent as a result of immigration.

Now let me tell you why that is not completely sensible. Somebody else's wage must have changed in the opposite direction. Who was that somebody else? Immigrants. For native wages to go up by one to two percent, the average wage of immigrants must have gone down by like 15–20 percent. That's just so outside what we know about labor demand that it puts the whole paper into question. They chose to focus on natives knowing the fact that whatever you do for natives, the immigrant wage must have fallen by like 15–20 percent, which would make the whole thing impossible. So they chose to ignore that.

But, you know, some people like the theory that immigrants "increase wages"— even though we know from theory that immigrants cannot increase wages.

Brimelow: *The Economist*, of course, is fanatically pro-immigration. In the article you just mentioned it also attempted to downplay your critique of current immigration policy. It said about you that

> Immigration's critics therefore count Mr. Borjas as an ally. But hold on. These figures take no account of the offsetting impact of extra investment. If the capital stock is assumed to adjust, Mr. Borjas reports, overall wages are unaffected and the loss of wages for high-school drop-outs is cut to below five percent.

That's actually purely hypothetical—mathematical theory, isn't it? It has nothing to do with the data?

Borjas: Yes. All these results are based on a theory of labor markets. It states the following: If the U.S. economy has constant returns to scale, namely, you double inputs, you double outputs, which is the key assumption we all make in this, then immigration cannot have an impact on the average wage, in the long run. That's the mathematical theory.

The way an economist finds the short run is, he holds everything else equal. So holding everything else equal, ten million that are let into the country, what happens to wages?

The long run, basically, is the complete opposite. We know that when immigrants come in, wages go down in the short run. Then capitalists build factories to exploit the cheaper labor and so on. So in order to find the long run, we suppose that every expansion that could take place actually does take place.

Now, let me emphasize, neither the short run nor the long run has really been proved. In the real world, things do adjust, but they don't adjust completely. So the best way to look at these extremes is as bounds of what the effect could be. You know, the short run is going to happen, and then, who knows when—Keynes said that in the long run we're all dead—everything adjusts completely. Nobody knows exactly how long the process takes.

But economic theory predicts unambiguously that if you have constant returns to scale production function, the average impact of immigration on wages in the long run has to be zero. Because everything adjusts completely. Capital adjusts enough to account for the extra labor.

But that doesn't mean that every group's wage is unaffected. It just means that the average wage effect is zero.

Now, I would say that the short run assumption is not completely plausible in the real world because it holds everything else equal. When you're living in the real world, people adjust. On the other hand, the long run assumption, that everything adjusts completely, is also not very plausible in the real world either, because not everything adjusts completely.

I will give you an example. Take Puerto Rico. It's part of the U.S., right, with very sizeable labor outflows, and very sizable capital inflows. It still hasn't had everything completely adjusted after 40–50 years of migration. The wage in Puerto Rico today should be the average wage in the U.S. today. Is it? No. There is still a huge wage gap between Puerto Rico and the U.S.

Brimelow: Why?

Borjas: A good question. That's one of the problems with economics. Things don't adjust completely. There are frictions. In theory Puerto Rico should be empty now, because the wage is much higher in the U.S., right? But it's not. In theory, capital flows would have equalized in Puerto Rico with the average in the U.S. market. It hasn't. There are these frictions that we don't really fully understand.

What I'm saying is that, we can do it mathematically, we can look at the marketplace and we can look at the extremes, we can look at the short run and we can look at the long run. But it is very hard to tell where the truth is in the middle. We can say, however, that right now, immigration is impacting wages.

Brimelow: How does this paper by Davis and Weinstein[9] fit in? (Columbia economists Davis and Weinstein estimated in 2002 that, by sharing their technological base with immigrants, U.S. natives suffer a loss of some 0.8 percent of GDP.)

Borjas: It doesn't really fit in. They have a different kind of argument that is much more familiar to trade economists than to labor economists. There are sort of field divisions in economics. People who study immigration tend to be labor economists. Labor economists tend not to be very well trained on international trade theory.

Brimelow: How important is their argument?

Borjas: It's pretty important, but the problem is that there's no evidence. They create a model and get a number out. If the model is correct, then the number is very important. But nobody is going the extra step of trying to see whether the model is correct or not.

Brimelow: But that's equally true for the labor economists, isn't it?

Borjas: No, because, for example, all the wage impacts that we've talked about actually come from data. That was the major contribution of our 2003 paper. I actually went out and looked at the data on wages and wage impact.

The Davis and Weinstein thesis needs more empirical work and nobody's doing it as far as I know.

Brimelow: No Ph.D. students feel compelled to do it?

Borjas: They had a very hard time publishing the paper. People don't like the result. Even ignoring the fiscal impact, they find a huge negative loss to the U.S., and that's not a kind of result that most trade economists like to hear. Most trade economists argue that free trade is great, that labor mobility's great, and so on. This goes very much against the grain.

Brimelow: What is the distinction made between trade and immigration from a theoretical standpoint?

Borjas: From a theoretical standpoint, there is actually very little distinction in the sense that both are importing resources into the country.

From a broader standpoint—people are not machines. We can import a car from Japan and not have a particular effect on the economy. We could import 25 Japanese who make that car, and that has a very different impact on the economy, because they're people. The machine will not incur schooling costs for the children, the machine will not incur Medicaid costs when it gets sick, right?

It goes back to the Milton Friedman quote you got in your *Forbes* interview,[10] right? It's not possible to combine mass immigration and the welfare state.

Brimelow: What about the claim we couldn't run the economy without illegal immigrants?

Borjas: It's complete nonsense. If there were no illegal immigration, and the demand was still there for gardeners and nannies, the price of those things would go up.

Illegal immigration is very highly regionalized, just like legal immigration. Does that mean that the rest of the country, between the two coasts, doesn't function because there are no immigrants? That's ridiculous. There are cabs in the middle of the country, believe it or not, there are gardeners.

It's like the argument that immigrants do jobs that natives won't do. That's complete nonsense too. It's a question of price. And one good by-product of all the current immigration controversy, I think, is that people now are getting that it's complete nonsense.

Brimelow: As I understand it, the data seem to indicate that incomes have stagnated for 30 years.

Borjas: The average real wage in the U.S. hasn't risen that much. The top has increased a lot. The bottom has decreased a lot. And immigration is part of that. It's clear that at the bottom end of the distribution, in other words, the high school dropouts, immigration has had an impact.

And, because the immigration in the U.S. is very bimodal—a lot of low-skilled people and some high-skilled people—you're starting to see an impact at the upper end too. And at the upper end, immigration, even though it's lowering wages there, is also fighting the whole trend of the U.S. economy, the increasing payoff for skills. So we don't quite see the impact as clearly.

Is immigration the only thing that is going on? No. But one thing I've noticed in the newspapers recently are statements like "Well, everybody agrees that at the very low end, immigration lowers wages." Well, since when did we agree on that? We were arguing about that six months ago.

Brimelow: Why are we arguing about wages anyway? It's a very narrow way of looking at immigration. The real issue is: What's immigrant surplus? How much better-off are the native-born?

Borjas: I agree. And then compare that with the cost of services if you really want to do a cost-benefit analysis.

But suppose that number is zero, which I think is pretty close to being true. Then you still might want to care about the wage impact because of the distributional effect. It's making the rich richer and the poor poorer.

Brimelow: If the total impact of immigration is a wash, then there is no economic rationale for immigration. What's America's need for immigration?

Borjas: No economic rationale in the context of this model. You can see a slight loss if you look at the transfer payments.

I wouldn't go so far as to say immigration is completely useless. There are loss and gain at specific sectors. In terms of potential benefits, think of Silicon Valley. It may well be the case that the large migration of high-skilled workers into a very clustered geographic region somehow created this energy. Now, nobody has actually proved that.

Brimelow: And revisionists point out all the original founders of Silicon Valley were Midwestern farm boys.

Borjas: Well, I'm willing to believe that, okay? But whatever synergy that exists with high-skilled immigration, you clearly cannot make that argument for low-skilled immigration.

Brimelow: As an economist, do you think immigration is necessary?

Borjas: For what?

Brimelow: Economic growth.

Borjas: For economic growth? Of course, the U.S. can grow without it. But it can be beneficial. A country that pursued a rational immigration policy of selecting the most skilled people could actually do pretty well.

Brimelow: What kind of numbers?

Borjas: Our current immigration policy leads to an immigration surplus of, like, $10 billion a year, right? If you had an immigration policy that was mainly skilled workers, you could easily get a number like $100 billion a year.

But there's no free lunch in immigration. There are gains, but somebody has to pay the cost of those gains. Immigration doesn't happen and then all of a sudden everybody gets manna from heaven. People are displaced. Not everybody's better off.

Brimelow: At the moment, native-born Americans of all races have apparently decided that there are enough Americans. Their birth rates are down to replacement levels and the population is spontaneously stabilizing. But it's being driven upward dramatically through government policy. Is there any economic reason to have a growing population?

Borjas: No. I've wondered why people worry about this. Assuming constant returns—if you double input, you double output—it wouldn't really matter what population level we're at. What matters for an economy's wealth is not the number of people but the kind of people we have.

In Europe, people worry about that a lot. But I don't quite understand why cutting the population by ten percent would imply that they are ten percent poorer. Per capita income needn't fall at all.

Brimelow: What about the argument that there's a demographic structure problem and the Baby Boomers need immigrants to pay for their retirement?

Borjas: That's a different issue. That problem exists because of the way that we have built our insurance system for the elderly. We have a security system that is basically a Ponzi scheme. We need more people to pay the benefits.

But immigration is still not a solution for two reasons: One, the kind of immigrants we get on average need government services. So even if the immigrants provide for retirement costs, we have to support their social assistance programs.

Two, what's going to happen when the immigrants retire? Do we have to let more immigrants in to pay for them too? It's not a viable long-run solution. Laurence Kotlikoff wrote a paper[11] with a simulation about the European Union and Japan that shows it's just impossible for immigration to do very much about it.

Brimelow: There are really two issues, aren't there? One is we don't actually know how long the Baby Boomer generation can work; health care has changed so much. The second is mechanization, robotics.

Borjas: The Japanese are very interesting. They basically had a choice between low-skill immigration and mechanization. And they did not choose low-skill immigration. Which is better for economy in the long run? That's a paper waiting to be written. It will be a very important paper. My gut reaction would be that mechanization is probably not a bad idea because it would lead to more discoveries and economic growth, but I could be completely wrong. I'm willing to be completely open until I see the data coming in.

Brimelow: Does economics give an answer as to how big a population should be?

Borjas: No. Economics to this day has not given an answer to even simpler questions, such as how many immigrants should there be. Economics gives an answer to which kind of immigrants we should get, if we have a choice: skilled immigrants. Economics does not give an answer as to how many skilled immigrants we should have.

Brimelow: But Tamar Jacoby would tell you that we need immigrants, that's why they're coming in. She would say the market is telling us we need immigrants.

Borjas: That's ridiculous. The U.S. has a wage level that is many times higher than that faced by four billion people in the world at least. That means Jacoby would continue to admit immigrants until the wage in the U.S. is the same as the wage where those four billion people live. That's a completely nonsensical definition of the market.

Brimelow: Well, I can see why that would be unfortunate for Americans, particularly working Americans. But why is it nonsensical from an economic standpoint? Say to a libertarian, who doesn't accept the legitimacy of the national community anyway?

Borjas: I think that the answer is the following: We have an economic answer, and we have a political answer—and they're intertwined. Who should U.S. policy makers care about when they decide immigration policy? If the answer to that is we should care about the four billion poor in the rest of the world, then by all means we should open the borders. But if we should care about the 300 million people who are here already, then letting in four billion people is not in their interest.

Brimelow: You don't have a lot of libertarians around here, do you? You must miss them.

Borjas: I—no. I don't really miss them, actually. They're crazy. They have no definition of what a country is!

Brimelow: Even if we were to open the borders to try to maximize the wealth of the world, there's a prudential question of whether it would work.

Borjas: Of course. It assumes no cultural conflict of any kind, only economics. It requires a movement of four to five billion people to three parts of the world: Japan, parts of North America, and Western Europe. You have to consider the cost of that kind of mobility. I don't mean just the plane, I mean the whole notion of what it entails to the culture, to the people themselves. So it's not actually clear that it's better off for the world as a whole to have no borders. I mean it's true that world GDP will go up, but what about mobility costs? Those could be even greater.

Brimelow: Of course, in fact, everybody would not move.

Borjas: Right. An example: Puerto Rico again. Since 1946 or so, people have been coming freely to the U.S. There's no legal restrictions of any kind. There are huge wage gaps that haven't narrowed. Puerto Rico should be empty. Yet only a quarter of Puerto Ricans left. That's telling me that a big fraction of the world would prefer to live where they are.

Brimelow: The Open Borders people would say that's an argument why we could have open borders—not all people would move.

Borjas: But what would the U.S. look like if we let in even just 25 million Mexicans and only 250 million Chinese? It would still be the U.S., but it wouldn't be the U.S. really.

Brimelow: Do you think that there is an answer in economic theory as to what the optimum level of immigration is?

Borjas: One can answer that question using economics.

Brimelow: Why?

Borjas: Because it is really an economic question. How do we allocate resources? How do you allocate people? It is at heart an economic question.

The problem is while it is an economic question, you need an objective function. And you have to work it out logically and consistently and mathematically. And that's a harder question to address than you think it is.

Brimelow: I don't think it is an easy question, but I do think it's an important question. In fact, I think it's the only important question when it comes right down to it.

Borjas: How many and who? Yeah, I agree. The "who?" we know the answer to—skilled immigrants. "How many?" is a harder question.

Brimelow: Is there work done on that?

Borjas: No.

Brimelow: Isn't that odd?

Borjas: It's odd, but I think it's a hard problem. It's an interesting problem, but it's very hard.

And if you were to do it, very few people would believe you. Because—think about an academic's career. You have to make sure you do things that are interesting, publishable, and have an impact. And you have to be convincing on the way.

To answer the question of how many immigrants there should be, you have to have a model at the very beginning that says, the world should look like this. It's your own objective function. Well, there's no natural objective function that could be pleasing to a lot of people.

One could imagine the following, and it would be a good place to start: Maximize the net gain to natives by having immigrants come in, and subtract out the cost of social assistance programs, right? You maximize that model and say, this is the true number of immigrants we should have. But I suspect that is harder than it sounds.

Brimelow: But it's astonishing on its face that no one is asking it, when you think about that Congress is on the verge of legislating this tremendous nation—altering public policy—doubling or tripling legal immigration. Americans are spending three percent of GDP on higher education and much of that goes to research, and there is who knows how much spent on research in Washington. So what are they waiting for?

Borjas: [*Chuckle*] Again, there's an academic's career to think of. You have to worry about getting tenure, you have to worry about . . . how many immigrants should there be? I agree. That is a very sensible question to ask. And, in theory, in principle, it is an answerable question. Just a very hard question to address. Somebody, someday, will come up with a very clever way of looking at it.

It will not be infinite. It will not be infinity. It will not be zero. There will be some number that is optimal for the U.S. And I can't tell you, right now, what is the optimal number.

Brimelow: Well, what other research is going on?

Borjas: A lot of people are starting to look more closely at Mexican immigration, because it is so large. There will be a lot of work coming out on the wage impact, which number is closer to the true impact of immigration—is it a short-run impact or a long-run impact?

Brimelow: I continue to regard that as a trivial question, myself.

Borjas: Well, the reason people will look at that is because it is a technically interesting question, which is answerable in theory by looking at data. The whole notion of capital adjustments and how capital adjusted to immigration— that's an answerable question if you have the data. Again, it's not the question you want answered, but it's a specific question that is answerable, given the tools we have.

Brimelow: What about your students?

Borjas: I discourage them from studying immigration.

Brimelow: Why?

Borjas: Because, given that I'm working with them, people will think that I'm doing most of the work, or that I gave them the idea or something.

Brimelow: Normally speaking, academics develop disciples, don't they?

Borjas: I know, and I don't have that. I don't have the need. Let me put it that way.

Brimelow: Would it do them any good?

Borjas: I don't think it would do them much good.

Brimelow: Even though there is interest in the subject now.

Borjas: Right.

Endnotes

[1] James P. Smith and Barry Edmonston, eds., *The New Americans: Economic, Demographic, and Fiscal Effects of Immigration*, Washington, DC: National Academy Press, 1997.

[2] George J. Borjas, Richard Freeman, and Lawrence F. Katz, "Searching for the Effect of Immigration on the Labor Market," *American Economic Review*, May 1996, pp. 246–251.

[3] Paul Krugman, "North of the Border," *New York Times*, March 27, 2006.

[4] George J. Borjas and Lawrence Katz, "The Evolution of the Mexican-Born Workforce in the United States," NBER Working Paper 11281, April 2005.

[5] George J. Borjas, "The Labor Demand Curve Is Downward Sloping: Reexamining the Impact of Immigration on the Labor Market," *Quarterly Journal of Economics*, 2003.

[6] George J. Borjas and Lawrence Katz, "The Evolution of the Mexican-Born Workforce in the United States."

[7] Gianmarco I. P. Ottaviano (University of Bologna) and Giovanni Peri (University of California–Davis), "Rethinking the Gains from Immigration: Theory and Evidence from the U.S.," January 2006.

[8] "Myths and Migration," *The Economist*, April 6, 2006.

[9] Donald R. Davis and David E. Weinstein, "Technological Superiority and the Losses from Immigration," National Bureau of Economic Research Working Paper No. 8971, June 2002.

[10] Milton Friedman, in an interview with Peter Brimelow, *Forbes*, 1998.

[11] Lawrence Kotlikoff, "Avoiding a Fiscal/Demographic/Economic Debacle in Japan," Chapter 11 in *Tackling Japan's Fiscal Challenges*, Keimei Kaizuka and Anne O. Krueger, eds., Palgrave Macmillan, 2006.

5

BIG BUSINESS AND IMMIGRATION: INSIDE THE MIND OF THE CORPORATE ELITE

by Peter Brimelow

They stood closely and spoke intensely but quietly, obviously not eager to attract attention. But there were more of them than usual gathered around at the podium after I had finished a contentious debate. And their message was the same: Whatever the economics of mass immigration, they were really worried about its social consequences. And they wanted to tell me their cogent reasons.

It was the summer of 1995. The issue of immigration was enjoying one of its brief moments in the sun of public attention—now forgotten, but very similar to the moment it enjoyed more recently, in the spring of 2006, when it was surfaced by the Bush Administration's fanatical and foolish determination to ram an illegal alien amnesty through Congress before the mid-term elections. Such moments are ultimately due to the relentless accumulation of foreigners in the United States that is occurring because of public policy, both of commission and omission, and the consequent inexorably-mounting problems. But the story is not one that the mainstream media wants to cover, and it takes something specific for it to break free of the news managers' control.

The Big Breakout

The earlier cause was the stunning victory in 1994 of California's Proposition 187, where a grassroots movement overcame the intense opposition of the state's entire political elite, liberal and "conservative," to vote restrictions on taxpayer-funded services to illegal aliens, followed by the reports (interim 1994, final 1997) of the U.S. Commission on Immigration,[1] headed by the black former Congresswoman Barbara Jordan (D-Texas), who recommended significant reductions in legal immigration. With this perfect cover, the newly Republican-controlled Congress had actually embodied Jordan's recommendations in legislation, the Smith-Simpson bill, which it appeared poised to pass. (In 2006, in sad contrast, American patriots were strictly playing defense—struggling to stop amnesty and other legislation that would have made America's epochal immigration disaster even worse.)

I was then a senior editor of *Forbes*. I had just finished speaking at one of the magazine's CEO (Chief Executive Officer) conferences. On the podium with me was George Gilder, the famous author of the 1980 book *Wealth and Poverty*, which had made the philosophical case for Ronald Reagan's supply-side tax cuts. Gilder was then in the process of becoming even more famous—and wealthier, alas briefly—as the messianic guru of the high-tech investing boom that was to go bust so dramatically in 2000.

I had never been allowed to write about immigration in *Forbes* (more about this later), and it had been clear to me that I was not to mention it at the conference. But I had just published a book, *Alien Nation: Common Sense About America's Immigration Disaster*, which had benefited from the issue's moment in the sun— "one of the most widely discussed books of the year," according to *Newsweek*'s Jerry Adler.[2] In fact, I had loyally come off the promotion circuit at the magazine's command to appear at the conference. And George Gilder, always something of an innocent in the context of *Forbes'* internal politics and bursting with simplistic messianic enthusiasm for Silicon Valley and all of its works, could not restrain himself at the thought of anything that would get in the way of people like his heroes (Intel's Andy Grove, Oracle's Larry Ellison) and their desire to import more computer programmers.

So Gilder attacked me on immigration anyway. The audience of CEOs immediately erupted, as invariably happens when Americans realize they are going to be allowed a brief holiday from political correctness in which to discuss this most incorrect of issues.

Gilder's enthusiasm for Silicon Valley is widely shared in Congress—or possibly the enthusiasm is for campaign contributions. An entire immigrant category, the H(1)(b) "temporary worker" visa, has been created to allow the importation of software engineers because of an alleged "shortage" of programmers. Since 1995, over one million have been imported with their families; most, of course, stay. Naturally, "shortages" are now being loudly descried by opportunistic employers of other unfortunate American professionals, notably nurses and teachers. Of course, economists, unlike businessmen, don't believe in "shortages"—they think it's just a question of setting a price—raising wages— that will call forth supply or redirect demand. Typically, this subtlety was lost on Gilder. When I pointed out that many U.S. software engineers are actually unemployed or have been driven out of the field by immigrant competition, he yelled: "Because they're no good!"

I don't remember that the CEOs who came up to me afterward had raised their concerns from the floor. I do remember saying something rueful about our joint failure to stay away from immigration to Kip Forbes, one of the numerous sons of Malcolm swanning about with some grand but obscure function at the magazine. He responded with ominous bad grace.

But my CEOs' arguments were telling. One told me he owned a ranch in Florida. The work used to be done by African Americans, he said. But now the workers were all Hispanics, and the African Americans were on welfare. Another was on the board of a big city school. The influx of immigrants was overwhelming its resources and making it impossible to maintain standards for the native-born.

Where, they wondered, would it all end?

The "Basis" for Immigration Enthusiasm

Needless to say, I am sure that George Gilder had supporters gathered around him, too. And I know, from long experience, what they must have been saying—some variant of "There's never been any real basis for opposing immigration but racism, in one form or another."[3]

That's actually what Michael A. Leven, CEO of U.S. Franchise Systems Inc., franchiser of hotels and motels, told Sanford Ungar, according to Ungar's 1995 book *Fresh Blood: The New American Immigrants*. Ungar apparently did not know that the Indian immigrant businessmen whom Leven has profitably helped invade the U.S. innkeeping niche—a process sometimes described as "hotels, motels, and Patels"—are heavy users of cheap affirmative-action finance, courtesy of the federal Small Business Administration (and hence, of course, the American taxpayer). Also, the immigrants were not shy about cashing in on U.S. affirmative action programs. Though in no sense disadvantaged, Patels qualified as a "minority" and tapped below-prime financing offered by the Small Business Administration.[4]

In other words, there is, in fact, a very "real basis" for opposing immigration: helping Leven enrich himself at the public's expense, while displacing American motel owners.

Leven, of course, must have known this, even if he did not tell Ungar.

At least, you would think so. But very few people are conscious hypocrites. My observation is that the beneficiaries of privilege, both private and public, are remarkably good at rationalizing their good fortune. It is just possible that Leven simply had not thought through the ways in which he was doing well by doing (as he saw it, no doubt) good.

A classic example of this occurred in the summer of 2006. Congressman Mike Pence (R-Indiana) was somehow persuaded to break with the House Immigration Reform Caucus and to espouse a modified version of President Bush's amnesty plan—"amnesty with a trip home tacked on,"[5] as Immigration Reform Caucus leader Tom Tancredo (R-Colorado) aptly described it. Pence's plan was obviously a clumsy trick. But what was interesting was that Pence felt comfortable heaping public praise on the plan's supposed originator, Loctite heiress and Colorado horse farm owner Helen Krieble, for Krieble had been astoundingly explicit about her motives:

> I think I'm one of the few people involved in the immigration, public policy issue who actually has hired guest workers," she said, describing the bureaucratic nightmare the horse farm faces when it tries to get seasonal work visas. Krieble explained that farmers, ranchers, and businesspeople around the country are unable to find American workers for certain jobs, even when they raise wages. She believes some are faced with a difficult choice: go out of business if they can't find "affordable, legal workers," or hire illegal immigrants. "To criminalize those people— both the worker and the employer—for doing what's necessary in each of their lives without providing any legal way for it to work is immoral in my view," she said.[6]

Notwithstanding this, according to the *Rocky Mountain News*, Pence actually called his patron "the Harriet Beecher Stowe of this issue." The reference, of course, is to the 19th-century author of *Uncle Tom's Cabin*, whose writings exposing the evils of slavery helped set the stage for the Civil War. It's said that when President Abraham Lincoln met Stowe, he famously quipped: "So this is the little lady who made this big war." Pence said that Krieble smiled when he told her she stirred the immigration fight the same way. (Her part-time home in Connecticut is not far from Stowe's historic residence.)

It might seem crass enough for Pence to trivialize the historic plight of America's slaves by comparing it with that of illegal immigrants—especially when African Americans today are clearly among the principle victims of displacement caused by the current alien influx (African American unemployment has actually risen during the post–2002 economic recovery).[7] But it shows a truly sublime innocence to raise the specter of slavery, when, from an economic standpoint, Mrs. Krieble is the exact analytical equivalent of the antebellum slaveholders:

self-righteously and blindly insisting on the employer's right to import labor in total disregard of the political and social consequences.

What the market is telling Mrs. Krieble, of course, is that her horse farm is too expensive. She should either scale it back, subsidize it herself (she might have to give up that second home in Connecticut), or figure out some imaginative way of making working on it more attractive. Perhaps she could work some part-time deal with a local college, simultaneously solving her problem and the parallel problem of students' graduating with crushing debt. But, in any event, this is hardly the end of the world. Her farm is, after all, a hobby.

Even if her farm were not a hobby, there is constant change in the pattern of American economic activity. The great strength of the American economy is that business owners generally do adapt—but they certainly will not do so if they can find some pliant politician offering to fix public policy to subsidize them. Immigration policy is such a subsidy. (And, incidentally, because immigration policy is currently so lax, American students are not merely ignored by employers like Krieble but are now being driven out even of traditional seasonal work, for example, in the summer colonies of Nantucket and Martha's Vineyard.)

Why Business Support Is Not Monolithic

So I have begun this story at the end: The monolithic support of the business class for mass immigration, legal and illegal, is not quite so monolithic as it appears. Businessmen live in the United States—even if, notoriously, they are retreating to gated residential communities. In the end, they will start to be alarmed by a policy that is destroying the country in which they live, and in which they hope their children and grandchildren will live.

Moreover, as the cases of Mrs. Krieble and the hotel franchiser Michel Leven illustrate, the business supporters of immigration are in a state of prelapsarian innocence about their activities. This is not to say they will behave differently when their eyes are opened. But they will have to take the trouble to hide their activities.

Flagrantly, both Leven and Krieble are being subsidized by public policy. And this does not merely take the implicit form of importing "willing workers" from other countries. It has tangible, pecuniary form. In Leven's case, for example, he benefits from taxpayer-underwritten finance of small businesses owned by "minorities"—a category which, because of the paradoxical interaction of Third World immigration and affirmative action, includes immigrant foreigners who qualify for a finance break. In Krieble's case, taxpayers are making working on her horse farm more attractive to immigrants by paying for the education of their children—and per pupil spending in the public schools now averages $9,000 a year. She also benefits from federal law mandating that hospitals provide Emergency Room[8] and other care to the indigent without payment. This means the hospitals have to pass on the cost to Americans who do have health insurance, driving up their premiums.

Indeed, there is an unimaginable cornucopia of government subsidies to immigrants, even illegal immigrants, and thereby to their employers. A case study: The Federal National Mortgage Association, colloquially known as Fannie Mae, has boasted on its foundation's Web site[9] of a "financial literacy education" program in Rogers, Arkansas, that enabled Tyson Foods, Inc. to stabilize turnover in its poultry processing plant where the workforce is described as "largely immigrant," some 500 families to purchase homes, and a local bank, First National Bank and Trust Company, to take in $5 million in deposits and more than $20 million in loans.

Naturally, this is very nice for the immigrants, First National Bank, and for Fannie Mae. But it is not at all nice for the American taxpayer, who in effect gets to guarantee the mortgage. And this guarantee is a serious risk: There is widespread speculation on Wall Street that both Fannie Mae and also the competing Federal Home Loan Mortgage Corporation ("Freddie Mac") are financially troubled and will ultimately require a taxpayer bailout perhaps even bigger than the 1980s Saving and Loan disaster.

It is because of this cross-subsidization, endemic in the modern mixed economy, that the late Milton Friedman, Nobel Laureate and clearly the outstanding economist of the 20th century, told me in one of our interviews in *Forbes* magazine: "It's just obvious that you can't have free immigration and a welfare state."[10] Friedman, of course, did not simply mean welfare—handouts to the poor—but transfer payments of all sorts.

Another example of the state of utter naiveté about immigration politics in which much of the business elite still operates—and its dangerous consequences—came in the summer of 2005. A story[11] in the *Los Angeles Times* reported, wide-eyed, the "broad coalition of business groups and immigrant advocates" (a.k.a. economic and ethnic special interests) that the Bush White House was mobilizing to support the amnesty drive that it unleashed the next year. According to the *LA Times*: "Those courted include Microsoft Corp., Wal-Mart Stores, Inc., and groups representing academic institutions, restaurants, hotels, landscaping firms, hospitals, and nurses. Organizers say this is the first time an effort has been made to bring these disparate groups together to focus on immigration issues. Admission into the new coalition costs between $50,000 and $250,000. . . ."

This extraordinary frank admission of business self-interest, and the role of opportunistic Washington lobbying firms in catering to it, explains a great deal about the mechanics of the Bush Administration. But it could not possibly have been made in a climate where there was elementary media awareness of the essential venality of this motive. It is simply too vulnerable to riposte.

In fact, this is exactly what happened to one member of the coalition. Craig Regelbrugge, a lobbyist for the American Nursery & Landscape Association, passed from frankness to open arrogance: "You're never going to please them all [Republican supporters]. . . . That's the difficult thing for the White House on this. They don't want to anger anyone. But the party's going to have to choose between the closed-minded restrictionists and the business base. . . . Who's really the base of the base? Farmers and businesspeople, or the others?"

"Others," in this context, means voters. And, apparently, enough of them called to educate Regelbrugge on this point that, a few days later, his office reportedly fended off yet another critic with the threat that the FBI had been alerted. Of course, it is typical of the prelapsarian political state that any criticism is assumed to be illegal. But it is doubtful that Craig Regelbrugge will be quite so indiscreet again.

None of which is to minimize the powerful economic nexus underlying the business community's support for immigration. Its outline has been clear in the labor economics technical literature for at least 15 years, since the change in U.S. immigration policy following the 1965 Immigration Act began to show up in the data. It was confirmed by The New Americans[12] 1997 technical appendix to the Jordan Commission, prepared by the National Research Council of the National Academy of Sciences.[13]

The Marxist Interpretation of Immigration Enthusiasm

In summary: The post–1965 immigrant influx has brought essentially no net aggregate benefit to native-born Americans. In fact, if the effect of government transfer payments is factored in, there is a small but significant net loss—Americans are paying to transform themselves. On the other hand, immigration causes a very substantial redistribution of income within the native-born community. For example, Harvard University economist George. J. Borjas (see interview, page 75) has estimated that about two percent of Gross Domestic Product is transferred from labor to the owners of capital because of the impact immigrants have on wage rates. (Similarly, immigration causes further redistribution within the native-born community because of its impact on transfer payments, which are ultimately funded by taxes.)

The stark fact is that current immigration policy lends itself to explanation in the crudest Marxist terms. Quite simply, it is a savage attack by the American rich on the American poor (and middle class), by American capitalists on the living standards of the American working class. This divide is confirmed very dramatically in opinion polls. Thus, the Chicago Council on Foreign Relations, which has a long tradition of polling to find differences between the public and opinion leaders, conducted a survey in the summer of 2002, which was summarized in this dramatic way:

> The results of the survey indicate that the gap between the opinions of the American people on immigration and those of their leaders is enormous. The poll found that 60 percent of the public regards the present level of immigration to be a "critical threat to the vital interests of the United States," compared to only 14 percent of the nation's leadership—a 46 percentage point gap.
>
> The poll results indicate that there is no other foreign policy-related issue on which the American people and their leaders disagreed more profoundly than immigration. Even on such divisive issues as globalization or strengthening the United Nations, the public and the elite are much closer together than they are on immigration.
>
> When asked a specific question about whether legal immigration should be reduced, kept the same, or increased, 55 percent of the public said it should be reduced, and 27 percent said it should remain the same. In contrast, only 18 percent of opinion leaders said it should be reduced, and 60 percent said it should remain the same. There was no other issue-specific question on which the public and elites differed more widely.
>
> The enormous difference between elite and public opinion can also be seen on the issue of illegal immigration. The survey found that 70 percent of the public said that reducing illegal immigration should be a "very important" foreign-policy goal of the United States, compared to only 22 percent of elites.
>
> Also with respect to illegal immigration, when the public was asked to rank the biggest foreign policy problems,

the public ranked illegal immigration 6th, while elites ranked it 26th.[14]

Of course, not all of these "opinion leaders" are capitalists and corporate executives, although it appears obvious from this description that many are:

> Included in the survey of leaders were top executives of the Fortune 1000 corporations; presidents of the largest labor unions; TV and radio news directors, network newscasters, newspaper editors and columnists; leaders of all religious faiths, chosen proportionate to the number of Americans who worship in each; presidents of large special interest groups and think tanks with an emphasis on foreign policy matters; presidents and faculty of universities; members of the U.S. House and Senate; and assistant secretaries and other senior staff in the Administration.

This remains the central reality that confronts immigration critics when talking to the business elite today. Thus, a year or so after *Alien Nation* was published, George Borjas and I were invited to address a meeting of major Republican donors on the opposite coast. My late wife took a dim view of weekends away from the family and, having ascertained that the organization was prepared to pay only expenses (cheapskates!), vetoed the trip. However, Borjas went, being an educator and possibly of a more charitable disposition. When he came back, he called to give me the news: "We've lost!"

Apparently, the assembled fatcats had been appalled at Borjas's demonstration that there was no economic rationale, on net, for the current policy of mass immigration. They had fiercely resisted his message.

But the specific term Borjas used stuck in my memory: "They were *dismayed*," he said. This goes to my earlier point about prelapsarian immigration enthusiasts. Even fatcats don't want to face the fact that the policy they prefer has no noble justification—that they are really just profiting at the expense of their fellow Americans. For one thing, they know that, in a democracy, it's going to be a very hard sell.

Breaching the Business Barrier

Nevertheless, the business barrier to ending America's immigration disaster is far from unbreachable. Class politics are actually relatively rare in American history. Sectional rivalries and, above all, ethnicity have usually determined political allegiances. Jews, for example, are significantly more likely to favor immigration than other Americans.[15] (Among the capitalists quoted previously, Grove, Ellison, and Leven are all Jewish.) There will be divisions within the business elite along these lines and between the business elite and other groups of "opinion formers" along other lines. The national argument about immigration will eventually play into these divisions.

It is a general truth that no one really has the faintest idea what is politically possible, least of all the professional politicians. They appear to have been designed by evolution to snuffle along like blind shrews, following their exquisitely sensitive snouts from one day to the next, reacting savagely if asked about next week, let alone year, and thus able to perform 180-degree turns without rupturing their consciences.

Or even noticing. On innumerable issues—wage and price controls,[16] welfare policy, the efficacy of military intervention overseas—the American conventional wisdom has changed out of all recognition over relatively short periods of time, without the conventionally wise seeming to feel much need to reproach themselves for being wrong.

Equally, the business elite is surprisingly flexible over time. Thus, it is unlikely that any corporate executive 50 years ago could have imagined that his modern successors must constantly mouth platitudes about "diversity," or that they now feel compelled to employ whole departments of bureaucrats devoted to "affirmative action," that is, discrimination against white men. The business elite is simply not into stands on principle. It just wants to be left alone. So it sometimes responds very quickly to friendly hints dropped by politicians. Similarly, if offered a carrot like a true guest worker program—that is, not an amnesty for illegal aliens already here and coupled with reform of the Fourteenth Amendment's "citizen-child clause" so that the American-born children of guest workers are not automatically citizens—the business elite would almost certainly ditch the rest of its "opinion-former" allies without a qualm.

Bottom line (to use an appropriate term): In the 30-year struggle that culminated in the legislated cutoff of the last Great Wave of immigration in the 1920s, it was the business elite's fear of mounting social disorder that caused it to change sides. The scars from the little-remembered anarchist bombing outside J.P. Morgan, Inc. on September 16, 1920, which killed 33 people and injured 400, are still visible[17] on the façade of 23 Wall Street. The crime was never solved, possibly because the immigrant chief suspect returned to his native land. All this can happen again. America's Second Great Wave of immigration can be broken. And the business community will go bobbing along with the flow.

Endnotes

[1] U.S. Commission on Immigration Reform website, http://www.utexas.edu/lbj/uscir/

[2] Jerry Adler, "What Is an American?" *Newsweek*, July 10, 1995.

[3] Sanford Ungar, *Fresh Blood: The New American Immigrants*, 1995, p. 383.

[4] Joel Millman, "Patel, Inc. (Hospitality Franchise Systems, Inc.) (Company Profile)," *Forbes*, August 14, 1995, p. 156, n.4.

[5] Tancredo Press Release, http://tancredo.house.gov/press/PRArticle.aspx?NewsID=1198

[6] M. E. Sprengelmeyer, "Coloradan Rides into Immigration Fray." *Rocky Mountain News*, July 3, 2006.

[7] Edwin S. Rubenstein, National Data, "Why Has Black Unemployment Risen (Yes, Risen!) in The 'Bush Boom.' " http://www.vdare.com/rubenstein/050504_nd.htm

[8] The EMTALA Statute, US CODE: Title 42,1395dd. http://www.law.cornell.edu/uscode/html/uscode42/usc_sec_42_00001395—dd000-.html

[9] http://www.fanniemaefoundation.org/programs/hff/v2i2-sidebars.shtml, accessed November 17, 2006.

[10] Milton Friedman, in an interview with Peter Brimelow, *Forbes*, December 29, 1997.

[11] Peter Wallsten and Nicole Gaouette, "Immigration Rising on Bush's To-Do List," *Los Angeles Times*, July 24, 2005.

[12] The New Americans. The full text is available online at http://fermat.nap.edu/books/0309063566/html

[13] For an updated summary, see Peter Brimelow's interview with Harvard's George Borjas, the leading economist in the field, on pp. 75-88.

[14] Roy Beck and Steven A. Camarota, "Elite vs. Public Opinion: An Examination of Divergent Views on Immigration," Center for Immigration Studies, December 2002. http://www.cis.org/articles/2002/back1402.html. accessed on November 17, 2006.

[15] See the 2006 Annual Survey of American Jewish Opinion, http://www.ajc.org/site/apps/nl/content2.asp?c=ijITI2PHKoG&b=2174431&ct=3152889 and compare it with the Fox News/Opinion Dynamics poll of May 16–18, 2006, http://www.foxnews.com/projects/pdf/FOX226_web.pdf

[16] http://www.pbs.org/wgbh/commandingheights/shared/minitextlo/ess_nixongold.html

[17] Pictures can be seen at http://web.honorscollege.cuny.edu/student-projects/2005/neighborhoods/10/terrorism.htm

6

IMMIGRANTS IN AMERICA: A STATISTICAL OVERVIEW

by Edwin S. Rubenstein

More than 35 million immigrants currently live in the United States. This is the largest foreign-born population in the country's history. Although the annual inflow declined somewhat following the 2001 terrorist attacks, it has averaged 1 million per year for the last 15 years, very high by historical standards.

Throughout American history, immigration has come in waves, followed by troughs that sometimes extend for many years. During the peak decade of the 1880–1920 "Great Wave" (1900–1910), the foreign-born population rose to 3.2 million, or considerably less than the 4.1 million increase over just the last five years alone (see Table 1). (The abnormally large 11 million increase of the 1990s reflects

Table 1: U.S. Immigrant Population, 1900-2005

Year	Total (in millions)	Change From Previous Period (in millions)	% of Population
1900	10.3		13.6%
1910	13.5	3.2	14.7%
1920	13.9	0.4	13.2%
1930	14.2	0.3	11.6%
1940	11.6	(2.6)	8.8%
1950	10.3	(1.3)	6.9%
1960	9.7	(0.6)	5.4%
1970	9.6	(0.1)	4.7%
1980	14.1	4.5	6.2%
1990	19.8	5.7	7.9%
2000	31.1	11.3	11.1%
2005	35.2	4.1	12.1%

Sources: Steve Camarota, "Immigrants at Mid-Decade: a Snapshot of America's Foreign-born Population in 2005," Backgrounder, CIS, December 2005 (1900-1990; 2005) http://www.cis.org/articles/2005/back1405.pdf ; Census Bureau, "The Foreign-born Population: 2000," December 2003 (2000).

the mass amnesty initiated by the Immigration Reform and Control Act [IRCA] of 1986. The amnestied were already here but not counted as immigrants.)

While the number of immigrants is at a record high, the foreign-born share of the U.S. population was higher during the first few decades of the 1900s. Thereafter, World War I and the immigration quotas enacted in the 1920s caused the foreign-born share of the U.S. population to fall, until mass immigration resumed following the 1965 Immigration Act.

Note, however, that today's foreign-born population share is the highest since the 1920 census. And if native and foreign-born populations continue growing at the average annual rates of 2000 to 2005, the foreign-born share of U.S. population will surpass the 1910 record high in 2017.

Demographers prefer to express immigration as a proportion of population growth. Population growth, of course, is determined by the birthrate (which has been declining for decades) less the death rate (also declining), plus net immigration (up since 1965 immigration law). Juxtaposing total population growth alongside the change in foreign-born population, we calculate immigration's contribution to U.S. population growth (see Table 2).

Table 2: Immigration's Contribution to U.S. Population Change, 1900-2005

Year	Population (in millions)		Change From Previous Period (in millions)		
	Total	Foreign-Born	Total	Foreign-Born	Foreign-Born as % Total
1900	76.0	10.3			
1910	92.0	13.5	16.0	3.2	20%
1920	105.7	13.9	13.7	0.4	2.9%
1930	122.8	14.2	17.1	0.3	1.8%
1940	131.7	11.6	8.9	(2.6)	(29.2%)
1950	151.3	10.3	19.6	(1.3)	(6.6%)
1960	179.3	9.7	28.0	(0.6)	(2.1%)
1970	203.3	9.6	24.0	(0.1)	(0.4%)
1980	226.5	14.1	23.2	4.5	19.4%
1990	248.7	19.8	22.2	5.7	25.7%
2000	281.4	31.1	32.7	11.3	34.6%
2005	290.9	35.2	9.5	4.1	43.2%

Sources: CIS and Census Bureau. Foreign-born contribution calculated by author.

In the first five years of the 21st century, immigration accounted for a record 43.2 percent of U.S. population growth—more than twice what it was during the 1880–1920 Great Wave. Think about that the next time you hear immigration enthusiasts prattle on about the foreign influx being really quite low.

Foreign Stock

Immigration's contribution to population growth does not tell the whole story. Immigrants have children after they arrive in the United States. The immigrants, by definition foreign-born, and their U.S.-born children together constitute what demographers call "foreign stock."

Immigrants seem to have children at a faster pace than native-born Americans. Fertility rates (births per 1,000 women of child bearing ages, 15 to 44) in 2002[1] were 102 births per 1,000 immigrants, 59 births per 1,000 native-born.

Although fertility is falling for both natives and the foreign-born, the share of immigrant females in child-bearing ages is rising, while a smaller share of native-born females are in this bracket. As a result, absolute numbers of births to immigrant mothers have quadrupled over the past three decades:

- 228,486 in 1970 (6.1 percent of all births)
- 339,662 in 1980 (9.4 percent of all births)
- 621,442 in 1990 (14.9 percent of all births)
- 915,800 in 2002 (22.7 percent of all births)

Even in 1910, during the peak of the Great Wave, only 21.9 percent of births were to foreign-born mothers, according to a Center for Immigration Studies report.[2]

And back then, of course, the native birth rate was much higher than it is now, while immigration was poised to decline. Illegal immigration was a rarity—a situation generally conducive to assimilation. This is not the case today. Births to illegal alien mothers—aka "anchor babies"—accounted for a whopping 42 percent of all immigrant births in 2002. That may sound surprising until you consider that illegals account for at least one-quarter of the total foreign-born population and a still larger share of foreign-born females in the prime childbearing years, 18 to 39. Moreover, their fertility rate—average number of births per mother of childbearing age—is higher than that of legal immigrants.

The share of U.S. population growth attributable to foreign stock—immigrants and their U.S.-born children—rose each decade since 1970. Overall, foreign stock accounted for more than half (50.7 percent) of U.S. population growth between 1970 and 2004, as shown in Table 3.

Table 3: Foreign Stock's Share of U.S. Population Growth, 1970-2004

Year	Total Population (in millions)	Total Post 1970 Immigrant Stock (in millions)	Post-1970 Change in Foreign Stock as % Population Growth	% Change, 1970-2004
1970	203.3			
1980	226.5	8.6	36.9%	
1990	248.8	19.9	51.0%	
2000	281.4	38.3	56.1%	
2004	293.6	45.9	61.9%	50.7%

Note: Census Bureau estimates for 2004 population differ from the Current Population Survey figures in previous tables.

Sources: Joy Lee, Jack Martin, Stan Fogel, "Immigrant Stock's Share of U.S. Population Growth," Federation for American Immigration Reform, 2005. Appendix A. *http://www.fairus.org/site/DocServer/immstock_report. pdf?docID=462.*

The foreign stock is distributed unevenly among the states. In several states, it accounted for more than 100 percent of population growth, owing to a decrease in the native born population (see Table 4).

Table 4: States in Which Post-1970 Immigrant Stock Accounted for the Highest Percentage of Total Population Growth, 1970-2004

Rank	State	% of total population growth
1	New York	541.2%
2	New Jersey	134.8%
3	Massachusetts	134.6%
4	Illinois	134.0%
5	Rhode Island	117.9%
6	Pennsylvania	110.4%
7	Connecticut	102.2%
8	Iowa	99.3%
9	North Dakota	94.6%
10	California	86.2%

Sources: Joy Lee, Jack Martin, Stan Fogel, "Immigrant Stock's Share of U.S. Population Growth," Federation for American Immigration Reform, 2005. Table D. *http://www.fairus.org/site/DocServer/immstock_report.pdf?docID=462.*

While much of the concentration of foreigners is in traditional immigrant gateway states, the impact has spread to hinterland locales such as Iowa and North Dakota. More than one-quarter of the 1970–2004 population growth in Nebraska and Kansas is also attributable to foreign stock.[3]

Illegal Immigrants

In January 2004 President Bush proposed granting "guest worker" status to the millions of illegal aliens working in the United States. This de facto amnesty would enable workers and their family members to remain in the country until they became naturalized citizens.

How many illegals are we talking about?

- 8.7 million, according to the 2000 census
- 10.3 million, according to the Pew Hispanic Center
- 12 million according to Homeland Security[4]
- 20 million, according to Bear Stearns[5]
- **Fact #1:** No one knows how many illegal aliens are living in the United States.
- **Fact #2:** Anecdotal evidence suggests the census estimates are way too low.
- **Fact #3:** Mexicans make up by far the largest group of illegals—57 percent of the total, according to the March 2004 census survey.

Illegal aliens are loath to fill out the questionnaires on which the Census Bureau bases its population figures (surprise! surprise!). For the Census Bureau, and the groups that use its figures, such as the cottage industry of illegal alien estimators at work inside the Beltway, undercounts are inevitable—which is why the Census Bureau estimate has been repeatedly revised upward.

The Mexicanization of Immigration

Another unique feature of today's immigration is its increasing lack of diversity. Mexicans alone accounted for 30.7 percent of all foreign-born in 2005, up from 28 percent in 2000, 22 percent in 1990, and 16 percent in 1980. In 1970, Italy—the top country of origin—accounted for only ten percent of the foreign-born population. In 2005, Mexico accounted for almost six times as many immigrants as the combined total for China, Taiwan, and Hong Kong. As recently as 1970, Mexico had only the fourth highest foreign-born population—behind Italy, Germany, and Canada.

Moreover, Mexicanization of U.S. immigration is accelerating. Here is the share of entrants from the top five countries of origin in the 2000–2005 period:

- Mexico: 36.0 percent
- India: 5.8 percent
- China/Hong Kong/Taiwan: 4.5 percent
- Philippines: 3.3 percent
- El Salvador: 2.6 percent

The large inflows to the United States have resulted in a significant share—about nine percent—of the Mexican-born population of the world actually residing in the United States. The number is expected to increase from 10.8 million in 2005 to more than 22 million in 2050. At that time more than one in seven (15 percent) of persons born in Mexico are expected to be living in the United States.[6]

Ethnic Mix of U.S. Population

Whites are the largest racial group in the country, but their grip on that status is weak by historic standards and is rapidly getting weaker. Of the nearly 294 million people in the country in 2004, about 198 million, or 67.4 percent, identified themselves as white and non-Hispanic. As recently as 1990, 76 percent of Americans called themselves non-Hispanic white.

It's not that whites are fewer in number, but that minority groups are increasing rapidly due mainly to a surge in immigration. While the white population grew by 9.5 million since 1990, or about five percent, all other categories grew by 35.3 million, about 58 percent. Since 1990, nonwhite minorities have accounted for nearly 80 percent of U.S. population growth, according to census data.

Table 5: Immigrant Stock Increases by Race/Ethnicity, 1970-2004

Ethnic Group	1970 Population (in thousands)	Post-1970 Immigrant Stock	
		Increase (in thousands)	as % of 1970 population
Asian/Pacific Islander	1,538.7	11,994.6	779.5%
Mexican	4,532.4	16,208.6	357.6%
Other Hispanic	5,056.8	8,224.3	162.6%
Black	22,580.3	3,710.1	16.4%
White, non-Hispanic	169,023.1	4,399.3	2.6%

Sources: Joy Lee, Jack Martin, Stan Fogel, "Immigrant Stock's Share of U.S. Population Growth," Federation for American Immigration Reform, 2005. Table D. *http://www.fairus.org/site/DocServer/immstock_report.pdf?docID=462.*

This increase in Hispanic and Asian populations parallels the rapid rise of immigrants from Mexico and China.

But the foreign influx is only part of the reason for the rapid growth of these ethnic groups. The other reason is the generally higher fertility rates among them.

Table 5 illustrates the population increase attributable to immigrant stock for major ethnic/racial categories.

The fastest-growing immigrant stock has been Asian, and the largest increase has been Mexican; non-Hispanic whites lag in both numbers and growth. It should come as no surprise, then, that the Census Bureau projects that minorities will account for nearly 90 percent of the total growth in the U.S. population over the 2000 to 2050 period, and that by 2050 the non-Hispanic white share of the U.S. population will drop to 50.1 percent.[7] (These shares reflect the population of individuals who categorize themselves as "non-Hispanic white alone." Multi-racial non-Hispanic whites are not included.)

More striking is the decade-to-decade decline in white population growth. By the 2040s, the number of non-Hispanic whites will actually start to decline, according to Census Bureau projections (see Figure 1).

Comparisons with previous census counts are not exact because the methods of counting different races have changed significantly throughout the years.

Figure 1: Non-Hispanic White Population, 2000-2050
(Census Bureau Projections; *www.census.gov/ipc/www/usinterimproj/*)

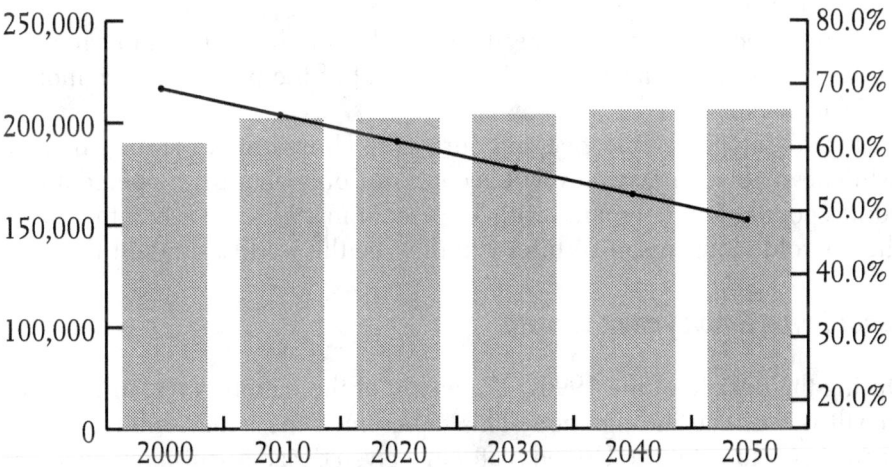

Population (thousands; left axis)
Population share (%; right axis)

But it is clear that, for most of our history, whites were the dominant share of America's population, as well as a growing one. The first census, in 1790, for example, found that almost 81 percent of the country considered itself white. That number had risen to 89 percent by 1950.[8]

There are 14 U.S. states in which whites account for more than 85 percent of the population. All but two of them are in the Midwest or Northeast. The two "whitest" states are Maine (96.1 percent) and Vermont (96.0 percent). At the other extreme are the four states—Texas, New Mexico, California, and Hawaii—in which non-Hispanic whites are already a minority. Hawaii, 23 percent non-Hispanic white, is the least white state.

Immigration and domestic migration trends are increasing the regional disparities in white population densities. Newly arrived immigrants tend to cluster in long-established ethnic enclaves, where their native language is spoken and community institutions are run by earlier immigrant cohorts. Immigration laws also foster clustering, since family reunification is a priority in legal immigration.

Places that attract immigrants have the opposite effect on people who can afford to move out—mainly nonimmigrant whites. Whites are moving out of California. Seven of the nine leading immigrant metropolitan destinations saw more nonimmigrants move out than move in over the past decade. Race is not necessarily the reason for this white flight. As demographer William Frey has written: "Domestic migrants are leaving immigrant magnets, not as a response to immigrants per se, but because of the increasing congestion and high costs of living in highly urbanized metro areas."[9] To which we add: Their displacement by low-wage immigrants is another factor behind the exodus of whites from large metropolitan areas.

Our projections indicate a steady rise in the number of states in which non-Hispanic whites will account for less than half of the population, as indicated in Table 6.

From a global perspective, of course, the United States is still an oasis of "whiteness." By 2010, whites will account for only about nine percent of the world's population, compared with 17 percent in 1997, according to demographer Harold Hodgkinson. Whites will then be the world's smallest minority.[10]

Labor Force/Employment Growth

During the decade of the 1990s, 47 percent of the nation's civilian labor force growth was due to immigration. This represented the largest influx of foreign workers ever to enter the United States in a given decade—substantially exceeding the number that came here during the Great Wave of 1890 to 1910.[11] Records are made to be broken, nowhere more so than in U.S. immigration stats. During the 2000 to 2005 period, foreign-born individuals accounted for:

- 37 percent of U.S. population growth
- 51 percent of U.S. labor force growth
- 82 percent of U.S. employment growth

Table 6: States Where Whites Are/Will Be a Minority, 2004-2050
(non-Hispanic white % in parenthesis)

2004 (actual)	2025 (projection)	2050 (projection)
Texas (49.8%)	Texas (36.1%)	Texas (22.4%)
California (44.5%)	California (33.6%)	California (22.7%)
New Mexico (43.5%)	New Mexico (37.2%)	New Mexico (30.3%)
Hawaii (23.3%)	Hawaii (25.9%)	Hawaii (29.2%)
	Florida (47.8%)	Florida (30.7%)
	Maryland (47.6%)	Maryland (33.5%)
	Georgia (47.0%)	Georgia (32.0%)
	Arizona (46.1%)	Arizona (29.4%)
	Nevada (39.0%)	Nevada (19.9%)
		Mississippi (50.0%)
		Virginia (49.4%)
		North Carolina (48.7%)
		Illinois (45.3%)
		Colorado (44.7%)
		Delaware (40.7%)
		New Jersey (36.1%)

Note: Projections were derived by extrapolating each state's 2000 to 2004 average annual white and non-white population growth rates.

The underlying numbers are presented in Table 7.

The foreign-born share of the labor force grew from 12.6 percent in 2000 to 14.8 percent in 2004. Thus, it took about 225 years of nationhood for the foreign-born share of our labor force to reach 12.6 percent—and only five additional years to reach 14.8 percent. If the immigrant and U.S.-born labor forces continue growing at their 2000–2005 rates, the foreign-born share will reach the following levels:

- 2010: 17.3 percent
- 2025: 26.8 percent
- 2050: 48.2 percent

By contrast, at the peak of the "Great Wave" in 1910, the foreign-born share of the U.S. labor force was slightly more than 15 percent. (Estimate assumes the same foreign-born labor force/population ratio as in 2005.)

Unfortunately, the government's monthly employment report does not track immigrant workers. But the BLS does track Hispanic employment, and, because so many Hispanics are immigrants or the children of immigrants, their employment history is a good proxy for that of immigrants. Similarly, the ratio of Hispanic to non-Hispanic employment growth is a good indication of native worker displacement.

Table 7: U.S.-Born Versus Immigrant Population, Labor Force, and Job Growth, 2000-2005

	2000	2005	Increase, 2000-05	% of Increase, 2000-05
Population				
Total	209,699	226,082	16,383	7.8%
U.S.-born	183,173	193,525	10,352	5.7%
Foreign-born	26,527	32,558	6,031	22.7%
% of total	12.7%	14.4%	36.8%	
Labor Force				
Total	140,863	149,320	8,457	6.0%
U.S.-born	123,158	127,278	4,120	3.3%
Foreign-born	17,705	22,042	4,337	24.5%
% of total	12.6%	14.8%	51.3%	
Employed				
Total	135,208	141,730	6,522	4.8%
U.S.-born	118,254	120,706	2,454	2.1%
Foreign-born	16,954	21,022	4,068	24.0%
% of total	12.5%	14.8%	82.4%	

Notes: All figures in thousands unless noted.

Sources: Census Bureau, Current Population Survey. Unpublished tables sent to author by BLS economist Abraham Mosisa, (202) 691-6346.

The following graph shows month-to-month growth in Hispanic and non-Hispanic employment since the start of the Bush administration, as well as the ratio of the two growth rates—which we call the VDARE.COM Worker Displacement index (VDAWDI). (See Figure 2.)

Figure 2: Vdare.com's American Worker Displacement
Index (VDAWDI) January 2001-January 2007
(January 2001 = 100.0)

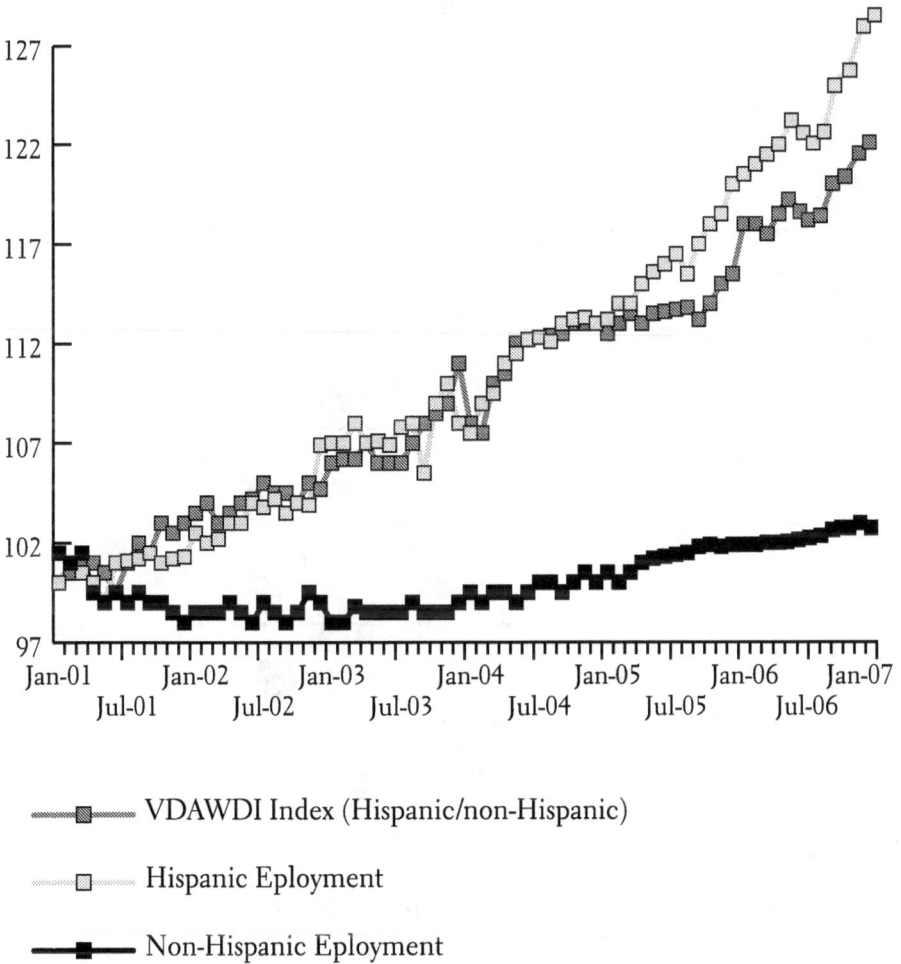

——■—— VDAWDI Index (Hispanic/non-Hispanic)

········□········ Hispanic Eployment

——■—— Non-Hispanic Eployment

- Hispanic employment rose 4.10 million (+25.5 percent)
- Non-Hispanic employment rose 4.08 million (+3.4 percent)
- VDAWDI displacement index rose 20.8 percent, to 120.8

Displacement of black workers by unskilled immigrants is suggested by the widening gap between black and Hispanic unemployment rates (see Figure 3).

Figure 3: Unemployment Rates by Race/Ethnicity, 1990-January 2007

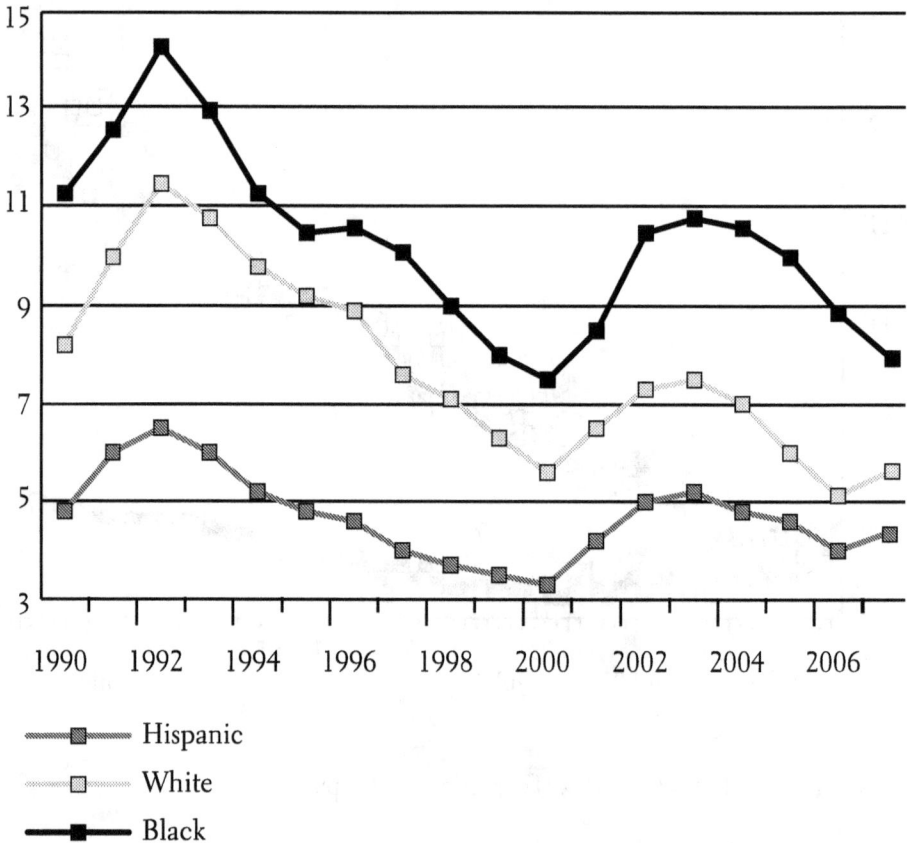

In 2000, the black unemployment rate was 1.9 points above the Hispanic rate; in 2006, the black unemployment rate was actually 3.7 points above the Hispanic rate—although the former was a recession year, and the latter four years into an economic recovery. By contrast, white and Hispanic unemployment rates were lower.

Historically, black unemployment shrank more rapidly than white and Hispanic unemployment during economic recoveries, reflecting the overrepresentation of blacks in manufacturing and other highly cyclical sectors of the economy. The trend held in the early 1990s; it abruptly ended with the Bush II economic recovery.[12]

Why the persistently high black unemployment rate? Discrimination may be the best explanation—but not the sort of discrimination affirmative action is designed to combat. The most racist policy in this country for the past quarter century has been immigration policy. U.S. companies knowingly employ millions of illegal immigrants while the government looks the other way. The illegals are paid less than comparable native minorities, but they obviously cannot sue their employers.

The onslaught of poorly educated, mainly Hispanic immigrants has stymied good-faith efforts of low-income Americans—minority and white alike—to climb up the economic ladder.

Importing Poverty

Census Bureau figures for 2004 show incomes stagnated, poverty was up, and the uninsured population reached a record high.[13] This occurred despite an economic recovery now in its fourth year. The Bush Administration responded by saying, in effect, "Wait till next year," when the recent spurt of job creation and new health insurance legislation will be reflected in the data. Perhaps. But the numbers already in hand show that U.S. immigration policy has weakened this recovery and put future gains at risk. It is increasingly clear that uncontrolled immigration is damaging the economic position of native-born U.S. workers.

Immigrants and their U.S.-born children are far more likely to be poor than U.S. natives. The March 2005 Current Population Survey found the following results:[14]

- 17.1 percent of immigrants are poor.
- 12.0 percent of natives are poor.
- 18.4 percent of immigrant stock (including U.S.-born children) are poor.

If you simply exclude poor immigrants and their children, the poverty population would decline by 8.5 million, or to 28.5 million. The overall poverty rate would fall to 11.7 percent.

But, of course, this static effect is only part of the impact of immigration on the poverty rate. There is also a dynamic effect. If these poor immigrants were not present in this country, wage competition would arguably be reduced—and even fewer Americans would be in poverty.

There are large variations in poverty among immigrants from different countries (see Table 8).

At 26.4 percent, the poverty rate for Mexicans is twice that of Koreans and more than five times that of persons from Canada or the Philippines.

Given the increased Mexicanization of the immigrant population, and the perverse tendency of American immigration policy to favor the poorest, least-skilled, and least versed in English, increases in immigrant poverty rates are inevitable.

Table 8: Immigrant Poverty Rates Ranked by Country of Origin, 2004

Country of Origin	In Poverty (in thousands)	In Poverty (%)
Mexico	2,847	26.4%
Dominican Republic	174	25.1%
Russia	107	20.6%
Guatemala	110	20.6%
Haiti	117	20.6%
Honduras	76	20.1%
Cuba	161	17.0%
Colombia	78	16.3%
Brazil	55	15.4%
El Salvador	164	14.7%
Vietnam	142	14.3%
Korea	89	13.2%
All Immigrants	6,006	17.1%
All Natives	30,991	12.0%

Sources: Steven Camarota, "Immigrants at Mid-Decade: A snapshot of America's Foreign-born Population in 2005," CIS, December 2005. Table 10. (Percentages calculated by author.) *http://www.cis.org/articles/2005/back1405.pdf.*

Dependency

The 1996 federal welfare reform law prohibits immigrants who entered the United States after August 22, 1996, from receiving most types of public assistance. (The ban is lifted when the immigrant becomes an American citizen.) Nevertheless, most states have filled the gap, enacting programs that grant welfare eligibility to new arrivals. As a result, immigrants continue to receive every major welfare program at higher rates than native-born Americans.

An analysis of Census Bureau survey data reveals that in 2004:

- 28.6 percent of immigrant households received at least one major welfare program.
- 18.2 percent of native households received at least one major welfare program.

And remember, the native-born rate is boosted by troubled subgroups like blacks and Hispanics. The dependency rate of white, non-Hispanic households is significantly below that of the other groups, as indicated in Table 9.

Table 9: Welfare Recipiency Rates by Race/Ethnicity, 2001

Program	All Races	White non-Hispanic	Black	Hispanic
	% of households receiving benefits			
Any Means-Tested Non-Cash Benefit	20.0%	14.0%	39.0%	41.8%
Medicaid	14.5%	10.4%	27.3%	28.6%
Food Stamps	5.4%	3.6%	13.5%	9.5%
Subsidized Housing	4.6%	3.0%	12.9%	6.2%
School Lunch	7.3%	3.8%	16.5%	22.7%

Sources: U.S. Census, Current Population Survey (CPS), Annual Demographic Survey, 2001. *http://ferret.bls.census.gov/macro/032002/noncash/nc1_000.htm.*

Only 14 percent white households received means-tested benefits in 2001. That was about one-third the dependency rate of Hispanic households (41.8 percent) and less than half that of black households (39.0 percent).

Dependency rate differences primarily reflect differences in poverty rates. In 2001, the poverty rate for blacks (22.7 percent) and for people of Hispanic origin (21.9 percent) was nearly three times the poverty rate for non-Hispanic whites (7.8 percent).[15]

Dependency by Country of Origin

As with poverty, there are enormous variations in welfare dependency among immigrant groups. The most recent survey shows

- *First place:* Immigrants from the Dominican Republic. Nearly three in five (57.2 percent) Dominican immigrant households received at least one means-tested program in 2004.
- *Runner-up:* Immigrants from Mexico. Over two in five (43.4 percent) of Mexican immigrant households are on welfare.
- *Dead last:* Only about 1 in 30 (3.4 percent) immigrant households from Italy receives benefits.

The welfare dependency rates for 25 countries of origin are found in Table 10.

The data was extracted from a March 2005 Census Bureau survey by the enterprising Steven Camarota of the Center for Immigration Studies. The table is not comprehensive, however. It omits, for example, 1990's two most dependent immigrant groups, whose countries of origin were Cambodia and Laos. In that year, their welfare participation rate was nearly twice that of Dominican immigrants—reflecting the presence of profoundly troubled subgroups, like the Hmong.[16]

But this 2004 list does include the largest immigrant blocs. For example, Mexican immigrants and their U.S.-born children now comprise about 4.2 percent of total U.S. population and 10.2 percent of all persons in poverty. One reason for high welfare usage is that some national groups include many refugees—for example, Russian and Vietnamese immigrants (40 and 32 percent on welfare, respectively). Refugees are immediately entitled to welfare, and it's addictive. Even after 20 years, refugees are still more likely to be on welfare than either native-born Americans or nonrefugee immigrants.

The most immigrant-subsidizing benefit of all was not even addressed by the 1996 welfare reform. The Earned Income Tax Credit (EITC) is not a welfare program but part of the tax code. It provides cash refunds to low-income workers with children. Technically, only immigrants with legal work status are eligible for EITC.

Table 10: Welfare Participation by Country of Birth of Household Head, 2004

Country	Major Means Tested Programs (Percent receiving benefits)	Earned Income Tax Credit (Percent receiving benefits)
Dominican Republic	57.2%	40.1%
Mexico	43.4%	49.9%
Russia	39.8%	12.5%
Honduras	37.5%	42.4%
Guatemala	35.7%	49.5%
Haiti	35.3%	40.6%
Cuba	33.0%	17.2%
Vietnam	31.8%	28.4%
Jamaica	31.3%	33.2%
Colombia	29.7%	29.1%
El Salvador	29.7%	42.3%
All Immigrants	**28.6%**	**30.0%**
Ecuador	23.1%	19.2%
Iran	21.9%	19.2%
Brazil	21.9%	26.8%
Peru	20.6%	30.8%
China	18.5%	22.5%
All Natives	**18.2%**	**15.8%**
Korea	17.4%	13.1%
Philippines	15.6%	18.1%
Japan	13.4%	16.8%
Canada	12.2%	7.1%
Poland	10.8%	9.7%
Great Britain	10.8%	13.6%
Germany	9.1%	11.7%
India	7.9%	15.4%
Italy	3.4%	4.7%

Sources: Steven Camarota, "Immigrants at Mid-Decade: A snapshot of America's Foreign-born Population in 2005," CIS, December 2005. Table 13. *http://www.cis.org/articles/2005/back1405.pdf*

But, in fact, the IRS, with its celebrated kind-heartedness, allows immigrants to claim EITC benefits retroactively for up to three years before they obtain legal work status. This, in effect, gives refunds to people for work they performed while here illegally—work on which they very well may not have paid taxes. At $30 billion per year, EITC is the nation's most expensive means-tested cash benefit program.

Overall, the latest results validate one of George Borjas's key conclusions from his 1991 study: National origin matters.[17] In general, immigrants from Europe participate in means-tested programs at about one-third the rate of immigrants from Mexico and the Caribbean.

Fiscal Burden

We have shown that immigrants are poorer and more likely to receive public benefits than natives. It follows, then, that they are taking more from the various levels of government than they are paying in taxes.

Yet immigration enthusiasts deny this. Julian Simon, for example, in his book *The Economic Consequences of Immigration*, claimed that "an immigrant family is an excellent investment." In a July 13, 1993, cover story, *Business Week* reported that immigrants pay $90 billion in taxes and get only $5 billion in services. The $5 billion, however, referred to cash benefits only—ignoring noncash means-tested benefits like Medicaid, EITC, housing subsidies, and food stamps. In 2005, the largest means-tested cash benefit, TANF, cost taxpayers $22 billion, while the largest noncash benefit, Medicaid, cost about $300 billion.

There has been little objective analysis on the fiscal burden imposed by immigrants. The most comprehensive study is still that in *The New Americans*, the National Research Council's 1997 study of immigration's economic and demographic impact. The NRC staff analyzed California's state and local government expenditures on programs such as Medicaid, AFDC (now TANF), and SSI, as well as the cost of educating immigrants' foreign- and native-born children. Their analysis also included the immigrant household's estimated share of costs related to police and fire-fighting forces, public works, general health, recreation, higher education, and municipal assistance.

The NRC concluded that immigrants generated a fiscal deficit of $3,463 per household—that is, they received $3,463 (1996 dollars) more in state and local spending than they paid in state and local taxes. In 2005 dollars, NRC's deficit is $4,151 per immigrant household. Using California as a proxy for the national average, we estimate the state and local deficit attributable to immigrants to be approximately $58.9 billion (14.2 million immigrant households × $4,151).

Immigrants also exacerbate the Federal deficit. Illegal aliens receive more than $26.3 billion in Federal services while paying only $16 billion in Federal taxes, adding about $10.3 billion to the deficit.[18] That works out to a deficit of $2,972 per illegal alien household. Applying this deficit to all immigrant households, the net drain on the Federal budget due to immigrants is $42.2 billion (14.2 million households × $2,972). Adding the two deficits, we can safely conclude that immigrants receive about $101.1 billion more in government benefits that they pay in taxes. In other words, natives are forced to pay about $100 billion in additional taxes to support immigrants.

Taxes Lost Due to Lower Native Income

A study by Harvard University Professor George Borjas finds that each ten percent increase in the U.S. labor force due to immigration reduces native wages by about 3.5 percent.[19] Foreign-born workers account for about 15.0 percent of the U.S. labor force. If Borjas is right, immigrant workers reduce average native wages by 5.25 percent (15.0/10.0 × 3.5 percent).This obviously will reduce revenues from personal-income taxes, payroll taxes, sales, and excise taxes. By contrast, corporate-income tax receipts will probably rise, because cheap immigrant labor reduces costs and increases profits of U.S. corporations.

A "quick and dirty" way to estimate lost revenues is to assume that taxes sensitive to personal income decline at the same rate as personal income. If U.S.-born workers suffer a 5.25-percent reduction in income, total personal income will fall by about 4.6 percent, the difference reflecting the fact that native-born workers receive 88 percent of personal income. (In 2004, U.S.-born workers accounted for 85 percent of the workforce and an estimated 88 percent of personal income. Median weekly income of U.S.-born workers in 2003 was $688; foreign-born workers earned $511 per week.)

Using this model, immigrant workers generate the revenue losses detailed in Table 11.

Based on these calculations, native-born workers pay $98.4 billion less in taxes, owing to their immigrant-related wage losses.

The total fiscal losses from immigration are thus estimated at nearly $200 billion—101.1 billion direct and $98.4 billion from the displacement of native workers.

Economic Bottom Line: A Loss

American economists have made relatively little effort to measure the overall economic effects of immigration. But when they have, the answer is clear: Immigration does not contribute much to economic growth. The consensus: the economic surplus (benefits less costs) generated by immigrants and accruing to native-born Americans is very small—about one-tenth of one percent of GDP.

Table 11: Tax Revenues Lost From Displacement of U.S.-Born Workers by Foreign-Born Workers

	Total Revenues (in billions)	Revenue Loss (in billions)	Percentage Loss
Federal Tax Revenues (2004)			
Individual Income Taxes	$809.0	$37.2	(4.6%)
Social Security Taxes	$733.4	$33.7	(4.6%)
Excise Taxes	$69.9	$3.2	(4.6%)
Subtotal-Federal	$1,612.3	$74.2	(4.6%)
State and Local Tax Revenues (2002)			
Individual Income Taxes	$202.8	$9.3	(4.6%)
Sales and use taxes	$324.0	$14.9	(4.6%)
Subtotal-State and Local	$526.8	$24.2	(4.6%)
TOTAL-Fed., State, Local	$2,139.1	$98.4	(4.6%)

Sources: Federal Revenues (2004): OMB; State and Local Tax Revenues (2002): Tax Foundation. Revenue loss estimates calculated by author.

One-tenth of one percent of GDP translates to a $12.5-billion immigration surplus. But if immigration imposes a fiscal loss on native taxpayers of $200 billion—as we calculated previously—that means that its net economic effects are a negative $187.5 billion.

American society is being transformed by a policy that, at the end of the day, makes us slightly poorer.

Of course, not all of "us" lose. By pushing down wages, immigration triggers a substantial redistribution of income from native-born workers to native-born owners of capital. Borjas calculates that this redistribution amounts to about two percent of GDP, or a whopping $250 billion at current levels.

Native elites gain this sum at the expense of native workers.

Education

Low education levels are a major factor behind the above-average poverty and dependency rates of immigrants. The share of adults (25 to 64) who have less than a high-school degree, and have at least a BA degree in 2005, are as follows:[20]

- Less than HS degree: immigrants: 31.0 percent; natives: 8.7 percent
- BA or more: immigrants: 27.9 percent; natives: 30.0 percent

The percentage of 16- to 24-year-olds who are out of school and who have not earned a high school credential, such as a General Educational Degree (GED), is called the "status dropout rate" in EdSpeak. In 2002, the status dropout rate for Hispanics was 25.7 percent, or more than twice the rate for blacks (11.3 percent), and about four times the white rate (6.5 percent). And younger Hispanics show no sign of catching up. Although Hispanic dropout rates have declined by 7.3 percentage points since 1972 (the first year of available data), other ethnicities have experienced greater improvements over that period, and the relative dropout rate disadvantage of Hispanic students has widened.

Immigrants are responsible for most—but not all—of the stubborn trend. Buried in the Department of Education's The Condition of Education 2005 is a revealing fact: First-generation Hispanics are four times more likely to drop out of high school than other first-generation immigrants, as Table 12 reveals.

Table 12: Dropout Rates by Recency of Immigration, 2002

Immigration Status	Hispanic	Non-Hispanic	Hispanic/ Non-Hispanic
Born Outside the U.S.	41.4%	5.3%	7.8 times
First Generation	14.4%	3.5%	4.1 times
Second Generation	11.3%	7.8%	1.4 times

Note: Dropout rates are the percentage of 16 to 24 year olds in each group who are not enrolled in high school and lack a high-school credential.

Sources: Dept. of Education, "The Condition of Education 2005," Table 19-2. *http://nces.ed.gov/programs/coe/2005/pdf/19_2005.pdf.*

The horrific dropout rate for foreign-born Hispanic youth—41.4 percent—may, in fact, understate their educational disadvantage. More than half of them never enrolled in a U.S. school but are counted as high-school graduates if they completed high school in their country of origin.

At the other end of the educational spectrum, natives now have a slight advantage in having at least a BA degree. Historically, immigrants had a significant BA-advantage. In 1970, for example, before the 1965 Immigration Act had time to bite, 18 percent of immigrants (25 to 64) had at least a BA degree versus 12 percent of natives. But, in 2005, the share of native-born adults with a BA degree or better (30.0 percent) was slightly higher than that of immigrants (27.9 percent). Because education is so important to economic and social success, this does not augur well for the future of immigrants in America.

Pro-immigration groups understandably downplay the declining quality of new immigrants. Exhibit A: a 2005 Pew Hispanic Center study by Jeffrey S. Passel.[21] The report claims that illegal aliens—now apparently "unauthorized migrants" in Pewspeak—are "like most Americans" in terms of education. To quote one gushing press account: "Around a quarter of the unauthorized population has some college education and the numbers of high school degree holders—over half— among the subset is greater than that of their documented peers."[22]

Of course, even the Pew study has to concede that nearly half (49 percent) of the illegal population has not completed high school, as opposed to one-quarter of naturalized immigrants and less than a tenth (nine percent) of native-born Americans, as shown in Table 13.

Table 13: Educational Status: Natives Versus Immigrants, 2004

Population Age 25-64 , 2004	Percentage of Population
Less than HS Graduate	
Natives	9%
Naturalized Citizens	25%
Illegal Immigrants	49%
College Degree or Beyond	
Natives	30%
Naturalized Citizens	32%
Illegal Immigrants	15%

Sources: Jeffrey S. Passel, "*Unauthorized Migrants: Numbers and Characteristics,*" Pew Hispanic Center, June 14, 2005, pp. 23-24.

But do 15 percent of illegal border crossers really have a "college degree or beyond"? Do more than one-half have HS degrees? No: A neat bit of statistical legerdemain forced these results.

Between 25 and 40 percent of the individuals counted as "unauthorized" in the Pew report are actually "overstays"—persons admitted on temporary visas who either stay beyond the expiration date of their visa or otherwise violate the terms of their admission. This group includes high-tech workers admitted under the H–1b visa program, medical doctors with J–1 visas, and even tourists who travel here for the express purpose of seeking asylum in the United States: hardly your middle-of-the-night border crosser.

Statistical chicanery aside, the plain fact is that the relative education and incomes of successive cohorts of immigrants have deteriorated.[23]

Jobs Americans Won't Do?

When unveiling his guest work proposal a few years ago, President Bush urged Americans to "legalize the process of people doing jobs Americans won't do." Illegal immigrants, in this view, are essential to the country's economic growth. Nothing could be further from the truth.

There are an estimated seven million illegal aliens working in the United States, or about 4.5 percent of the civilian labor force. Certain occupations have abnormally high concentrations of illegals, for example:[24]

- Drywall/ceiling tile installers, 27 percent
- Gardeners, 26 percent
- Maids and housekeepers, 22 percent
- Construction laborers, 20 percent

Yet illegals make up only 13 percent of hotel industry workers, 13 percent of food-manufacturing industry workers, 11 percent of workers in food preparation and serving, and eight percent of workers in production. Clearly, millions of Americans are, in fact, doing precisely the same jobs. And countless others were working in these fields before being displaced by foreign-born workers.

It's also obvious that native workers need these jobs: 19 million U.S.-born adults do not have a high-school degree. Only 7.1 million of them are in the labor force, and 684,000—nearly ten percent of this labor force—are unemployed.[25] American workers in building cleaning and maintenance have an 11-percent unemployment rate, as do 13 percent of native construction workers and nine percent of those in food preparation. There appears to be no dearth of American workers, but rather wages and working conditions that sink lower with each arriving wave of illegal aliens.

U.S. Economy Dependent on Illegals?

The share of GDP generated by the illegal alien workforce is considerably less than their numbers would suggest.

Foreign-born Hispanic workers (legal and illegal) in the United States less than ten years made $321 per week in 2004, or just 55 percent of the median weekly wage of U.S. natives.[26] More than half, 57 percent, of Mexican immigrants who work in manufacturing, and 60 percent who work in agriculture, made less than $300 a week. If these workers are supporting a family of four, they are living below the poverty line, according to a recent Pew Hispanic Center study.

And illegals surely make less than the average immigrant. If they earn, say, 40 percent of what natives make, the share of GDP attributable to illegal alien workers would be a mere 1.8 percent (4.5 percent × 40 percent).

Immigrants are also more likely to be out of work. Unemployment rates for foreign-born noncitizens—a category that includes legal guest workers as well as illegal immigrants—averaged 6.3 percent versus 5.5 percent for natives in 2004. Put differently, 94.5 of every 100 natives in the labor force actually work, compared to 93.7 of every 100 foreign-born noncitizens.

So illegals are likely to produce less than 1.8 percent of GDP.

And even this estimate has to be qualified. It doesn't take into account the taxes that native-born Americans pay to finance government programs available to illegals—Medicaid, welfare, education for their children, and so forth.

Also, it doesn't factor in the wages lost by displaced native-born workers. Each one percent rise in U.S. labor force due to immigration reduces native wages by about 0.35 percent, according to research by Harvard economist George Borjas.[27] It follows, then, that illegal immigrant workers reduce native wages by approximately 1.6 percent (4.5 × 0.35 percent). This translates to more than $90 billion in lost wages in 2005.

Criminal Aliens

Criminal aliens—noncitizens convicted of crimes—are a growing reality.

(The criminal alien category does not completely capture the criminal consequences of immigration because criminal immigrants can be citizens. But, not for the first time, government statistics are not really trying to reflect what's going on.)

In 1980, Federal, state, and local correctional facilities held fewer than 9,000 criminal aliens. But at the end of 2003, approximately 267,000 noncitizens were incarcerated in the United States, as follows (see Table 14).

Noncitizens account for 7.2 percent of the total U.S. population, according to a 2003 census survey.[28] Their share of the prison population that year was 12.9 percent, more than half as large.

Approximately 27 percent of all prisoners in Federal custody are criminal aliens. The majority (63 percent) are citizens of Mexico. Other major nationalities include those from Colombia and the Dominican Republic, seven percent each; Jamaica, four percent; Cuba, three percent; El Salvador, two percent; and

Table 14: Non-Citizens Incarcerated in Federal, State, and Local Prisons, 2003

	Total	Non-Citizens	Citizens
Number of Inmates			
Federal	170,365	46,063	124,302
State	1,221,501	74,000	1,147,501
Local	678,000	147,000	531,000
Total	2,069,866	267,063	1,802,803
Percent of Total			
Federal	100.0%	27.0%	73.0%
State	100.0%	6.1%	93.9%
Local	100.0%	21.7%	78.3%
Total	100.0%	12.9%	87.1%

Sources: GAO, Letter to Representative John Hostettler, April 7, 2005. *http://www.gao.gov/new.items/d05337r.pdf* (non-citizens); U.S. Dept. of Justice, "Prison and Jail Inmates at Midyear 2003," Bulletin, Bureau of Justice Statistics, May 2004. *http://www.ojp.usdoj.gov/bjs/pub/pdf/pjim03.pdf* .

Honduras, Haiti, and Guatemala, one percent each. The remaining 11 percent are from 164 different countries. Diversity is strength!

The Federal government spent $1.34 billion to incarcerate criminal aliens in fiscal year 2003. This total includes $280 million of reimbursements made to state and local governments under the State Criminal Alien Assistance Program (SCAAP).[29]

The total cost of incarcerating SCAAP criminal aliens in fiscal year 2003 is estimated at $3.46 billion, allocated as follows (based on the author's analysis of data in GAO letter to Congressman John Hostettler):[30]

- Federal: $1.34 billion
- State: $1.40 billion
- Local: $0.72 billion

Although state and local outlays are reimbursable under SCAAP, the program is underfunded—resulting in an onerous fiscal burden placed on state and local governments. Making matters worse, many localities have decreed themselves "sanctuaries" and do not allow local law-enforcement officials to ask foreign-born inmates their legal status. As a result, less than 25 percent of the full cost of incarcerating criminal aliens in state and local correctional facilities is covered by SCAAP funds, according to the GAO.

Still, the public costs of incarcerating aliens are trivial alongside the private costs they impose on their victims. The GAO recently analyzed the rap sheets of more than 55,000 illegal aliens incarcerated in federal, state, and local facilities during 2003.[31]

It found these results:

- The average criminal alien was arrested for 13 prior offenses.
- 12 percent were for murder, robbery, assault, and sexually related crimes.
- Only 21 percent were immigration offenses; the rest were felonies.
- 81 percent of their arrests occurred after 1990.

In a word, criminal aliens are not casual law breakers. Most are recidivists—aka career criminals. The economic burden they impose on victims, including loss of income and property, uncompensated hospital bills, and emotional pain and suffering, has been estimated at $1.6 million per property and assault crime offender.[32]

Moral: The benefits of incarcerating criminal aliens far outweigh the costs.

Public Health Consequences

They come in uninsured[33] and often with infectious diseases.[34] But, because new immigrants are generally younger than natives, on a per capita basis they use 55 percent less health care (1,139 vs. $2,546 per capita). This was the conclusion of Dr. Sarita A. Mohanty of the University of Southern California in a study she did for the express purpose of making immigrant health care costs look good.[35] However, thereafter things get worse, not for the first time in the immigration debate.[36] Long-term exposure to U.S. culture appears to be dangerous to immigrant health, and to the health of their U.S.-born children. Result: Immigration-imported health care costs are a ticking time bomb.[37]

Obesity: Some eight percent of immigrants who have lived here for less than a year are obese. But this figure jumps to 19 percent among those who have been here for at least 15 years.[38] Treating an obese person cost $1,244 more than treating an individual of normal weight in 2002 (the latest year of available data).[39] Obesity increases the risk of acquiring diabetes, especially for certain immigrant groups: Latinos, particularly Mexican-Americans, incur diabetes at close to twice the rate of whites. Nor are Asians immune.

Diabetes: The cost of treating a patient with diabetes in the United States is two to three times that of treating one without that condition.[40]

Mental Health: Although immigrants appear to have lower rates of mental illness than natives, many studies find that second- and third-generation immigrants are at higher risk for psychological distress.[41] This finding may simply reflect underdiagnosis in first-generation individuals due to the stigma associated with such problems in immigrant cultures, as well as to linguistic barriers.

Safety: We have documented the above-average propensity of U.S.-born Hispanics to die in automobile accidents and in the workplace.[42] Similar risks are found in regard to pedestrian injuries and deaths (twice as likely to kill Hispanic than non-Hispanic white children), homicides, and violence against family members.[43] The National Violence Against Woman Survey finds, for example, that Hispanic women are significantly more likely than non-Hispanic women to report that they were raped by a domestic partner at some time during their lifetime.[44]

Childhood Diseases: Finally, foreign-born children are estimated to be almost 45 percent less likely to be immunized for diphtheria, pertussis, tetanus, influenza, and Hepatitis B. Since the late 1990s, most confirmed cases of congenital rubella have occurred in children of foreign-born rather than U.S.-born mothers.[45] Because of their sheer numbers, immigrants are already responsible for a disproportionate share of the annual rise in health spending. From 2000 to 2004, the immigrant stock (immigrants and their children) accounted for about 62 percent of U.S. population growth and about 45 percent of the growth in health spending. This growth will inexorably increase.

English Language Proficiency

Inability to speak proficient English is often associated with poverty, inadequate health care, depression, and—most obviously—alienation from the mainstream American culture. The economic penalty imposed by poor English skills has been quantified: Immigrants who are not proficient in English earn 17 percent less than immigrants of similar backgrounds, experience, and education, who are proficient in English.[46]

The census has a term—"linguistic isolation" (LI)—for individuals who lack basic English skills. A linguistically isolated household is one in which "no adult speaks only English; and no adult speaks English 'very well.'"

More than one-fifth (21.9 percent) of all non-English speaking households were classified as LI in 2000. English competency varies greatly with the language spoken at home. Specifically, Linguistic Isolation afflicts:

- 2.6 million, or 23.9 percent, of Spanish-speaking households
- 855,000, or 7.9 percent, of European-language households
- 805,000, or 29.2 percent, of Asian-speaking households

Spanish speakers now form the largest LI community in the United States, comprising about 60 percent of those who do not speak English well.

Among the foreign-born, there are enormous differences between Spanish and non-Spanish language groups, as Table 15 indicates.

Table 15: English Language Proficiency of Immigrants Speaking a Language Other Than English at Home, 2000

Speaks English	Spanish	Non-Spanish
Very Well	28.1%	50.0%
Well	23.9%	28.9%
Not Well	28.6%	16.7%
Not at All	19.4%	4.4%
Total	100.0%	100.0%

Note: Population five years and older.

Sources: Census Bureau, Census 2000, Detailed Tables, Table PCT 12. *http://factfinder.census.gov/servlet/DTTable?_ts=81279693520.*

Only 52 percent of the Spanish-speaking immigrants are fluent in English (i.e., speak it "well" or "very well"), compared with about 80 percent of non-Spanish language groups. Or to put it another way, 48 percent of Spanish-language immigrants lack English language fluency, compared to only 20 percent of the other language groups. Moreover, 19.4 percent of the Spanish-speaking immigrants reported that they could not speak English at all, compared to only 4.4 percent of the non-Spanish immigrant group. The relative disadvantage of Spanish-speaking immigrants in speaking English is apparent even when the data are adjusted for age and citizenship status.

Conclusion

Through commission and omission, Federal government policy has steered the United States into the greatest immigration storm in its history. The historic American nation is being displaced, to the considerable economic disadvantage of the majority of its citizens, although greatly to the benefit of certain elite groups. At the same time, federal policy is effectively importing various social pathologies and divisiveness, which experience suggests will last for generations. There is no economic rationale for this policy. As to whether there is a political or moral rationale, I leave readers of this chapter to judge for themselves.

Endnotes

[1] Steven A. Camarota, "Births to Immigrants in America 1970 to 2002," Center for Immigration Studies, July 2005. http://www.cis.org/articles/2005/back805.html.

[2] Ibid.

[3] Joy Lee, Jack Martin, Stan Fogel, "Immigrant Stock's Share of U.S. Population Growth," Federation for American Immigration Reform, 2005. http://www.fairus.org/site/DocServer/immstock_report.pdf?docID=462.

[4] Jerry Seper, "Ridge Rapped for Immigration Views," *Washington Times*, http://www.washington-times.com/national/20031211-120505-1795r.htm, December 11, 2003.

[5] Robert Justich and Betty Ng, "The Underground Labor Force is Rising to the Surface," Bear Stearns Asset Management, January 3, 2005. http://www.bearstearns.com/bscportal/pdfs/underground.pdf.

[6] Jeffrey S. Passel, "Undocumented Migrants: Numbers and Characteristics," Pew Hispanic Center, June 14, 2005, http://pewhispanic.org/files/reports/46.pdf.

[7] U.S. Census Bureau, "U.S. Interim Projections by Age, Sex, Race, and Hispanic Origin," 2004. http://www.census.gov/ipc/www/usinterimproj/.

[8] Sean Scully, "Minorities Gain Ground," *Insight on the News*, May 28, 2001.

[9] William H. Frey, "Zooming in on Diversity," *American Demographics*, July/August 2004.

[10] Nat Irwin II, "America's Increasing Diversity," *Futurist*, March/April 2004, p. 21.

[11] Andrew Sum, et al., "Foreign Immigration and the Labor Force of the U.S.," Center for Labor Market Studies, Northeastern University, July 2004. http://www.nupr.neu.edu/7-04/immigrant_04.pdf.

[12] Edwin S. Rubenstein, "Why Has Black Unemployment Risen (Yes, Risen!) in the Bush Boom?", VDARE.COM, May 5, 2005. http://www.vdare.com/rubenstein/050504_nd.htm.

[13] Census Bureau, "Income, Poverty, and Health Insurance Coverage in the United States: 2004," August 2004. http://www.census.gov/prod/205pubs/p60-229.pdf.

[14] Census Bureau, "Income, Poverty, and Health Insurance Coverage in the United States: 2004," August 2004. http://www.census.gov/p5pubs/p60-229.pdf.

[15] Census Bureau, "Income, Poverty, and Health Insurance Coverage in the United States," August 2005. Table B-1. http://www.census.gov/prod/205pubs/p60-229.pdf.

[16] See Peter Brimelow's *Alien Nation*, HarperPerennial, 1996. Appendix 3.

[17] George J. Borjas and Stephen J. Trejo, "Immigrant Participation in the Welfare System," *Industrial and Labor Relations Review*, January 1991. http://ksghome.harvard.edu/~GBorjas/Papers/Borjas-Trejo_1991.pdf.

[18] Steven A. Camarota, "The High Cost of Cheap Labor: Illegal Immigration and the Federal Budget," Center For Immigration Studies, August 2004.

[19] George J. Borjas, "The Labor Demand Curve Is Downward Sloping," *Quarterly Journal of Economics*, November 2003. http://ksghome.harvard.edu/~GBorjas/Papers/QJE2003.pdf.

[20] Steven A. Camarota, "Immigrants at Mid-Decade," *Backgrounder*, CIS, December 2005, p. 19.

[21] Jeffrey S. Passel, "Unauthorized Migrants: Numbers and Characteristics," Pew Hispanic Center, June 14, 2005. http://pewhispanic.org/files/reports/46.pdf.

[22] Brendan Coyne, "Undocumented Immigrants Live Like Most Americans, Study Says," *The New Standard*, June 17, 2005. http://newstandardnews.net/content/?action=show_item&itemid=1947.

[23] Peter Brimelow, "Time to Rethink Immigration," *National Review*, June 22, 1992. http://www.vdare.com/pb/time_to_rethink.htm.

[24] Jeffrey S. Passel, "Unauthorized Migrants: Numbers and Characteristics," Pew Hispanic Center, June 14, 2005, P. 26. http://finance.aol.com/usw/portfolios/view?pid=1.

[25] Current Population Survey, 2004. Table 4. (Unpublished statistics provided to author.)

[26] Rakesh Kochhar, "Latino Labor Report, 2004: More Jobs for New Immigrants but at Lower Wages," Pew Hispanic Center, May 2, 2005. Tables 5(a) and 9. http://pewhispanic.org/files/reports/45.pdf. Calculations by author.

[27] George J. Borjas, "The Labor Demand Curve Is Downward Sloping," *Quarterly Journal of Economics*, November 2003, http://ksghome.harvard.edu/~GBorjas/Papers/QJE2003.pdf.

28 U.S. Census Bureau, Current Population Survey, Annual Social and Economic Supplement, 2003 Immigration Statistics Staff, Population Division. http://www.census.gov/population/www/socdemo/foreign/ppl-174.html#cit.

29 Terry Graham, "Victimizing Peter to Pay (For) Paco," VDARE.COM, February 12, 2005. Available at http://www.vdare.com/misc/graham_050212_scaap.htm.

30 http://www.gao.gov/new.items/d05337r.pdf.

31 General Accountability Office, "Information on Certain Illegal Aliens Arrested in the United States," letter to Congressman John N. Hostettler, May 9, 2005. http://www.gao.gov/new.items/d05646r.pdf.

32 Anne Morrison Piehl and John J. DiLulio, "Does Prison Pay," http://www.safe-nz.org.nz/Articles/prispay.htm.

33 Edwin S. Rubenstein, "RAND Study Concedes Immigrant Health Care Burden—But Not Enough," VDARE.COM, November 15, 2005. http://www.vdare.com/rubenstein/051115_nd.htm.

34 Edwin S. Rubenstein, "Give Me Your Tired, Your Poor, . . . Your Infectious Diseases?" VDARE.COM, September 30, 2004. http://www.vdare.com/rubenstein/diseases.htm.

35 M.A.J. McKenna, "Immigrants Subsidize Care," *Atlanta Journal-Constitution*, July 27, 2005. http://immigration.campustap.com/blog/entry/view.aspx?lid=108164.

36 Edwin S. Rubenstein, "Looking (in Vain) For Latino Assimilation," VDARE.COM, July 13, 2005. http://www.vdare.com/rubenstein/050713_nd.htm.

37 Joe Guzzardi, "Illegal Aliens: The Health Cost Dimension," VDARE.COM, January 23, 2003. http://www.vdare.com/guzzardi/health_care.htm.

38 Mita Sanghavi Goel, MD, MPH, et al., "Obesity Among US Immigrant Subgroups by Duration of Residence," *Journal of the American Medical Association*, December 15, 2004. http://jama.ama-assn.org/cgi/content/abstract/292/23/2860.

39 Nanci Hellmich, "Health Spending Soars for Obesity," *USA Today*, June 26, 2005. http://www.usatoday.com/news/health/2005-06-26-health-spending-obesity_x.htm.

40 Symposium on Diabetes Economics, "The Costs of Diabetes in the Americas," September 2004, http://www.paho.org/English/AD/DPC/NC/dia-alad-background.pdf.

41 Joe Guzzardi, "View From Lodi, CA: In Immigration's Tower of Babel, Even Less Incentive to Learn English," VDARE.COM, November 24, 2005. http://www.vdare.com/guzzardi/051124_vfl.htm.

[42] Edwin S. Rubenstein, "Why Mexicans Make MADD Mad," VDARE.COM, August 25, 2005. http://www.vdare.com/rubenstein/050825_nd.htm; and "Hispanic Immigrants are Dangerous to Workplace Safety," VDARE.COM, July 10, 2004. http://www.vdare.com/rubenstein/workplace_safety.htm.

[43] Alan Wall, "For Fox, Dead Mexicans More Equal Than Others," VDARE.COM, September 9, 2002. http://www.vdare.com/awall/death.htm.

[44] National Institute of Justice, "Findings From the National Violence Against Women Survey," July 2000. http://www.ncjrs.gov/pdffiles1/nij/181867.pdf.

[45] Rubenstein, op. cit., September 30, 2004.

[46] B. R. Chiswick and P. W. Miller. "Language in the Immigrant Labor Market," in *Immigration, Language, and Ethnicity: Canada and the United States*, American Enterprise Institute, Washington, DC, 1992.

7

THE COSTS OF ILLEGAL IMMIGRATION TO TEXAS

by James A. Bernsen and the Lone Star Foundation

When people talk about illegal immigration, one of the biggest concerns they raise is how much illegal immigrants are actually costing the American taxpayer. But it is not on the federal government, but rather on the states, especially the border states, that the burden of illegal immigration lies heaviest. Although much of the taxes that immigrants pay goes to Washington, the cost of services falls in great part on the state government through numerous entitlement programs, health care costs, and, most crucially, education.

Texas, which accounts for about half of the U.S. border with Mexico, has been particularly hard hit by the costs of illegal immigration. The state has experienced an extraordinary growth in immigration generally over the last few decades. In 1970, there were only 310,000 foreign-born citizens in the state. By 1990, that number had increased 391 percent (1.5 million). Immigration since then has exploded. According to a 2004 U.S. Census Bureau estimate, the number of foreign-born residents of Texas in that year was 3.45 million—1,100 percent of the 1970 number. In 1970, the foreign-born population of Texas was three percent. In 1990, it was eight percent. In 2004, foreign-born residents represented 15.7 percent of all Texans. Although Texas has seen widespread migration from within the United States as well, this wave of external immigration comes with much more profound social and fiscal consequences. The majority of this increase comes from legal immigrants; but a large, and proportionately growing, percentage comes from illegal immigrants. Texas, according to the Census Bureau, is now home to 15 percent of all illegal immigrants in the United States. Since 1993 the illegal population has doubled, by conservative estimates. Some studies have estimated that it has even tripled.

While much is said about the benefits that immigrants bring to this country, most of the experts agree that immigrants, particularly illegal ones, are a net loss. In a survey of 13 studies on the costs and benefits of immigration, the U.S. General Accounting Office found only one that showed a net gain to the states.[1] So what is the cost to Texas from illegal immigration? The answer, at best, is only an estimate. Illegal immigration costs defy comprehensive evaluation because so much of the data needed to analyze and define the problem simply doesn't exist. Accurate statistics on the immigration problem in Texas are difficult to come by, while those that are available require many caveats and qualifications.

One obvious reason for this is that illegal immigrants don't want to be found. Living in the United States illegally, illegal immigrants rarely identify themselves. Yet so many of the ways that governments verify citizenship status presuppose self-identification. Furthermore, illegal immigrants shy away from agencies that inquire about their status. State bureaucrats concerned with protecting and expanding their programs don't want to risk driving away potential beneficiaries of those programs. In some instances, such as emergency room acceptance, it is impossible to verify citizenship status before the state expends money on a patient. In many cases, however, state agencies go well beyond the dictates of common sense (indeed, they go to excessive lengths) not to record data, even though no clear procedural reason exists for failing to do so. Also, as the voluminous data recorded concerning every other aspect of agency programs indicate, it is not likely that program administrators are simply lazy. The obvious conclusion is that such data are not kept because the agencies do not wish to know the extent to which their programs are being patronized by illegals. Or, as is even more likely, they don't want others to know.

Take, for instance, the Texas Education Agency (TEA). Although independent research points to education as being by far the single largest expense the state of Texas incurs from illegal immigration, TEA doesn't keep account of the relevant numbers—this despite the fact that the state requires school districts in Texas to track immigrant students, having ordered TEA to establish, and all school districts to participate in, a database called the Public Education Information Management System (PEIMS).[2]

The PEIMS is a massive database containing a variety of personally identifiable information concerning students. PEIMS serves a variety of functions in the Texas education system, including verifying districts' claimed attendance levels (relevant to the amount of state funding they receive), tracking dropouts, providing data to policy makers, and assisting with school accountability. This database also requires school districts to determine whether a student is an "immigrant" as defined by the federal No Child Left Behind Act (according to the NCLB, immigrants are "individuals who are ages three through 21; were not born in any state; and have not been attending one or more schools in any one or more states for more than three full academic years").[3] But the database does not explicitly instruct the agency to record whether such immigrants are legal or illegal. Given this loophole, TEA makes clear it considers less information to be better information: The agency expressly advises school administrators that, "Districts should not assume responsibility for determining the extent to which students are legal or illegal immigrants under INS regulations."[4]

Given these impediments, identifying the costs of illegal immigration to Texas, whether in education or health care, is difficult but not impossible. Various statistical analyses, assumptions based on the census records, and other proxies can fill in the gaps to provide a consistent portrait of the problem. About one thing, there is no doubt—immigrants consume many of Texas's resources, at cost to the taxpayers. Some of these costs are direct, and others are hidden costs. An increase in population strains all resources of the state, as well as those of counties and cities, and most of Texas's dramatic population growth in the last two decades has come from immigrants.

Many expenditures would have occurred regardless of Texas's illegal immigrant population, and separating costs incurred by foreign and domestic immigrants is often impossible. Other state programs have no direct cost, because they are paid for through user fees. For example, immigrants contribute to traffic congestion in Texas, but they also pay the gas taxes that subsidize Texas roads (although, in recent years, revenues from fuel taxes have declined to the point that they are needing to be replaced with other funds, or by toll road fees).

Additional costs, difficult to calculate, are incurred every time a state agency hires a translator or establishes a new program geared to immigrants. Texas, for example, recently received a $340,000 grant to help educate immigrants on U.S. traffic laws.[5] Although the program is paid for with federal money, the problem it highlights is a state one. Immigrants' ignorance of U.S. laws, customs, and culture incurs costs to the state each time a foreigner drives without auto insurance or doesn't wear a seatbelt. Another cost is the money immigrants remove from the Texas economy. Money transfers to foreign countries from Texas immigrants—called "remittances"—total about $3.2 billion a year[6] sent primarily to Latin America. Unlike wages paid to U.S. workers, which stay in the United States and turn over several times in the economy, remittance money does not generate additional economic impact—or the related sales tax benefits.

But the impact of immigrants is the most profound in the areas of education, health and social services, and criminal justice. These costs will be the focus of this chapter.

How Many Are Here?

We've already seen the increase in the total immigrant population in Texas. Now let's look specifically at that of the illegal one.

In 1993, government estimates of the illegal immigrant population in Texas ranged from 390,000 to 500,000. In 2000, the Immigration and Naturalization Service offered a conservative estimate of this population at 1,041,000. This estimate, however, failed to include certain categories of immigrants. In a study that did include those categories, the Migration Policy Institute estimated an illegal alien population in Texas of 1.2 million. The Urban Institute put the number at 1.1 million and the Federation of American Immigration Reform much higher—at 1.5 to 1.8 million.[7]

As is often the case with such a high-profile issue, different studies come out with different numbers reflecting the biases or assumptions of the study authors. However, the Pew Hispanic Center estimates an illegal immigrant population nationwide, that, if extrapolated to Texas using census estimates, would amount to 1.8 million people.[8] For an organization that generally takes a moderate stand on immigration issues to come up with a number close to FAIR's high-end estimate is telling. However, for the purpose of this study, we will assume an estimate of 1.5 million illegal immigrants in Texas. This estimate is slightly higher than the INS and census numbers (acknowledged by their agencies to be based on incomplete data), while falling roughly midway between the low estimates and the high ones offered by nongovernmental researchers.

Several attempts have been made to estimate the costs of immigration to Texas; as with the population estimates, the results are often skewed by the perspectives and assumptions of their authors. In 1992, Rice University economist Donald Huddle estimated the total nationwide cost of immigration (legal and illegal) at $14.4 billion, and to Texas at $4.6 billion, of which $1.02 billion was attributed to illegal immigration. In response, the Urban Institute countered later that year by proposing a much lower nationwide cost of $6.9 billion. Huddle then did another study the following year, encompassing many other costs previously not measured, that put the bill at $29 billion (nationwide). One reason for the dramatically higher figure is that Huddle included many new costs, such as displacement of American workers, to obtain it.

In 1996, Professor Huddle took still another look at the costs of immigration to Texas.[9] Huddle found that immigration to Texas cost taxpayers a net $7.2 billion and the state 248,000 jobs. About $1.5 billion of this sum he claimed was owing to illegal immigrants. Even more startling, however, were Huddle's projections for the future. Estimating an immigrant population growth that proved to be very close to the actual number, Huddle predicted an annual cost of $10 billion by 2006. Assuming the same proportionality between legal and illegal immigration, Huddle predicted Texas could spend $2.1 billion a year annually. In fact, research done since Huddle's study indicates that number is likely a low one. The most recent, conducted by FAIR in mid-2004, found a cost of $4.7 billion arrived at by looking only at the three distinct areas of cost—health care, education, and criminal justice, offset by an estimated tax benefit of $1 billion, for a net cost of $3.7 billion to Texas. When one analyzes the numbers in depth, FAIR's number holds up pretty well.

The Costs of Illegal Immigration to Texas

There are basically three areas in which large-scale identifiable costs can be attributed directly to illegal immigrants: education, health and human services, and criminal justice. Among these, education is the largest cost driver in the Texas budget. This makes sense, as education is the single biggest line item in the state's budget, yet the cost of illegal immigration is disproportionately represented in education, which in fact, represents 84 percent of the total cost to Texas of illegal immigrants living there.

The reason is that while health care costs, incarceration costs, and other expenditures are attributable only to some to illegal immigrants, education is an entitlement for which all immigrant children are eligible. Moreover, control over the cost of this entitlement is entirely out of the legislature's hands, owing to a decision by the U.S. Supreme Court in 1982 prohibiting the state of Texas, and others, from denying educational services to people who are in this country illegally.[10]

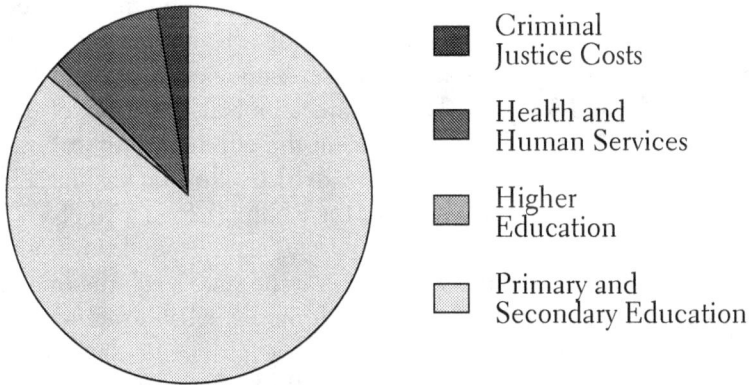

- Criminal Justice Costs
- Health and Human Services
- Higher Education
- Primary and Secondary Education

Primary and Secondary Education

Because reliable statistics are not kept regarding the number of illegal (or, for that matter, legal) immigrants in Texas schools, most studies on this topic have tried to estimate the number, the commonest technique being to come up with a guess as to the number of illegal immigrants of school age and then to multiply that number by the per-student cost of educating a child. This method is subject to two criticisms. First, not all children of illegal immigrants enroll in the public schools, while very little data exist to determine what proportion do. Second, most published national statistics on the per-student cost of public education underestimate that cost, usually by omitting classes of administrative cost from the calculation.[11] Furthermore, there is the additional cost of bilingual education. Although we cannot automatically assume all bilingual costs are attributed to aliens, since some second-, third-, and fourth-generation Americans in Texas also have limited English proficiency, a large portion, if not the majority of the costs, are attributable to immigrants.

The effect of the first objection would be to skew the data in an upward direction, while the latter two would both skew them downward. Nonetheless, such an analysis provides the only available estimates of the number of illegal children in the Texas school population.

Not only must we consider children who themselves are illegal. Because children born in this country are U.S. citizens regardless of the status of their parents, children born to illegal immigrant parents after they arrive are nonetheless reflective of the cost of illegal immigration, despite their legal status.

In a report on school costs, FAIR,[12] using an analysis of data from the Urban Institute,[13] estimated a school-age population of 1.5 million illegal immigrants nationwide, plus an additional two million U.S.-born children of illegal immigrants. Since approximately 15 percent of the illegal immigrant population resides in Texas, the respective state numbers, using Census Bureau percentages, would be 224,000 and 300,000. That means about 11.6 percent of the student-age population of Texas as a whole represent the children of illegal immigrants.

At a cost of $7,136 per pupil,[14] Texas spends $1.6 billion on the illegal immigrant children and an additional $2.1 billion for their siblings, for a total of $3.7 billion.

It is also instructive to examine federal and state expenditures on programs that serve primarily immigrant populations. At the state level, the finance system provides extra dollars to students deemed Limited English Proficient (LEP) and to low-income students who qualify for free or reduced-cost lunch programs (known as "compensatory education"). Not all of these students are children of immigrants: Some, in fact, are native-born U.S. citizens who have nonetheless failed to master English despite their families having lived for several generations in the United States.

Although compensatory education includes a large percentage of native-born students, LEP has fewer of them. In the case of this program, the Urban Institute has estimated that 40 percent of LEP students in the United States are foreign born.[15] Using conservative estimates, about 30 percent of those students are illegal immigrants or their siblings. The cost to Texas, therefore, is at least $12 million a year. Though the expense is significant, it is not large enough to change the overall education costs dramatically.

This $3.7 billion cost to the state represents about 10.5 percent of the entire budget of Texas's school districts, amounting to the entire federal portion of the state's education budget, which in 2004 was $3.6 billion.[16]

Higher Education

Unlike the elementary and high school education systems, higher education collects and publishes significant information. Universities report exactly how many foreign students are in their programs and what their immigration status is. All public institutions of higher learning in Texas report their data to the Texas Higher Education Coordinating Board. The board has set up its own Web site, http://www.txhighereddata.org, where voluminous statistical information about Texas public colleges and universities is kept.

In-state tuition for illegal immigrants

In 2001, the Texas Legislature passed, and Gov. Rick Perry signed, House Bill 1403, a Democratic bill that nonetheless had wide bipartisan support. The bill allows illegal aliens who graduate from Texas high schools to receive in-state tuition, provided they graduated from a Texas high school and sign an affidavit that they will apply for permanent residency as soon as they are eligible.

The coordinating board tracks the number of students who get residency status through House Bill 1403, but it does not release that information to the public. (The authors obtained that information through the Texas Public Information Act.) In fiscal year 2005, 3,150 illegal immigrants received in-state tuition at Texas four-year universities, and 8,300 of them at Texas two-year colleges. In general, most of the schools benefitting from House Bill 1403 are not located along the Texas-Mexico border. Of the four-year schools, the University of Texas at Dallas had the most beneficiaries, and Houston Community College led among two-year schools.

Costing out the state educational benefits

Higher education in Texas is funded by a series of complex formulas. These formulas differ in respect to four-year universities and two-year colleges. (The description here is a summary of state funding formulas. The Legislative Budget Board has produced a more detailed treatment of the subject, from which most of this description is taken.)[17] In accordance with these, the state pays for Instructions and Operations of campuses, infrastructure, teaching experience, and a small institutional supplement. Additional funding comes from "special items," usually determined by political manipulation, and a series of infrastructure endowments, such as the Available University Fund that Texas universities receive in addition to tuition.

Thus, it is impossible to calculate exactly the per-student subsidy a student receives without knowing the exact course load that student shoulders. To calculate that part of the total cost to the state attributable to immigration, the best estimate available is to take the average biennial appropriation per student and multiply it by the number of illegal immigrants receiving in-state benefits. (The figures for students availing themselves of HB 1403 benefits represent the total number of students, while per-student appropriations are given on a full-time equivalent (FTE) basis. This could lead to a slight overestimate of the costs involved, because the state does not disseminate figures on course-loads taken by HB 1403 students.) In fiscal year 2003, the average biennial appropriation per FTE student was $7,112. In fiscal years 2004 and 2005, that amount was estimated by the state at $6,960. Table 1 presents a cost estimate.

Table 1: State Subsidy for Illegal Immigrants at State Universities

Fiscal Year	HB 1403 Students	Average State Appropriation	Total
2003	1,670	$7,112	$11,877,040
2004	2,433	$6,960	$16,933,680
2005	3,150	$6,960	$21,924,000
Grand Total			**$50,734,720**

Foreign students at Texas universities who immigrate legally on student visas must, unlike their illegal counterparts, pay out-of-state tuition. The state does not set per-student subsidy rates for out-of-state students. But given the dramatic rise in tuition nationally in recent times, it is likely that foreign students do not receive subsidies from state taxpayers. Hence, legal immigrants pay their full cost; illegal immigrants do not.

Two-year community colleges are funded differently than state universities—primarily through a local college district tax and by tuition—while their students take fewer course hours than do regular college students. In fact, each community college student represents the equivalent cost of one-third that of a full-time student. Using those percentages, we can assign a cost deriving from illegal immigration to community colleges. In fiscal year 2003, 4,021 illegal immigrants received in-state tuition at Texas community colleges. Multiplying the resulting product times the per-FTE subsidy gives us an estimated subsidy for illegal immigration at Texas two-year colleges and universities of $6,465,188 in fiscal year 2003.

Table 2: Total Subsidy Received at Texas Public Community and Technical Colleges for Illegal Immigrants Getting In-State Tuition

Fiscal Year	HB 1403 Students	Estimated HB 1403 FTEs	Subsidy per FTE	Total
2003	4,021	1,395.29	$4,633.58	$6,465,188
2004	5,949	1,986.97	$4,635.66	$9,210,917
2005	8,300	2,766.67	$4,622.61	$12,789,236
Grand Total				$28,465,341

Financial Aid

Legal immigrants are also eligible, under some circumstances, for financial aid. However, most illegals are not. Generally speaking, only persons who have permanent residency or have been granted asylum are eligible for most federal financial aid programs.[18]

The state of Texas has a variety of student aid programs. (Chapter 56 of the Texas Education code establishes almost all state financial aid programs and contains the eligibility standards.) However, while it is possible for illegal immigrants to receive state-funded financial aid, most programs require students to meet the federal financial aid qualifications, which would eliminate immigrant eligibility.

Here again, however, the state of Texas does not disseminate statistics on the immigration status of financial aid recipients. As with secondary education, we know that there must be a cost, but it is nonetheless very difficult to calculate an exact cost of financial aid provided to illegal immigrants.

Human Services

Although welfare reform has made dramatic reductions in the eligibility of immigrants for entitlement benefits, a corresponding decrease in the welfare rolls has not been achieved.

The 1996 welfare reform law, Personal Responsibility and Work Opportunity Reconciliation Act (PRWORA), stripped most immigrants of their eligibility for various welfare and other entitlement programs. Prior to that act, noncitizens were eligible for such programs as Aid to Families with Dependent Children (AFDC), Food Stamp, and Supplemental Security Income and Medicare without restriction. However, with the passage of PRWORA, Congress tightened eligibility requirements on noncitizens, thus causing an overall drop in the number of immigrants using social services.

Nonetheless, immigrants still avail themselves of welfare benefits at higher rates than native citizens. In Texas, it is estimated that 30.6 percent of immigrant households (418,000) received welfare benefits in 2004.[19] This includes temporary assistance to needy families (formerly AFDC), supplemental security income, food stamps, public/subsidized housing, or Medicaid. In comparison, only 18 percent of native headed households (1.22 million) received welfare benefits in 2004.

One reason for these numbers is the practice known as *grandfathering*. Legal immigrants who resided in the United States before August 22, 1996, remain eligible for many social services. Qualified immigrants in most circumstances include refugees, asylum seekers, and Cuban and Haitian immigrants. In addition, immigrants who are veterans or on active military duty and their families, battered spouses who qualify under the Violence Against Women Act, victims of a severe form of human trafficking like slavery, and legal permanent residents with 40 qualifying annual quarters of work are eligible.[20]

Another reason for high immigrant use of welfare programs is that immigrants are also much more likely to live in poverty. In Texas, 29.5 percent of immigrants are statistically impoverished compared to only 13.1 percent of native citizens.[21] Even more immigrants live in what is called "near poverty," defined as an income of less than 200 percent of the poverty threshold. According to the Center for Immigration Studies, 59.5 percent of immigrants and their children live in poverty or near poverty in Texas, compared to 32.2 percent of natives and their children.[22]

The socioeconomic status of immigrant families in Texas is directly related to the level of educational attainment. In Texas, 46 percent of immigrants older than 18 do not have a high school diploma, compared to only 12.6 percent of natives.[23] Consequently, it is not surprising that a higher proportion of the immigrant population, as compared to the native one, in Texas, receives state and federal assistance through social service programs.

A Look at a Few Entitlement Programs

Temporary Assistance to Needy Families (TANF) is a block grant program that provides cash assistance to recipients. With the passage of PRWORA, states were given the option to bar Legal Permanent Residents (LPR) who were in the state before August 22, 1996, from receiving TANF benefits if they were not currently receiving benefits. However, Texas chose to continue to allow LPRs to receive benefits.

If LPRs received TANF benefits before August 22, 1996, they were eligible to continue receiving benefits. LPRs who entered the country after the enactment of PRWORA are barred from receiving TANF benefits unless they become U.S. citizens. Exceptions to this rule include the qualified immigrants described earlier.

There are varying estimates on how many immigrants use social services in Texas. The Urban Institute estimates that 10,000 noncitizen families received TANF in 2000 (6,700 legal and 3,300 undocumented). The study points out that immigrants are more likely to remain on welfare than U.S. citizens.[24] The Governor's Office on Immigration and Refugee Affairs estimates that 5,687 legally admitted aliens received TANF in 2002.[25] However, according to the House Ways and Means Committee Green Book, 8,305 adult noncitizens received TANF benefits in fiscal year 2000–2001.[26]

The state pays about 30 percent of the cost of TANF, while the federal government pays the rest. For 2002, the state outlay for illegal immigrants on TANF was around $1.65 million and the federal costs, $3.5 million; those for legal recipients of TANF were double that amount.[27] Noncitizens who are eligible to receive food stamps include the same population that is eligible for TANF. The Food Stamp Program also accepts individuals under age 18 or age 65 and older. Approximately 117,000 noncitizens in Texas received food stamps in fiscal year 2004.[28] Noncitizens make up 5.2 percent of Texas Food Stamp recipients, for a cost of $107.4 million. The benefits are 100 percent federally funded, so there is minimal cost to the state (using the statewide average of 2.6 people per household for food stamps).

Supplemental Security Income (SSI) is a federal cash assistance program for the blind, aged, and otherwise disabled individuals of low-income status. The requirements are the same as for other programs. In 2004, 60,716 noncitizens received SSI in Texas, of a total of 472,347 SSI recipients. Thus, noncitizens amount to 12.9 percent of the SSI recipient population.[29] There is minimal or no cost to the state for this program.

Health Care

After education, health care is the single biggest cost accruing to Texas from illegal immigration. But beyond the economic costs are the uncountable burdens placed on an already stressed health care system, with their potential effects on the health and well-being of all Texans. Consequently, use of health care by immigrants—legal and illegal—in the United States is heavily debated. Almost all research has shown a large cost to the system from immigrants. Nonetheless, there are dissenters. A study in the *American Journal of Health* in 2005 discounted immigrants as a cost-driver in the U.S. health care system.[30] The authors cite costs that show that the average immigrant receives half as much health care as the average native citizen. Those numbers, however, are disputed by researchers like Stephen Camarota at the Center for Immigration Studies, who claims the sample is not representative and the conclusions do not follow from the data.

Such studies are also belied by the Texas data, however, which show heavy effects of aliens on the health care system. Despite some successes welfare reform has had in eliminating immigrants from entitlement programs, immigrants still enjoy limited access to those programs. One of the biggest costs, however, is in emergency room care. Owing to federal law as well as to practicality, no one checks immigration status at the emergency room door. Additionally, policy makers fear that even so much as inquiring about a patient's immigration status will deter immigrants with life-threatening conditions from seeking treatment.

When an immigrant without private health insurance shows up at an emergency room, one of two things happens. Either the federal government covers the procedure through the emergency Medicaid program, or the hospital absorbs the uncompensated cost. Because of the high cost of emergency room visits, these costs can be staggering.

Uncompensated Costs to Texas Hospitals and Emergency Medicaid

Trauma hospitals across the country absorb many of the costs for indigent care, whether for aliens or U.S. citizens. While some expenses are reimbursed by the federal government's Disproportionate Share (DSH) funding program, the remainder of funds are a loss to hospitals and result in overcrowding, diversions of patients to other hospitals, and increased cost to the paying patients. (DSH funding attributable to immigrants, legal or otherwise, is impossible to calculate because the number of U.S. citizens who are also a source of nonreimbursed trauma care is high, and the data to break the two groups out separately is not available.) Although tracking hospital costs is difficult, as we shall see, most estimates show illegal immigration having a profound impact. The Texas Hospital

Association reported that in 2002 the costs incurred by hospitals to treat undocumented aliens was $393 million.[31] That cost does not include legal noncitizens, a population almost twice as large as the illegal one.

Not all hospitals are impacted equally. Some are hit much harder, including those on the border. Brownsville Medical Center, for example, spends $500,000 a month on health care for illegal immigrants.[32] South Texas Health System, just west of Brownsville, spends $9 million a year on illegals in its two hospitals.[33] And inner city hospital systems spend even more, for example, $50 million by the Harris County Hospital District in Houston.

Some of that cost is reimbursed through DSH. Additionally, Texas was awarded a grant of $46 million to cover immigrant costs through the 2003 Medicare Prescription Drug bill. Still, those funds are insufficient to cover Harris County's expenses, let alone those of the entire state. And the funds come with limitations. Regardless of the length of a patient's stay, the federal money will pay for only two days' treatment. To help reimburse some of these costs to hospitals, Texas provides funds through a program called Emergency Medicaid, which, as the name implies, covers mostly emergency room visits.

An offshoot of the traditional Medicaid program, Emergency Medicaid doesn't contain citizenship restrictions similar to those imposed on Medicaid through the welfare reform act. Because of this, immigrants represent a much higher percent of the cost to Emergency Medicaid than do the native born. According to the Health and Human Services Commission, Texas spends just over $300 million a year, on average, for emergency Medicaid for noncitizens, of which at least a third—$100 million—is attributable to illegal immigrants.[34] Because the funds come out of its financial pool established for the traditional Medicaid program, a greater use of Emergency Medicaid decreases the funding the state has available to Medicaid itself. In accordance with matching formulas, Texas pays 40 percent of all Medicaid costs, and the federal government picks up 60 percent.

When the U.S. General Accounting Office, in a 2004 study, took a look at spending for Emergency Medicaid,[35] it found that in every state but one the GAO studied, Emergency Medicaid, in which immigrants can participate, was increasing faster than traditional Medicaid—in which new immigrants cannot. The GAO found some surprising results: "Although states are not required to identify or report to [the Centers for Medicaid Services] their Medicaid expenditures specific to undocumented aliens, several states provided data or otherwise suggested that *most of their emergency Medicaid expenditures were for services provided to undocumented aliens.*" Furthermore, in five of the ten states, the GAO reported, one half of emergency Medicaid expenses were for labor and delivery for birthing women. This amounts to a very large cost, as we shall shortly see.

Although a true accounting of the costs of illegal immigrants to health care facilities in Texas remains difficult given a lack of information on the scope of the problem, the GAO concluded that the new federal funds available to hospitals could act as an incentive to those hospitals to collect more reliable information regarding the illegal population.

Impact of Welfare Reform on Health Care Availability

While the impact of immigrants on emergency Medicaid appears to be increasing, traditional Medicaid is a different story. Because welfare reform limited access to those already in the program as of 1996, or those who have lived in the United States for at least five years, the pool of new applicants for Medicaid has substantially decreased. Initial numbers showed substantial declines. Between 1995 and 1999, the number of children enrolled in Medicaid and the Children's Health Insurance Program (CHIP) dropped by eight percentage points, while the number of immigrant children covered under Medicaid fell by 190,000.[36] Nonetheless, Texas still spends $108 million for illegal aliens in the Medicaid program, including those grandfathered into it.[37] PRWORA gave states the option to allow new immigrants to qualify for Medicaid after five years of residence in the country, but so far Texas has not passed legislation allowing that.

Not all health care costs of immigration, however, can be judged by limiting the scope of review to aliens on Medicaid. As we have seen with education, many of the "costs" are incurred by citizen children born to immigrants, including those of illegal aliens who are often eligible for coverage and are therefore not represented among immigrant statistics. This number is around 300,000, though how many children actually use such services is another question, one that cannot be accurately answered until better data are recorded by the state.

Statewide, Medicaid rolls in Texas have been growing rapidly, and in one area, in particular, the growth has been astounding. In 2004, the majority— 52 percent—of all births in Texas were paid for by Medicaid. This is a large factor in the costs of immigration as pregnancy is covered under the umbrella of Emergency Medicaid, which is open to all immigrants regardless of status. We may assume that immigrants are likely to take advantage of this benefit in numbers at least proportional to their population and birth rate. The reason for this is that birth is a nonelective procedure that also confers citizenship status on the child. When one further considers that immigrants in Texas account for 59 percent of the increase in the uninsured in Texas, it becomes clear that they, in fact, have even more incentive than do U.S. citizens to avail themselves of Emergency Medicaid to pay for childbirth.

In 1997, the U.S. General Accounting Office sought statistics on illegal alien births through Medicaid.[38] At that time, the GAO found that 24,000 Medicaid-funded births occurred to illegal alien mothers in Texas, which represented a doubling of the births from only three years before. Although no such study has been conducted recently, the population of illegal immigrants in Texas has approximately doubled itself since that date.

In fact, with birth costs between $3,000 and $4,000 based on most estimates, Texas could spend as much as $144 to $200 million on childbirth alone. The fact that this number is indeed larger than almost all estimates given for the total usage of emergency Medicaid by illegal immigrants should give us pause. The most likely explanation is that some of those costs are not being borne by emergency Medicaid but are instead represented in the hospitals' uncompensated care. Or, what is of even greater concern, illegal immigrants not legally eligible for traditional Medicaid may in fact be receiving it through fraud or lack of oversight.

Either way, it is clear that childbirth incurs the largest portion of emergency Medicaid costs paid on behalf of illegal immigrants. Here again, this is an area of public policy where clarity is lacking in result of a bureaucratic culture that discourages record-keeping on the residency status of patients. As in the case of the educational system, the state and its hospitals have decided selectively to ignore this one narrow issue of health care—while simultaneously recording copious statistics on every other area.

Although the future of Medicaid, owing to PRWORA, includes fewer recipients, the costs for each case will likely increase as a result of the overall increase in health care expenses. Additionally, Emergency Medicaid will continue to be exploited as long as the population of immigrants expands, and access to it is not curtailed. Furthermore, the population still on Medicaid through the grandfathering clauses of PRWORA will become more expensive to treat as it ages. Although the elderly only represent 11 percent of Medicaid beneficiaries, they represent 36 percent of the costs.[39] Since studies have shown that large numbers of immigrants continue to lack health insurance even after they become citizens, many of these grandfathered recipients will remain on Medicaid for years to come.

Children's Health Insurance Program

CHIP is a separate health care entitlement that covers children whose families are just outside of the income restrictions of Medicaid. Whereas Medicaid can be assumed to have a sizeable number of clients grandfathered under PRWORA,

CHIP is different. It would seem that because eligibility is limited to children under age 18, the pool of those eligible for grandfathering is limited to those children who were younger than age eight in 1995 and will continue to drop as children reach the age of maturity. However, because immigrant children born in the United States are considered citizens—as many as three out of five immigrant children—these children will continue to be eligible for CHIP. No numbers are available for the number on CHIP who are children of immigrant parents, but most experts believe it to account for a sizeable portion of the $700 million program.

Following welfare reform, noncitizen children of immigrants were cut off from CHIP. However, Texas chose to continue to provide services by foregoing federal funds through a special program called Immigrant Children's Health Insurance, at a cost of $18.1 million a year. Many of these children would have previously been enrolled in Medicaid or regular CHIP. However, prior to 1996, Texas would have received federal matching funds for these children. For CHIP, the match is a generous three to one.

Immigrant CHIP, however, does not pull down federal funds. Thus, if Texas were to redirect those funds to citizen children under regular CHIP, the state would draw down an additional $54.3 million from Washington.

Children With Special Health Care Needs

One program in which immigrants have a very profound effect on Texas health care expenditures is the Children With Special Health Care Needs (CSHCN) program.

CSHCN is a supplemental health care program designed to assist indigent children with extraordinary or chronic health care problems that are too expensive to treat in the traditional Medicaid system. Due to the nature of the program, a small number of patients incurs a large percentage of the cost. The only requirement for residency, as far as this entitlement is concerned, is that the child live in the United States and the parents state their intention to remain in the country. They do not have to be legal residents, though the children are supposed to be. However, the state's eligibility requirement is based on the honor system, so that no independent verification is made of the veracity of the beneficiaries' statements.

According to the Texas Department of State Health Services, in December 2005, 1,452 noncitizens were participants in the program, representing 68.82 percent of all clients and 78.9 percent of the total cost, or $29.9 million per year.[40] That amounts to over three quarters of the budget for the entire program that is spent on non-Americans.

Preventive Health Care Programs

For other health care programs, Texas does not keep any representative numbers. However, immigrants' use of all social services has been estimated by Camarota, who, as previously mentioned, found that about 30.6 percent of the immigrant population are beneficiaries of entitlement programs in Texas. Using those numbers, a researcher could estimate in theory the cost for other medical entitlements, although the actual numbers might vary widely from program to program. Additionally, the state funds a number of programs, such as immunization, infectious disease prevention, and education programs, and others are an expense to all Texans. Immigrants living in Texas are, of course, beneficiaries of such programs, and at least as likely to be struck by disease as Americans. Particularly in the case of tuberculosis, immigrants from Mexico are at a statistically higher risk because of the prevalence of that disease in their home country.

Criminal Justice

Illegal immigrants in Texas who commit crimes also represent a huge cost to the state. In a 1994 study, "Alien Offenders in the Texas Correctional System," and in subsequent reports, the Texas Criminal Justice Policy Council (CJPC) took a look at criminal aliens.[41] Its findings show that alien offenders are almost twice as likely to be convicted of violent crimes as nonaliens.

Estimating the total cost incurred by these offenders, however, is problematic. The state keeps a precise count of all alien inmates (legal and illegal) but requires prisoners to declare their status, thus calling into question the accuracy of that count. According to the Texas Department of Criminal Justice (TDCJ),10,254 offenders in Texas prisons claimed foreign citizenship in 2005. That number is likely low. Although the immigrant community amounts to 15 percent of Texas's total population, TDCJ's number represents just 6.8 percent of the prison population—a statistical improbability, especially given the immigrants' low income and education levels—historically accurate indicators of a propensity toward criminal behavior.

Additionally, half of the state's prison population is Hispanic, and 87 percent of the criminal aliens in Texas are Hispanic. Assuming that noncitizen Hispanics are not dramatically less likely than citizen Hispanics to commit crime, the true number of criminal aliens would likely be around 23,000, of whom 8,000 would be illegals. (Arguing against this methodology is the fact that many immigrants are deported after their sentencing, which should reduce the recidivism rate among alien offenders. A counter argument, however, is that noncitizen offenders are statistically more likely to receive prison sentences instead of parole than is the citizen population.)

In 1994, the CJPC study estimated that the 3,125 immigrants in Texas prisons at the time, plus another 1,343 immigrants backlogged in county jails, cost the state $74.3 million per year, a figure based on the total time served by those inmates. When that number was reduced to an annual figure, the cost worked out to $63.6 million for all noncitizen prisoners.

Moving forward to 2005, the numbers have risen dramatically. While the actual per diem expense for housing prisoners has dropped slightly (to $40.06 per day), that decrease is swamped by the massive increase in the alien prison population. Applying the earlier-used methodology to today's numbers, and accounting for the statistically more likely population estimate of 23,000, the cost comes to $336 million for all noncitizens, of which $117 million is incurred by illegal aliens. The Federation for American Immigration Reform, in a separate study using a different methodology, put the figure at around $150 million.

Another applicable cost is jail construction. The CJPC in 1994 identified an additional $150 million in expenses by including the cost to construct new jails to house that years' immigrant population. Although this cost is a one-time expense, it dramatizes just how big the problem is. For Texas to build enough prisons to house today's immigrant population alone would cost $750 million (based on a $250 million cost for a 2,750-bed unit, of which Texas would need three).[42] Even if these facilities had a pre-renovation lifespan of 30 years, the cost would still work out to $25 million a year—not including upgrades and debt service—which, in the unique world of prison construction, are very high. Texas is bearing this financial burden today: $55 million in new construction and annual repair of facilities, of which, it seems probable, a good portion is incurred by illegal immigrant inmates. Against the objection that these costs are exaggerated, one might suggest that they do not include such legal expenses as trials, public defenders, and appeals. As these vary widely from case to case, an estimate of these expenses is impossible. Clearly, however, in the case of a population as chronically trapped in poverty as illegal immigrants are, the cost in public defenders and defaults on assessed court fines must be considerably higher than those incurred by average Texans. Against all of these costs, the federal government has provided only $17 million to the state of Texas in payment for the incarceration of illegal immigrants, plus another $9 million to its counties. Moreover, even that number is falling, laying increased burden on the state.[43] The current reimbursement is less than half that received in 2002 through the Department of Justice's State Criminal Alien Assistance Program.

Alien Offender Costs to Counties

Even on the county level, the $9 million payment from the federal government is only a drop in the bucket in regard to costs. Texas counties incur expenses of their own beyond state costs, particularly those adjacent to the border and in major urban centers.

A 2001 study by the Border Counties Coalition found that Texas border counties alone spend $23.3 million a year in law enforcement, criminal justice, and health care for alien offenders.[44] This number includes illegal aliens only while excluding legal resident noncitizens, as the previous numbers for the state do. Border counties report that they are reimbursed for less than 12 percent of their expenditures in providing for illegal aliens.

Additionally, counties are on the hook for many of the costs of providing free defense counsel for the poor, amounting to $138 million in 2004.[45] That figure includes $11 million worth in state reimbursements. Although there are no data to tie a percentage of that cost to noncitizens, income and earnings data from immigrants suggest they are disproportionate to the population percentage. Moreover, indigent defense is available to all, regardless of citizenship status. Additionally, minor costs are incurred in the parole system, through parole diversions, and in the state's expenditures for special needs offenders.

Labor and Wages

Do illegal immigrants take jobs from American workers? If so, the loss is not only to those displaced workers, but also to the state of Texas and its taxpayers. According to economist Donald Huddle of Rice University, 248,500 low-skill Texas workers were displaced from their jobs in 1996 by illegal immigrant workers. Huddle defined the displacement rate as the number of American and legal immigrant workers who are not able to find work per 100 undocumented workers who have jobs. In a separate study, Huddle calculated the displacement rate for low-skilled U.S. citizens at 23 percent.[46] These displaced Texas workers cost the state $1.37 billion in unemployment insurance, Medicaid, AFDC, food stamps, and lost tax payments in 1996.[47] Huddle forecasted the displacement costs to total $1.53 billion in 2006.

In a separate study, he analyzed the effects of the Immigration and Naturalization Service's operation "Project Jobs." Over a five day period in 1982, 400 INS and Border Patrol agents apprehended 5,440 undocumented workers from targeted job sites in nine metropolitan cities, including Dallas and Houston.

At the time, the nation's unemployment rate was ten percent. The INS wanted to make the case that illegal aliens were working for more than minimum wage and that those jobs could be made available to unemployed Americans and LPRs.

Huddle's analysis shows that seven U.S. workers, on average, applied for each job vacated by an illegal alien due to the INS raids.[48] These jobs paid, on average, 45 percent higher than the minimum wage. After the raids, Huddle's team found that 60 percent of those jobs left vacant by the apprehended illegal aliens were filled with U.S. workers who had heard about the job openings from advertisements and newspaper accounts of the INS raids. The remaining 40 percent were held by undocumented workers. The study determined that, contrary to myth, American workers indeed were willing to take jobs similar in scope and in pay to those held by illegal aliens.

In addition, Huddle conducted three micro field surveys on job displacement due to immigration in Houston in 1983, 1985, and 1990. He found the displacement rate dependent partly upon the ups and downs of the business cycle, wage rates, and unemployment levels. In 1983, when unemployment was 10.2 percent in Houston, the net displacement rate was 53.1 percent. By 1990, the unemployment rate had dropped to 5.2 percent and the displacement rate fell accordingly to 22.4 percent, owing to American workers having become "more choosy about jobs."[49]

Does Immigration Depress Wages?

George Borjas has estimated the impact of the influx of immigrants between 1980 and 2000 on the wages of U.S. citizens. Borjas found that immigration during this period increased the labor supply of working men by 11 percent.[50] As a result, the average wage earned by the native worker with a high school diploma decreased by 3.2 percent, while that of the native worker with little education (that is, the high school dropout) fell by 8.9 percent.

The results are not specific to Texas, and the relevant costs are hard to estimate. However, Borjas's study suggests how immigration affects the wages of lower income Americans.

Benefit to Businesses from a Ready Supply of Immigrant Labor

As stated previously, the social costs of immigration on the Texas economy are indirect, as well as direct. However, businesses certainly benefit from employing low-skilled immigrants at low-wages. With a ready supply of immigrant labor, businesses can hold down their labor costs, to the extent that Steven Camarota argues that unskilled Mexican immigration acts as a subsidy for employers who avail themselves of low-wage labor.[51] The business lobby argues that employers are in need of immigrants because most Americans will not work certain kinds of jobs. However, economists like Borjas argue that low-skilled American workers are willing and able to work at some of the traditionally "Mexicanized" jobs like agriculture and farming, but only if the wages were higher.

Immigrant Taxes to Texas

Calculating the tax revenues governments generate from immigrants is inherently difficult. Many illegal immigrant laborers work in an underground economy, and those who work above-ground do so only through deceptive means, such as the use of fake social security numbers. Of the taxes that are paid, however, the majority go to the federal government, while the costs of immigration are born in great part by the states. Some illegal immigrants pay income tax, as well as social security tax—according to one estimate, up to $7 billion nationwide.[52]

All of this, however, is irrelevant to Texas. While the state has a higher proportion of illegal immigrants than most in respect of its general population, in addition to containing 14.9 percent of all immigrants resident in the United States, tax revenues, with the exception of a few immigration-related grants, are distributed equally among all the states, regardless of immigrant population.

Texas has no state income tax; the majority of state government funding comes from property taxes and sales taxes. Immigrants pay the former, but at a lesser rate since they are primarily renters, not owners of homes. Immigrants also pay sales tax, but presumably at a slightly lower percentage than nonimmigrants due to their lower income and the large portion of their salaries—in some cases as much as one-third—that is wired to their home countries and therefore not reflected in sales taxes. As for use taxes, such as the gasoline tax, the benefits are presumed to be eliminated by the service used. Since they are intended—at least in theory—to be neutral, they were not considered in relation to either side of the cost/benefit equation.

So what is the benefit to Texas from taxes paid by illegal immigrants?

As with other immigration-related statistics, lack of clear data forces researchers to rely on estimates, which allows for the introduction of bias. Pro-immigration groups generate lower figures in regard to the costs of immigration, higher ones in respect of tax benefits; organizations seeking to curb immigration do the opposite.

One figure that blends the two approaches is an update by FAIR of the 1994 Urban Institute numbers.[53] Adjusting the conservative 1994 estimate of $202 million for the increase in immigrant population and for inflation, FAIR came

Table 3: Net Cost of Illegal Immigration to Texas

Item	Costs (dollars)
Education—Elementary and Secondary	
Non-citizen children of illegal immigrants (224,000)	$1.605 billion
Citizen children of illegal immigrants (300,000)	$2.141 billion
Total school aged-children of illegal immigrants	$3.746 billion
Higher Education	
State colleges and universities	$21.9 million
Community and technical colleges	$12.6 million
Total higher education	$34.5 million
Total Education Costs	$3.781 billion
Health and Human Services	**STATE / FEDERAL**
Temporary Assistance to Needy Families	$1.65 / 3.5 million
Medicaid	$108 / 166.5 million
Emergency Medicaid	$100 / 154.2 million
Immigrant CHIP	$6 / (n.a.) million
Children With Special Health Care Needs	$9.9 / 15.3 million
Federal reimbursement	$(46) / 46 million
Uncompensated care to illegals (absorbed by hospitals)	$393 / (n.a.) million
Total Health Care Costs	$572.5 / 385.5 million
Criminal Justice	
Incarceration	$117 million
Prison construction	$25 million
Other criminal justice costs	$3 million
Federal reimbursements (State portion only)	$(26 million)
Total Criminal Justice Costs	$119 million
Total Cost of Illegal Immigration	$4.47 billion
Minus Tax Receipts (Sales—60%, Property—40%)	$965 million
Net Cost of Illegal Immigration	$3.51 billion

Notes: Unknowable costs include county incarceration costs, prosecution/appeals costs for illegal immigrant criminals, displacement costs for American workers (Huddle estimated $1.53 billion) and many others up with a tax income for Texas, from both sales taxes and property taxes, of $965 million. Those numbers hold up fairly well after further review. (The U.I./FAIR methodology used a 60/40 percentage split on property and sales taxes. Taking the IRS estimates of annual sales tax paid by Texans in the income bracket that most immigrants would likely fall into results in a calculation of $452 million for sales tax expenditures paid by illegal immigrants, suggesting a total tax income derived from them of $1.13 billion. However, this sum does not account for money remitted to the immigrants' home countries before it can be spent, and thus is likely high.) Clearly, there is a benefit, but, when weighed against costs that are over four and a half times as large, illegal immigration in Texas is still a losing proposition. With a net cost of $3.5 billion—not including many known expenses whose costs are impossible to measure—Texas's fiscal soundness will continue to be jeopardized by what amounts to a giant unfunded mandate from the federal government. With an explosion of illegal immigration in ever-expanding numbers, this gap in the Texas budget will only continue to widen. As the tax benefits of high-skilled, educated, English-speaking workers are canceled by the tax liability of low-skilled, poorly educated, non-English-speaking workers, the imbalance will further exacerbate the fiscal problems of a state wrestling with the problems of school finance and the increasing costs of health care.

Reflections on Findings

The costs to Texas of illegal immigration ultimately fall on the people of the Lone Star State. In recent years, the state's political landscape has been focused on skyrocketing property tax rates, which pay for funding the state's schools. Texans have complained bitterly of such property taxes. However, the cost of illegal immigration works out to $739 for each native-born household in Texas—an expense almost as high as the $890 median school property tax that Texans so vehemently protest. Looking at it another way: Each illegal immigrant costs the state almost $2,333 a year.

Nonetheless, there is a silver lining to this dark cloud—the Welfare Reform Act of 1996. This bipartisan response to the nation's welfare crisis has prevented a $3.5 billion hole in the Texas budget from enlarging further. While there is a strong possibility that this study's estimate of Medicaid, food stamps, and AFDC costs is low, owing to the incalculable cost of fraudulent claims by noncitizens enrolled in those programs, the costs to the state would certainly be much higher if noncitizens had direct access to these entitlement programs. Illegal immigration's cost to Texas is a crisis. Without welfare reform, it would be a disaster.

Solving the problem of illegal immigration is, to the perennial chagrin of state lawmakers, largely in the hands of the federal government, which so far has refused to enforce existing immigration laws.

But while Washington, DC, buzzes about amnesty and securing the border, the state of Texas shouldn't be bashful about facing up to its responsibilities. And, for once, Texas should consider that the people to whom the state is ultimately responsible are the taxpayers.

The first step toward reform is for the state to stop hiding and obfuscating data. A free country and a republican form of government are predicated on a free flow of information. Regardless of their political leanings, voters need accurate and reliable data on how their government spends their tax dollars in order to be able to make informed decisions. Where illegal immigration is concerned, they don't have that. Although the collection of data costs money, the expense is minimal compared to the cost of ignorance.

For a state like Texas—which collects voluminous, comprehensive (privacy advocates would say excessive) statistics for every other concern of public policy—to refuse to collect data in this one critical area is inexcusable: It is the equivalent of using high-tech satellites to map most of the surface of the earth to the nearest foot, while leaving a crucial portion of the planet a blank space marked "Here be monsters."

But Texans aren't interested in fairy tales. While bureaucrats in Austin may fear the truth, Texas taxpayers have consistently demanded to be given it—only to be frustrated by a perpetual parade of elected officials of both parties who refuse to demand accountability.

Only when state and federal bureaucrats step aside and allow accurate and adequate data be collected, can the true scope of the problem be grasped. That would pave the way for a solution to the burdens of illegal immigration—a solution based on reasoned policy and open and frank debate, rather than emotion. Only with an accurate budgetary map of Texas before them can the people of Texas perceive the size of the monster hiding there–and what its appetite really is.

William Lutz and Christine DeLoma of the Lone Star Foundation contributed research to this report.

Endnotes

[1] U.S. General Accounting Office. Illegal Aliens: National Net Cost Estimates Vary Widely. July 1995.

[2] Texas Education Code, Section 42.006.

[3] Texas Education Agency, PEIMS Data Standards, p. 3.59.

[4] Texas Education Code, Section 42.006.

[5] Tom Bower, "Traffic Safety Effort Aimed at Immigrants," *San Antonio Express-News*, November 25, 2005.

[6] Inter-American Development Bank. Remittances from the United States to Latin America, 2004.

[7] Federation for American Immigration Reform, The Costs of Illegal Immigration to Texans, April 6, 2005.

[8] Pew Hispanic Center, Size and Characteristics of the Unauthorized Migrant Population in the United States, March 7, 2006. Available at http://pewhispanic.org/reports/report.php?ReportID=61.

[9] Donald Huddle, The Net Costs of Immigration to Texas: The Facts, the Trends and the Critics, 1996.

[10] *Plyler v. Doe* 457 U.S. 202 (1982).

[11] See *The Lone Star Report*, May 31, 2002, for a more detailed description of the Texas Public School Finance System and the shortcomings of published per-student costs of education.

[12] Federation for American Immigration Reform. "Breaking the Piggy Bank: How Illegal Immigration is Sending Schools into the Red." June 2005. Available at http://www.fairus.org/site/PageServer?pagename=research_researchf6ad.

[13] Michael Fix and Jeffrey S. Passel, "U.S. Immigration—Trends and Implications for Schools." The Urban Institute, January 2003. Available at http://www.urban.org/UploadedPDF/410654_NABEPresentation.pdf.

[14] U.S. Department of Education, National Center for Educational Statistics, Common Core of Data, "National Public Education Financial Survey," 2002–2003.

[15] Ibid.

[16] Texas Education Agency, Division of Performance Reporting, "Snapshot Pocket Edition, 2004–2005, Texas Public School Statistics. Available at http://www.tea.state.tx.us/perfreport/pocked/2005/pocked0405.pdf.

[17] See Legislative Budget Board. *Financing Higher Education in Texas: A Legislative Primer*, Second Edition, January 2005. Available at http://www.lbb.state.tx.us/Education/Higher/HigherEd_FinancingPrimer_2ndEd_0105.pdf.

[18] U.S. Department of Education Web site. Available at http://studentaid.ed.gov/students/publications/student_guide/2005–2006/english/important-terms.htm#elegible_noncitizen.

[19] Steven Camarota, Immigrants at Mid-Decade: A Snapshot of America's Foreign-Born Population in 2005, December 2005, p. 23.

[20] Governor's Office of Immigrant and Refugee Affairs, New Americans in Texas, 2002, pp. 41–43.

[21] Camarota, Immigrants at Mid-Decade, p. 22.

[22] Ibid.

[23] Camarota, Immigrants at Mid-Decade, p. 22.

[24] Urban Institute, Immigrants and TANF: A Look at Immigrant Welfare Recipients in Three Cities, October 2003, Occasional Paper Number 69.

[25] Governor's Office of Immigrant and Refugee Affairs, New Americans in Texas, 2002, p. 44.

[26] House Ways and Means Committee, 2004, Green Book.

[27] Based on percentages from a study by Karen C. Tumlin and Wendy Zimmermann, "Immigrants and TANF: A Look at Immigrant Welfare Recipients in Three Cities." The Urban Institute, October 2003. The percentage of illegal immigrants receiving TANF was then multiplied into the formula provided by the Texas Health and Human Service Commission on a per-household basis.

[28] The Office of Analysis, Nutrition and Evaluation, Characteristics of Food Stamp Households: Fiscal Year 2004, Nutrition Assistance Program Report Series, Report No. FSP–05-CHAR, p. 77.

[29] SSI Annual Statistical Report, 2004.

[30] Sarita Mohanty, "Health Care Expenditures of Immigrants in the United States: A Nationally Representative Analysis." *American Journal of Public Health*, 2005, p. 95.

[31] Gary Martin, "Senators Addressing Health Care on Border." *San Antonio Express-News*, March 5, 2003.

[32] FAIR, The Sinking Lifeboat: Uncontrolled Immigration and the U.S. Healthcare System.

[33] Hernan Rozemberg, "Hospitals Glad to Get Immigrant Health Aid," *San Antonio Express-News*, May 11, 2005.

[34] Information provided via email from Stephanie Goodman, Texas Department of Health and Human Services, December 2, 2005, stating a cost of $310 million in 2003 and $296 million in 2004 for noncitizens.

[35] U.S. General Accounting Office. Highlights: Undocumented Aliens—Questions Persist about Their Impact on Hospitals' Uncompensated Care Costs.

[36] Center for Budget Policy Priorities. Health Coverage for Legal Immigrant Children, October 10, 2000.

[37] Texas Governor's Office of Immigrant and Refugee Affairs, New Americans in Texas, 2002, p. 44.

[38] U.S. General Accounting Office. Letter to the Honorable Elton Gallegly, U.S. Representatives. May 30, 1997. Available at http://archive.gao.gov/paprpdf1/158747.pdf.

[39] Texas Health and Human Services Commission, Texas Medicaid in Perspective, June 2004, pp. 4–7.

[40] Information provided via email by Fawn Escalante, Texas Department of State Health Services, December 23, 2005.

[41] Texas Criminal Justice Policy Council, Alien Offenders in the Texas Correctional System, August 15, 1994.

[42] Source: Texas Department of Criminal Justice.

[43] U.S. Department of Justice, State Criminal Alien Assistance Program Payment List. Available at http://www.ojp.usdoj.gov/BJA/grant/05SCAAP.pdf.

[44] U.S./Mexico Border Counties Coalition, Illegal Immigrants in U.S. Border Counties: Costs of Law Enforcement, Criminal Justice and Emergency Medical Services, February 2001.

[45] Texas Association of Counties, Uncontrollable Costs, 2005.

[46] Donald Huddle, Immigration and Jobs: The Process of Displacement, NPG, May 1995.

[47] Donald Huddle, The Net Costs of Immigration to Texas, Carrying Capacity Network, 1999, p. 19.

[48] Donald Huddle, Immigration and Jobs: The Process of Displacement, NPG, May 1995.

[49] Ibid.

[50] George Borjas, "The Labor Demand Curve Is Downward Sloping: Reexamining the Impact of Immigration on the Labor Market," *Quarterly Journal of Economics*, November 2003, p. 1370.

[51] Steven Camarota, Immigration from Mexico: Assessing the Impact on the United States, Center for Immigration Studies, July 2001, p. 10.

[52] Eduardo Porter, "Illegal Immigrants Are Bolstering Social Security with Billions," *New York Times*, April 5, 2005.

[53] Federation for American Immigration Reform, The Costs of Illegal Immigration to Texans. April 6, 2005.

8

NATIONAL SOVEREIGNTY GOES LOCAL

by Roger D. McGrath

> *This is my country! Land of my birth!*
> *This is my country! Grandest on earth!*
> *I pledge thee my allegiance, America, the bold,*
> *For this is my country to have and to hold.* *

While President George Bush has ignored the will of the great majority of American people and has tacitly encouraged illegal immigration into the United States from Mexico, citizens and their representatives have rallied on the local level in various efforts to protect American sovereignty. From the people themselves and from mayors and county sheriffs to governors and state legislators, there are signs of a rebellion against the President's dereliction of duty. It's about time.

Arizona Battlefront

Arizona is leading the way. In November 2004, Arizonans voted by a 56–44 margin to approve Proposition 200—The Arizona Taxpayer and Citizen Protection Act. The act denies public benefits not mandated by federal law to illegal aliens, requires public employees to verify the immigration status of those seeking benefits, and makes it a crime for public employees to fail to report illegal aliens. The act also requires proof of citizenship for those registering to vote and voters to show proper identification at the polls.

That the act was approved by a substantial margin came as a surprise to many. Arizona's two U.S. Senators, Republicans John McCain and John Kyl, and the state's governor, Democrat Janet Napolitano, and Attorney General, Democrat Terry Goddard, opposed the measure. So, too, did Arizona's Chamber of Commerce and both the Republican (George Bush) and Democratic (John

---

* Don Raye and Al Jacobs, *This Is My Country,* 1940.

168

Immigration and the American Future

Kerry) Presidential candidates for the fall election in 2004. All of the usual "immigrant rights" groups and Latino organizations were strongly opposed to the act, calling it "racist" and "xenophobic." About the only ones supporting it were the average Arizona taxpayers who had become fed up with the deterioration of their communities and the drain on the state treasury. By 2004, the Arizona-Sonora border had become the principal entry point for illegal immigrants, and in the preceding decade Arizona's Latino population had doubled.

Unlike Proposition 187 that was passed by California voters in 1994, Arizona's act has withstood several court challenges. Nonetheless, its effects thus far have been more symbolic than substantial. Governor Napolitano and Attorney General Goddard have been less than aggressive in enforcing the act. This led Phoenix attorney David Abney, representing the *Yes* on Proposition 200 Committee and others, in January 2006, to file a challenge in Arizona's Court of Appeals to Goddard's ruling that Proposition 200 only prohibits a small number of benefits to illegal aliens. Goddard opined that such programs as the state's health care for the poor was not covered by the proposition, and the state's department of housing was not required to verify legal residency. Randy Pullen, chairman of the *Yes* on 200 Committee, charged that Goddard and Napolitano "colluded and came up with a scheme in order to eviscerate implementation of Prop 200." Whichever way the court rules, it is likely that the case will go to the Arizona Supreme Court.

This is all reminiscent of the battle in California over Proposition 187, which was approved by a 59–41 margin. Far more rigorous in dealing with illegal aliens than Arizona's Proposition 200, California's Proposition 187 would have prohibited illegal aliens from attending public schools or receiving health care other than emergency services and would have required school districts and public agencies to verify the immigration status of students and parents. The proposition would also have required public employees to report suspected illegal aliens to state and federal authorities and have required police to verify the immigration status of every arrestee and report illegal aliens to federal authorities.

Proposition 187 faced court challenges immediately from such groups as the Mexican American Legal Defense and Education Fund (MALDEF), The League of United Latin American Citizens (LULAC), and the ACLU, and its implementation was suspended until the cases could be adjudicated. In 1999 a Federal District judge, Mariana Pfaelzer, ruled that 187 was unconstitutional, basing her decision on the 1982 Supreme Court decision in *Plyler v. Doe*. Many lawyers argued that Pfaelzer had clearly misinterpreted *Plyler v. Doe* and that if California appealed her decision to the Supreme Court, the state would very likely prevail. However, by 1999 a new governor, Democrat Gray Davis, had been elected to office.

After Mexican President Ernesto Zedillo met with Davis in both Mexico and in California, Zedillo said on a Spanish language television station, "I have a commitment from the governor that he will do whatever he can so that these catastrophic effects that were foreseen for Proposition 187 several years ago will not come to pass." In response to a reporter's question from the Spanish station, Davis replied, "In the near future, people will look upon California and Mexico as one magnificent region." Two months later Governor Davis announced that the state of California would not appeal Pfaelzer's decision. Many suspected that Davis failed to appeal the decision because he was afraid that the state would prevail. He was subsequently recalled from office and, in a special election, replaced by Arnold Schwarzenegger. But by then the damage was done. From 1999 through 2004, the population of Los Angeles County increased by a million people, mostly illegal immigrants from Mexico.

Despite Judge Mariana Pfaelzer and Governor Gray Davis frustrating the will of the California voters, Proposition 187 clearly inspired Proposition 200 in Arizona. Proposition 200, in turn, has forced Arizona Governor Napolitano to make some gestures to appease the aroused electorate. In August 2005 she declared a "state of emergency" in Arizona's four border counties in response to the thousands of Mexicans and Central Americans entering Arizona daily. The numbers are mind boggling, but in 2005 alone more than a half million illegal immigrants were apprehended in Arizona. The Border Patrol and others estimate that at least that number and perhaps many more got through. In January 2006, Napolitano ordered the state's National Guard to the border. Both the declaration of a state of emergency and the commitment of the Guard made headlines, yet only some 170 Guardsmen were actually deployed to the border. Their duty was limited to inspecting cargo shipments at legal entry points and monitoring surveillance cameras. "They are not there to militarize the border," Napolitano cried. "We are not at war with Mexico."

The Republican-controlled state legislature has forced the Democrat governor to reveal her true feelings time and time again. In April 2006 the legislature passed a bill that criminalized the presence of illegal immigrants in Arizona by expanding the state's trespassing law to allow local authorities to arrest such aliens anywhere in the state. Napolitano vetoed the bill saying that immigration arrests should remain a federal responsibility. Calling Napolitano the worst governor in the nation on immigration issues, state representative Russell Pearce of Mesa proposed another anti-illegal alien initiative for the November 2006 ballot. As of June 2006, momentum was building to bypass the governor once again.

Meanwhile, during May 2006 the colorful sheriff of Maricopa County, Joe Arpaio, known for his harsh treatment of county inmates, organized a volunteer posse for the apprehension of illegal aliens. Within days he had more than 300 volunteers, some retired deputies, searching the county's hinterland for "coyotes" and their human cargoes. "I have compassion for the Mexican people," said Arpaio, "but if you come here illegally you are going to jail." Both the volunteers and Arpaio's regular deputies have brought in more than 200 illegal aliens. Advocates for the jailed aliens have been vocal. "It's really an attempt to intimidate immigrants by threatening and imposing incarceration," said Victoria Lopez, executive director of the Florence Immigrant and Refugee Project.

Sheriff Arpaio's actions have not gone unnoticed in Mexico. The government there directed its consulate in Phoenix to retain Los Angeles-based immigration lawyer Peter Schey to represent the jailed Mexicans. "This sheriff is not the director of homeland security, but that is how he is acting," claimed Schey. Sheriff Arpaio said that before he acted he received the approval of Maricopa's County Attorney Andrew Thomas, who said that illegal immigrants could be prosecuted under an Arizona statute that makes it a felony to conspire with smugglers. According to Arpaio, those apprehended readily confessed to paying "coyotes" up to $2,000 apiece to guide them into Arizona. Thomas sent a letter to the State Department protesting Mexico's intrusion into Arizona affairs by hiring Schey, evidently with the intention of challenging Arizona's antismuggling statute.

In the meantime, Sheriff Arpaio, his deputies, and his posse are hard at work. "I am continuing to enforce this law despite the controversy surrounding it," he said. "If you get caught by immigration, you get a free ride back to Mexico in an air-conditioned bus. A free ride? Not in my county. I'm going to put them on chain gangs, in tents and feed them bologna sandwiches." Arpaio says that he has been forced into action by the inaction of President Bush. "I am a little disappointed," remarked Arpaio, "that the federal misdemeanor law that calls for up to six months in prison for anyone illegally entering the United States, has seldom been enforced in the past and is likely not be enforced in the near future. Now we have an Arizona felony law that allows the arrest of illegal immigrants and I am still the only agency enforcing that new state law."

Born in Massachusetts to Italian immigrants, Arpaio is no stranger to controversy. After a hitch in the Army during the early 1950s, he served on the police departments of Washington, DC, and Las Vegas, Nevada. He then spent more than 20 years with the Drug Enforcement Administration, including serving at posts in Turkey and Mexico. He served his last four years as head of the DEA's Arizona office. Elected Sheriff of Maricopa County in 1992, his provocative actions brought controversy and national attention. He issued pink underwear to jailed inmates, reduced their meals to subsistence level, prohibited smoking, coffee, pornographic magazines, and movies, and created chain gangs, saying "Jails should not be country clubs." The chain gangs work six days a week, cleaning streets, painting over graffiti, and burying the indigent dead in the county cemetery. In 1993, with Maricopa County's population growing and jails becoming overcrowded, he erected a tent city that houses more than 2,000 inmates. When temperatures hit 120 degrees during the summer of 2003, prisoners in the tent city complained that their incarceration was inhumane. "It's 120 degrees in Iraq and the soldiers are living in tents and they didn't commit any crimes, so shut your mouths," Arpaio told them. By then he was dubbed "America's Toughest Sheriff."

If any local official is equipped to tackle the illegal immigration problem, it is Joe Arpaio. "My message to the illegals is this: Stay out of Maricopa County, because I'm the sheriff here," declared Arpaio. In mid-June, a group calling itself Phoenix Copwatch demonstrated outside Sheriff Arpaio's headquarters, demanding that sheriff deputies stop arresting illegal aliens. Arpaio walked out of his headquarters in downtown Phoenix and told the demonstrators in no uncertain terms that his deputies and his volunteer posse would continue to hunt down and arrest illegal aliens.

Meanwhile, the state of Arizona has created a task force, including officers from the Phoenix police, the state Department of Public Safety, and the state Attorney General's Office to investigate human-smuggling operations and money laundering. "We are going after the leaders," said Phoenix mayor Phil Gordon. "Do we want to raid restaurants and arrest dishwashers? We need to arrest people at the top." During the spring of 2006 the task force seized dozens of weapons and vehicles, $4.8 million in cash, six real estate properties valued at nearly $2 million, small amounts of cocaine and marijuana, and more than 500 illegal aliens. "If we're going to cut off this poison," said Attorney General Terry Goddard, "we're going to do it by making it unprofitable to conduct human smuggling."

The efforts in Arizona to tackle illegal immigration are having an effect. "All I heard in Mexico was how much work there was to be had here," said Isaia Perez Sanchez to a reporter for *The Arizona Republic* in May 2006. "But then I get here to find out that police are cracking down on day laborers, so there's no work." Sanchez is an illegal alien from the Mexican state of Chiapas, where much of the work is done by illegal immigrants from Guatemala, who work for $3 a day.

One of the spots where illegal aliens, like Sanchez, had congregated seeking day labor was on Thomas Road in east Phoenix. However, complaints from residents and business owners in the area about traffic hazards, litter, trespassing, and public urination caused a group of businessmen to hire off-duty Phoenix police officers to chase away the illegal aliens. Soliciting work from the sidewalk is not illegal, but the other activities of the day-laborers are. The presence of a few off-duty cops has effected a change for the better. "It used to be really bad," said Santiago Romero, manager of a pawn shop at the corner of 35th Street and Thomas Road. "The business owners and neighbors really banded together to help turn this around and things have really improved."

Attitudes regarding day-laborers have changed dramatically in Phoenix as Arizona has become the principal entry point for illegal aliens. Several years ago, the city helped fund a day-labor center in the northeastern portion of the town but has since cut off public monies. Immigrant activists' calls for day-labor centers now fall on deaf ears and Phoenix is considering having on-duty police patrol the Thomas Road area.

Pressure to control illegal immigration in Arizona comes from the grassroots. In January 2006 Michelle Dallacroce, a 40-year-old housewife and mother, formed Mothers Against Illegal Aliens (MAIA). A six-year resident of Phoenix, she says that she has watched the schools and health care system deteriorate and fears for the well-being of her children. Attractive, outspoken, and energetic, Dallacroce represents a growing number of women who have been inspired to activism by the negative effects that the invasion of Mexicans has had on their children. Mountain men always said that the most dangerous animal in the wild was a she-grizzly defending her cubs. On radio and television interviews, Dallacroce appears to be just that. She makes some of the male anti-illegal alien activists seem timid and reserved. The mission statement of MAIA pulls no punches, saying in part:

> Our beautiful Nation has been turned into a jungle by the mass invasion of illegal aliens—the streets of America; the neighborhoods and communities where we live; the malls and stores where we shop; the schools where our LEGAL children attend—and, yes, even the churches where we worship—are now the Citadels of fear, bigotry, racism, physical danger and hate! The LEGAL children of America's 21st century have become the scapegoats and the victims of this invasion of illegal aliens. They have become—the get behind, the left behind, the back of the class, the back of the bus, the get off the playground, the get out my way—pawns and victims of peer abuse and societal indifference.

Dallacroce's rhetoric is reality for those who cannot flee to a protected suburb or afford the cost of a private-school education for their children. According to Tom

Horne, Arizona's state superintendent of public education and not a Dallacroce supporter, Arizona is educating at least 125,000 illegal alien children, at a cost to the state of $750 million a year. And David Engelthaler, Arizona's epidemiologist with the state's Department of Health Services, also no supporter of Dallacroce, noted that the foreign born account for 57 percent of the new cases of tuberculosis, of which Mexicans account for 64 percent.

For a time, Dallacroce thought about moving but decided to stay and fight. She has been vehemently denounced by supporters of illegal aliens and has suffered all the usual *ad hominem* attacks. At the same time, she and MAIA have been warmly embraced by older, more well-established anti-illegal immigrant organizations in Arizona, including Border Guardians, led by Laine Lawless of Tucson; Minuteman Civil Defense Corps, headed by Chris Simcox of Tombstone; Arizonans for Immigration Control, led by Wes Bramhall of Tucson; and American Border Patrol, led by Glenn Spencer of Sierra Vista.

Glenn Spencer is one of the pioneers of the fight against illegal immigration. I first met him during the 1990s when he was leading Voice of Citizens Together, a group of San Fernando Valley, California, residents concerned about the devastation wreaked by illegal aliens in what had been the heartland of white middle-class Southern California only a couple of decades earlier. While sharing a speaker's platform, I happened to ask him if he was any relation to Tim Spencer, a guitarist, vocalist, and songwriter for the Sons of the Pioneers, famous for their recordings of "Tumbling Tumbleweeds" and "Cool Water," among many other songs, and their appearances in dozens of "B" Westerns. It turned out that Tim Spencer was his uncle. Now, Glenn Spencer is a pioneer of another sort. He moved to Sierra Vista to be at the battlefront and put into operation the first of the aerial drones transmitting photographs of border activity to his computer center. The photos are posted on his Web site daily. The U.S. government, embarrassed no doubt by Spencer's initiative, finally got an aerial drone of its own in the air.

Reaction in the Rockies

The combined efforts of American Border Patrol and the other groups are not only making a difference in Arizona but also have inspired residents in Colorado to propose a ballot initiative similar to Arizona's Proposition 200. Citizen activists formed Defend Colorado Now and have prepared a ballot initiative that would prohibit illegal aliens in Colorado from receiving public services other than those directly related to public safety, emergencies, or those mandated by federal law. Illegal aliens would also be prohibited from receiving in-state tuition at public colleges. However, to preclude possible challenges over federal mandates and Constitutional questions, K–12 schooling for illegal aliens will continue at taxpayers' expense. At the same time, though, the initiative would prohibit illegal aliens from owning real property in Colorado and restrict county clerks from recording transfer of real property to those unlawfully in the country.

A petition drive was begun late in April 2006 to qualify the initiative for the November 2006 election. During May and early June signatures were pouring in by the thousands. With only some 68,000 signatures needed, it looked as if the initiative was destined for the ballot until opponents of the initiative, led by Manolo Gonzalez-Estay and keenly aware of the initiative's momentum and the mood of Coloradans, took the usual leftist course of going to the courts. In mid-June the Colorado Supreme Court ruled, in a five to two decision, that the initiative could not appear on the ballot on the ground of its being in violation of a state constitutional requirement that initiatives address a single subject only. Curiously, the Colorado Title Board approved the measure's language earlier. "This is outrageous judicial activism, Exhibit A in how courts disregard precedent to reach a political result," said Richard Lamm, former Colorado governor and current registered agent for Defend Colorado Now. "This isn't law—it's raw, naked politics." The dissenting justices, Nathan Coats and Nancy Rice, sharply criticized their colleagues, saying the court has inconsistently applied the single-subject requirement allowing the justices "unfettered discretion to either approve or disapprove virtually any popularly initiated ballot measure at will."

Coloradans can take heart, however, from the actions of their Department of Motor Vehicles (DMV) and Department of Revenue, and of their state legislature. Colorado's DMV and Department of Revenue have been investigating discrepancies between information provided for driver's licenses and Social Security records. Thus far, the DMV has canceled 2,000 licenses. Over the past two years, the agency, in comparing more than four million licenses in its database with Social Security Administration records, has found that names or birth dates on licenses do not match Social Security data, or that Social Security numbers as claimed by license holders have never been issued. These discrepancies have additionally caused the DMV to send warning letters to 53,000 license holders.

Although officials with the DMV and Department of Revenue claim that they are merely engaged in an effort to reconcile information, Latino activists claim the DMV is out to harass "undocumented migrants." Evidently, hundreds of Latinos have visited Centro Amistad, El Comite, and other Latino advocacy organizations to have the DMV letters translated for them. Rusty Denham, a caseworker for Centro Amistad, calls the DMV's reconciliation effort "institutional racism." "I don't see that there is any potential for targeting at all," said

M. Michael Cooke, director of the Department of Revenue. "It is our job to issue these documents to make sure drivers are competent, of age, and legally present. Once they meet those requirements, we issue. If there is an individual driving without it, that's unlawful."

For its part, the Colorado state legislature passed seven measures aimed at illegal aliens during the spring of 2006. The first of these, Senate Bill 90, requiring law enforcement officials to notify U.S. Immigration and Customs Enforcement (ICE) whenever they arrest an illegal alien, was signed into law by Governor Bill Owens in early May. The new statute also requires municipal and county governments to cooperate with state and federal officials in enforcing immigration laws. So-called sanctuary cities would lose grants from the state Department of Local Affairs.

The six other anti-illegal alien measures were signed by Governor Owens at the end of May or in early June. His signature on the bills was a very positive affirmation of a changed political climate in Colorado. He could have vetoed any one of the bills, of course, but he also could have allowed them to become law without his signature.

Senate Bill 206 makes it a felony, punishable by up to 12 years in prison, to smuggle someone into or through Colorado in violation of federal immigration laws. Each person smuggled would constitute an additional felony count. Senate Bill 207 makes trafficking in adult illegal immigrants a felony punishable by up to 24 years in prison. Senate Bill 225 creates a Colorado State Patrol immigration-enforcement unit. Senate Bill 110 establishes a $50,000 fine for anyone caught forging, counterfeiting, altering, or providing documents for illegal aliens to use in fraudulent verification of their eligibility to work in the United States. House Bill 1343 prohibits a state or local agency from contracting for goods and services from a business that knowingly employs illegal aliens, or that knowingly subcontracts with another business that employs illegal aliens. The bill also requires businesses with government contracts to verify their employees' work status through a Department of Homeland Security-sponsored computer database. Finally, House Bill 1306 requires the state to audit all state agencies and public colleges and universities to insure that they are in compliance with a 2003 law that establishes what constitutes "secure and verifiable" identity documents for public services.

California's Pockets of Resistance

Unlike the state legislatures of Arizona and Colorado, California's legislature is controlled by members who openly support, or give tacit consent to, illegal immigration. The most powerful coalition within the state legislature is the Latino Caucus, which did not exist before 1973. Now it has 27 members, including such professional Mexicans as Cruz Bustamante, Gil Cedillo, and Fabian Nunez, all three of whom have been strong advocates for such causes as driver's licenses, in-state tuition, and amnesty for illegal aliens.

When El Presidente Vincente Fox visited the California legislature, he was introduced by Assembly Speaker Nunez. "You know, as we do, that California and Mexico share so much more than a border and the language that many of us speak," said Nunez. "We share a common culture, a common history, and a common heritage." Nunez should have said "We Mexicans . . . ," as a majority of Californians would undoubtedly dispute his claims to a common culture, history, and heritage. Nunez concluded his introductory remarks by gushing, "President Fox—You are a champion of human rights, governmental reform, and economic progress. President Fox—Liberty, equality, and justice have been the hallmarks of your tenure—values that we hold dear in the State of California. You have fortified a political system that works, but, moreover, that people trust. I am proud to present to you, His Excellency, Vincente Fox Quesada, President of the United Mexican States." (Nunez, at least, inserted "Mexican" between "United" and "States.") Despite Nunez's sycophantic praise, four or five million more Mexicans have arrived illegally in the United States during El Presidente's term in office, and Mexico remains the same corrupt country it has always been.

With Nunez and his compadres voting as a bloc in the state senate and assembly, there is no hope of anything being accomplished through the legislature in California. On the state level, reform will have to come through the initiative process, or through Governor Arnold Schwarzenegger. Although the governor did veto a driver's license bill for illegal aliens, sponsored by Gil Cedillo, he has done little else. Like the bodybuilder and the actor he was, Schwarzenegger wants to be loved and admired by everyone. When a few of his proposals for reform—on issues not involving illegal aliens—met resistance, he ran for cover and apologized for his own initiatives. Heroic play-acting in movies is fine, but Schwarzenegger is no Conan in California.

Nonetheless, early in June 2006, the governor promised to send 1,000 California National Guard troops to the border as part of President Bush's plan to control illegal immigration. Schwarzenegger quickly added, though, that the Guard's border mission would end no later than December 31, 2008. Moreover, the troops will not be armed—just imagine: National Guardsmen, including veterans of Iraq, with rifles and sidearms!—and will not detain or arrest illegal immigrants. Instead, the troops will be tasked with fixing vehicles, repairing roads, operating cameras, and other such duties in support of the U.S. Border Patrol. "The mission that I will assign to our California National Guard will be significantly different from the plan laid out by President Bush," said Schwarzenegger. "We will assist in a manner that protects our troops and uses our men and women in the most effective and appropriate way possible." If it wasn't already clear that Schwarzenegger was uncomfortable with his commitment of the Guard to the border, he added, "It's not my preference to send the National Guard to do this mission." Schwarzenegger, I suppose, thinks he has now staked out the acceptable middle ground.

Fabian Nunez made no such attempt at appealing to all constituencies in California. He predicted that Latin American countries would consider the deployment of the Guard offensive. "When you deploy the National Guard to the southern border—but you don't do the same to the northern border—then you send a message that the problem is Latin America," said the Assembly Speaker. (So half of the five or six million illegal aliens in California are actually Canadians!) Nunez tried to disguise some of his opposition to deployment by citing supposed manpower shortages. Although he is a powerful figure in the state legislature, he cannot seem to perform simple calculations. There are 20,000 California National Guard troops. Some 2,000 are deployed overseas, mostly in Iraq, and, with 1,000 on the border, that leaves 17,000 for use in the case of an emergency in California. The governor and the Guard, said Nunez, "seem to feel confident we have enough manpower in the National Guard to respond to a natural disaster. I'm not totally convinced that's the case." Nunez's attempt at disguising his real agenda is embarrassingly transparent and insulting.

If Schwarzenegger's "girlie-man" governorship and the Latino Caucus give Californians little hope of immigration reform at the state level, there are nevertheless signs of local revolt against the illegal alien invasion. The action is hottest in the cities of Orange, Costa Mesa, and San Bernardino. The city of Orange is located, not surprisingly, in the heart of Orange County. In 1970 it had a population of some 77,000 and was virtually all white. Its population is now nearly 140,000, 32 percent of which is Hispanic. In 1989, the city established a day-labor center to keep those soliciting work off private property and to prevent public urination. The facility, which includes a bathroom and a bike rack, costs the city $38,000 a year to maintain. Yet, during the last few years day laborers have again become a public nuisance in Orange, congregating on private property, soliciting work, drinking alcoholic beverages, and urinating. During the summer of 2005, the Orange Police Department finally began making arrests and handing over illegal aliens to the U.S. Border Patrol. Under federal law the city is not required to do so, but Mayor Mark Murphy has promised, "If you break the

law in Orange and don't have legitimate ID, you will be cited and turned over."
Illegal aliens are beginning to worry. "I know the white people are thinking it's
wrong, because there are too many people and it looks bad," admitted illegal
alien Miguel Angel Vasquez, "but we need a job."

The parking lot of Home Depot is one of the most popular spots in Orange
for illegal aliens to gather. The store itself does not alert police—some people
have alleged that Home Depot stores throughout California cooperate with illegal aliens—but customers do, bringing Orange police to the site. On a Friday
morning in February 2006, for example, police arrested nine men in front of the
store for soliciting work. Eight of the nine had no evidence of legal U.S. residency and were taken immediately to a Border Patrol checkpoint at Dana Point.
"It is unusual, but I think it's wonderful," said Barbara Coe, Orange County
resident and chair of the California Coalition for Immigration Reform. "These
people are criminals in violation of federal immigration law."

Ten miles to the southwest of Orange is Costa Mesa, a city with a population
of nearly 110,000. Costa Mesa had fewer than 17,000 residents when it was incorporated in 1953. During the 1950s and 1960s the town was virtually all white.
Now the population is 32 percent Hispanic—76 percent of that Mexican—and
many are illegal aliens. Like Orange, Costa Mesa had established a day-labor
center in 1989 but the city's new mayor, Allan Mansoor, closed the place in
2005, calling it "city-subsidized competition" for the private sector, besides costing the municipality $100,000 a year. Costa Mesa has also authorized its police
to receive training in the enforcement of federal immigration law. "Just because
the federal government dropped the ball doesn't mean that we should sit idly
by," says Mansoor. "We need to stop making excuses as to why we're not uphold-
ing the law and start looking for ways to uphold our oaths of office."

The 41-year-old son of an Egyptian father and a Swedish mother, Mansoor
is quick to note that he is trying to reduce crime and illegal immigration, not to
harass legal immigrants. Costa Mesa police now check the immigration status
of those arrested on felony charges. Mansoor, who wants a greater police crackdown on illegal aliens, adds, "It's what I am able to do right now." Minuteman
Project cofounder Jim Gilchrist told Mansoor, "You are a dream come true."

The mayor has his critics, including many Hispanic business owners who
claim their customers are now afraid to come out of their houses. Vincente
Barajas, owner of the La Espiga de Oro bakery, says his business has declined
20 percent since the city council voted to implement Mansoor's plan. "People
think that just because of the way they look, you're going to get picked up by the
police and taken to jail," he said. "Even people from out of the city are afraid to
come in and support us." The Costa Mesa Chamber of Commerce also opposes

the policy, said Edgar Fawcett, its president. (Business first and foremost, it would seem.)

Mansoor seems unfazed by his critics, perhaps because he has been personally affected by the presence of illegal aliens. Ten years ago he bought a house on Costa Mesa's affordable west side. He has seen aging apartment buildings fill with illegal aliens, his neighborhood deteriorate, and Spanish become the predominant language there. Mansoor recalls that his Swedish grandmother, who lived with him and his mother, used to say, "We are in the United States now. We speak English." He and his brothers were raised as the Americans they were born, and his family has fully assimilated. This is not the case with illegal aliens, Mansoor argues.

Others in Costa Mesa have had the same experience. Ken Rasmussen, a 64-year-old retired restaurateur, has lived in the city, where his two sons attended the city's public schools, since 1968. He says he wouldn't have his children in the same schools today, as the illegal alien invasion has ruined them. "All of a sudden, it isn't the same city. I want my city back." Rasmussen notes that to the north of Costa Mesa is Santa Ana, which has become predominately Latino, poor, and crowded—one of the most densely populated cities in the United States. "Guess what's coming south," says Rasmussen. "Guess what's coming this way."

Before Mansoor became mayor in January 2006, Costa Mesa had last made headlines for its illegal alien problem in 1990, when the city council prohibited local agencies from receiving Housing and Urban Development (HUD) grant money if those agencies aided illegal immigrants. Jack Kemp, then secretary of HUD, called the policy "un-American" and issued an order against it.

That Costa Mesa's plan to do nothing more than have police review the immigration status of those arrested on felony charges is cause for controversy should be an alarm for Californians. It took a bill sponsored by Congressman Elton Gallegly of Ventura County in 1997 to send federal immigration officers into Ventura and Orange county jails to make immigration checks. It seems unbelievable, yet such was the case, that until then felonious illegal aliens were not identified and deported. One notorious illegal in Ventura County had been arrested three times for assault with a deadly weapon but not deported. The fourth time he used a deadly weapon in an assault, he succeeded in murdering his victim, a woman from the town of Santa Paula. Referring to his own county jail identification program, Gallegly remarked, "If this program had been in place at the time of his previous arrests, this killer would have been identified and deported and Isabela Guzman would most likely be alive today." Despite a powerful agricultural lobby in Ventura County, Gallegly has consistently been one of the few Republicans in the state who has not conceded the cause of national sovereignty to business interests.

Gallegly's program is still in operation at the Ventura County Jail, yet only two ICE agents are assigned to the lockup. They cannot interview all the suspected illegal aliens who are arrested and jailed for crimes daily. While 20 to 30 are identified each day, others pass through the system undetected. "There are many that we miss," admitted agent David Wales in July 2006, adding that agents prioritize their interviews, starting with those suspects who have committed the most heinous crimes. "There's nothing that is 100 percent, but we work very hard to keep those folks from getting back on the street." Why Ventura County sheriff's deputies have not been trained to interview suspected illegal aliens, Wales did not say.

The big battle in California is now occurring in the city of San Bernardino over the Illegal Immigration Relief Act, which would prohibit illegal aliens from renting or leasing property and subject landlords to fines for allowing them to do so. Under the act, police could impound vehicles used to transport illegal aliens, the city could deny permits, contracts, and grants to employers who hire illegal aliens, and all city business would be required to be conducted in English. Behind the initiative is Joseph Turner, the founder of Save Our State, a highly active organization opposed to the presence of illegal aliens in California.

Turner is 29 years old, married, the father of two children, and a graduate of the University of Southern California. He considers himself nobody special. "I guess you could call me a patriot," he told me in an interview. He grew up in Riverside, California, and has seen portions of his hometown, and the rest of the state, deteriorate dramatically with the illegal alien invasion. In 2004, with more enthusiasm than money, he founded Save Our State to address the issue. He has been called all the usual names—racist, bigot, xenophobe, Nazi—by the illegal alien lobby who, lacking good arguments, resort to *ad hominem* attacks. I found him sharp, articulate, and vitally concerned about the future of the country that his children will inherit.

In the city of San Bernardino, whose population is now nearing 200,000, Turner and other volunteers from SOS collected enough signatures to qualify the Illegal Immigration Relief Act for the ballot. Through a process peculiar to the San Bernardino city charter, the initiative first went before the city council during June 2006. When council members voted against it four to three, they simply set the stage for a citywide special election on the initiative. With 48 percent of San Bernardino's population Hispanic, it would seem that the initiative has little chance of succeeding. However, much of the Hispanic population is illegal and, presumably, will not be voting. Then, too, there are some old-time Mexican-Americans in

San Bernardino who, like their counterparts in other regions of California, are none too happy about the invasion of illegals.

The wild card in the election in San Bernardino is the city's blacks, who comprise about 16 percent of the population. While most black politicians try to link the plight of the illegal aliens with civil rights issues and white racism, there is a growing resentment in San Bernardino and other black communities in California of the Hispanic invasion. Nonetheless, the rhetoric of the politicians is something to behold. "You knew who the Klan was," cried black San Bernardino councilman Rikke Johnson. "They paraded in sheets." Now "they wear suits, they have Web sites, they have initiatives." The white mayor of the city is also against the initiative, although for more pragmatic reasons. "Burdening the taxpayers of San Bernardino with unnecessary costs simply because Washington, DC, has a failed immigration policy makes no sense at all," said Patrick J. Morris. The cost of enforcing the initiative could run to more than a million dollars a year. On the other hand, the cost of schooling illegal aliens and the American-born children of illegal aliens, together with the costs of dealing with the crime committed by illegal aliens, dwarfs the projected budget for the Illegal Immigration Relief Act.

Lawyers for the ACLU and MALDEF have already vowed to challenge the proposed ordinance in court, saying that it would infringe on the federal government's authority to regulate immigration and would pressure landlords to discriminate based on race. "It turns ordinary residents into immigration agents," exclaimed Hector Villagra, director of the ACLU's Orange County office. He added that the provision making English the required language for city government would deny residents the ability to petition the government as protected under the First Amendment.

For a time, it looked as if the initiative would be contested in the November 2006 election. However, in late June, Florentino Garza, represented by attorney Bradley Hertz, challenged the initiative on the basis of the number of signatures gathered. According to the city charter of San Bernardino, a petitioner must gather enough signatures to equal 30 percent of voters "at the last preceding city election at which a mayor was elected." When Turner began his petition drive during the fall of 2005, the last mayoral election was November 2001. Turner had his initiative title approved and in his words, "had dotted every 'i' and crossed every 't.'" By April, he had more than the requisite number of signatures gathered and the petition filed. The county registrar of voters verified the minimum number of signatures needed, plus one, and then stopped counting.

Garza argued that the number of signatures should have been based on a mayoral runoff election that occurred during February 2006, which would require more signatures than Turner had gathered. San Bernardino's city attorney, Jim Penman, reasoned that the initiative should remain on the ballot because Turner had legally begun the process long before the February election, and City Clerk Rachel Clark had told Turner at that time the number of signatures that he would need to qualify the initiative. Clark acted according to the California Elections Code, which explicitly states that the requisite number of signatures be determined when the notice to circulate a petition is published—something Turner did in November 2005. Although the language in the Election Code seems unequivocal and Turner's notice-to-circulate date indisputable, on June 26, Superior Court Judge A. Rex Victor ruled against the ballot initiative, saying the city had erred. "This is a case of an activist judge that took matters into his own hands," declared Turner.

Meanwhile, Joseph Turner was attacked while debating the initiative with members of the National Alliance for Human Rights in front of the San Bernardino Superior Court building. Evidently not considering free speech a human right, Roberto Valentine, a member of the group, struck Turner in the face. Sheriff's deputies cited Valentine for misdemeanor battery. If convicted, he could be fined or jailed. Valentine is probably wishing he could appear before Judge Victor.

Great Basin Efforts

Utah is one of the most conservative states in the Union, yet highly ambivalent about the presence of illegal aliens within her borders. There is an obvious explanation for this. The Church of Jesus Christ of Latter-day Saints holds that American Indians are descendants of the Ten Lost Tribes of Israel and that it is the Mormons' mission to save them. For that reason, the Mormons have had mostly good relations with various tribes and bands of Indians in the American West. Since the illegal immigrants from south of the border have varying degrees of Indian blood—many of them are mostly, or even purely, Indian—they are candidates for conversion. Moreover, many young Mormon men have spent their two-year missions proselytizing in Latin America. Hispanics, many of them, if not most, illegal, now represent about ten percent of Utah's population.

It was not by accident that Mexican President Vincente Fox began his June tour of the Western states with a visit to Utah, where he told a cheering crowd of a thousand Mexicans in West Valley, "Even though you are far from Mexico, you are an integral part of Mexico. We will never forget you. We love you." (Fox should have added, "as long as you keep sending money home and living off the largess of the gringos.")

Utah was one of the first states to give illegal aliens drivers' licenses and to grant them in-state tuition at public colleges. As the burden of illegal aliens on state services has increased, however, the mood has changed. Early in 2006, state legislators repealed the drivers' license bill and replaced it with a drivers' permit that allows illegal aliens to operate a vehicle on public roads, but does not allow them to use the permit as official government identification or for boarding airplanes.

In 2002, U.S. Representative Chris Cannon, a Republican, exclaimed to the audience at a MALDEF dinner, "We love immigrants in Utah. We don't make distinctions between legal and illegal." During April 2006, Cannon began circulating a video to party activists announcing that he was tough on illegal immigration and that the nation must have secure borders. Republicans in his district, unconvinced by his change of course, circulated a video of their own, showing Cannon at the MALDEF dinner. As a result, Cannon was forced into a runoff election in the Republican primary, an extraordinary indignity for a five-term incumbent in a safe district. His opponent, John Jacobs, a real estate developer, was running neck and neck with Cannon in opinion polls until late in June when Jacobs blundered badly by making nutty statements about Satan interfering in his business and admitting that he had no concrete plan for dealing with illegal aliens.

On the last Tuesday in June, Cannon won the runoff with 55 percent of the vote to Jacobs's 45 percent. "This is a big margin of victory," crowed Cannon. "It says a lot about Republicans getting together and solving this problem. I hope what it means is Republicans look at this and realize we don't have to be divided on the issue of illegal immigrants." In fact, the real significance of the election is that a five-term incumbent had 45 percent of his own Republican constituents vote against him with a weak unknown as the alternative.

Idaho is, perhaps, the most conservative state in the Union if party affiliation is any indication. Republicans outnumber Democrats 28–7 in the state Senate and 57–13 in the House. Democratic strength exists only in parts of Boise, Pocatello, Lewiston, and Ketchum. It is likely that Idaho will soon be passing bills aimed at illegal aliens, who have begun arriving in significant numbers to work on factory farms in the southwestern portion of the state and today are costing the taxpayers millions of dollars. When an illegal alien from Mexico gave birth to a premature baby in Caldwell, Canyon County was handed a hospital bill for $174,000. And a criminal illegal alien cost the county thousands more for incarceration in a motel room of his own, because it was feared his tuberculosis would be contracted by other jail inmates.

The all-Republican commissioners of Canyon County have responded to the illegal alien invasion by retaining attorney Howard Foster, a member of the Federation for American Immigration Reform, who, as an expert in using the RICO (Racketeer Influenced and Corrupt Organizations) Act, has filed a racketeering lawsuit against four large businesses in the area, alleging that they deliberately employ illegal aliens. Canyon County is the first municipality to file a suit under RICO for such employment practices. RICO allows plaintiffs in civil lawsuits to sue for triple damages. "Many of these illegal immigrants have committed crimes resulting in criminal justice expenses to the county," the lawsuit states. "Others have become public charges by seeking medical services, which the county had had to pay."

The lawsuit was dismissed by a federal district court in December 2005, on grounds that municipalities cannot expect to recoup the cost of services they provide in the normal course of business. The lawsuit is now before the U.S. 9th Circuit Court of Appeals. Foster, using RICO, won a case before the 9th Circuit in 2000 when he represented a cleaning company that sued a competitor for hiring illegal aliens. In three other cases, he is representing employees who allege that their employers kept wages artificially low by hiring illegal aliens.

The most outspoken of the Canyon County commissioners is Robert Vasquez, himself the grandson of legal Mexican immigrants. Elected to the county commission in 2002, he had the county send the Mexican government a $2 million bill for services Canyon had provided to illegal aliens from Mexico. Also, he asked Idaho Governor Dirk Kempthorne to declare Canyon County a disaster area, arguing that it needed emergency funds for costs attributed to illegal aliens, and proposed state legislation that would prohibit illegal aliens from receiving welfare. "For every dollar for an illegal alien, it's one less dollar in my constituents' pocket," says Vasquez. He plans to run for Congress, largely on the illegal immigration issue.

The town of Caldwell in the heart of Canyon County is now experiencing what so many California towns did during the 1970s and 1980s. "We have young guys, white and Hispanic, in here legally who want jobs—but companies give them to people who they can pay half the going wage," said Joyce Yelm, an Idaho native who grew up working in beet and potato fields. She says her old neighborhood has become a Spanish-speaking "shanty town."

Idaho's neighboring state of Oregon is not nearly so conservative, especially in her great population centers running down the Willamette Valley to Portland. However, east of the Cascades, in cowboy country, reside some tough conservatives who don't cotton to illegal aliens. One of them is John Trumbo, the tall Western-dressed sheriff of Umatilla County in the northeastern portion of the state. Until recently, the area was known for little else than a rodeo, the Pendleton Round-Up, held each year in mid-September. Now Trumbo has brought some attention to the county by writing Mexican President Fox to demand $318,843, the cost of incarcerating criminal illegal aliens in his county jail. (Trumbo added, "At this time, you will not be billed for medical, dental, and transportation costs. Your prompt attention to this request will be very much appreciated.") To date, Fox has not responded, let alone made a payment.

During the last 20 years the Hispanic population of Umatilla County has grown from less than one percent to more than 12 percent, most of the increase the result of illegal immigration from Mexico. Neighborhoods in several of the county's towns are called "Little Mexico." At many public schools, the majority of the children are illegal aliens or the children of illegal aliens—and their numbers are growing rapidly. So, too, are gangs, drug use, domestic violence, alcoholism, and nutrition programs. The illegal presence costs millions and the county is facing funding shortages. The county has a jail capacity for 252 inmates but can afford staff and services for no more than 135. Sheriff Trumbo, who should have 27 deputies on patrol, can afford only nine. From 2 A.M. to 8 A.M. there are no deputies at all on patrol.

"When people call the police, they expect to see the police," says Trumbo. "They see it on TV all the time. But there are times when I can't send anybody because I don't have anybody because I don't have the money." He says the money he should have goes to the apprehension and incarceration of criminal illegal aliens, among them Ever Alexis-Flores, a convicted robber and murderer, and Juan Flores-Romero, who has been in jail 20 different times, usually for burglary, and deported to Mexico again and again. "The old joke among the immigration agents who shuttled these guys back to Mexico was," says Trumbo, "'I hope we make it back to Pendleton before they do.'"

Fernando Sanchez Ugarte, the Mexican consul general for Oregon, dismissed Trumbo's letter as political posturing, as well as racist, adding, "If a visitor from Switzerland does something wrong while visiting Umatilla County, will Mr. Trumbo send a bill to the leader of Switzerland? I don't think so." Neither do I. Perhaps Ugarte's English is weak but he doesn't seem to draw a distinction between visitor and illegal alien, and he doesn't address the costly burden his countrymen have put on Umatilla County.

Texas Sheriffs Standing Tall

Like Trumbo in Oregon, county sheriffs in Texas are doing the job that the federal Immigration and Customs Enforcement authorities should be doing. The county top cops formed the Texas Border Sheriff's Coalition in 2005 to coordinate their efforts to halt illegal immigration and to seek reimbursement from the state for county funds expended in those efforts. Chaired by Zapata County Sheriff Sigifredo Gonzalez, the coalition has 16 county sheriff's departments as members. "The lack of federal response has left the counties with no other alternative than to join forces," said Gonzalez.

Late in March 2006, the Texas Border Sheriff's Coalition conducted meetings in El Paso with border sheriffs from New Mexico, Arizona, and California to form a second organization, the Southwest Border Sheriff's Coalition. "Basically, we're hoping to organize so we can all speak with one voice," Sheriff Gonzalez said. "It's true, there is strength in numbers. Instead of fighting each other, we are going to work together to protect the American people from what we see as a serious national-security risk." Gonzalez added that the federal government has virtually abandoned the 2,000-mile border with Mexico and that the resulting invasion of illegal aliens has become a "financial nightmare" for the border counties.

Lobbied by the Texas Border Sheriff's Coalition, Governor Rick Perry, in 2005, launched "Operation Linebacker," a $10 million program to aid the border counties. In June 2006, he announced a $5 million plan to install hundreds of night-vision cameras on private land along the Mexican border and put live video from the cameras on the Internet. Anyone with an Internet connection will be able to watch the video feed and report illegal border crossings to authorities on a toll-free hotline. "I look at this as not different from the neighborhood watches we have had in our communities for years and years," said Perry. Like many other politicians, Perry has changed his stance on the border issue during the last couple of years, having previously argued that illegal immigration was strictly a federal responsibility. Now he says, "Texas cannot wait for Washington, DC, to act."

Meanwhile, the border counties of Texas are running highway checkpoints to intercept illegal immigrants. In March 2006, Hudspeth County sheriff's deputies apprehended 75 illegal immigrants in 28 hours of operating a checkpoint. Two months later, Hudspeth deputies intercepted 54 illegal immigrants on Highway 62/180 near the Guadalupe Mountains after running another for no more than a few hours. Three trucks and one van were found packed with illegal aliens, including two men carrying Mexican military identification cards. One of the men with the military ID had been deported only two weeks earlier. "Makes you wonder what the military is trying to do over here," said Hudspeth County Sheriff Arvin West. He suggested that so simple an expedient as a checkpoint demonstrates that local law enforcement can be another line of defense along the border, and added that it was clear to him that the increase in illegal immigration is in response to an anticipated amnesty.

El Paso County sheriff's deputies apprehended 275 illegal aliens at highway checkpoints, gas stations, and rest areas during April and May 2006, resulting in the U.S. Border Patrol being called more than a hundred times. Consequently, the sheriff's department has been accused of "racial profiling." The ACLU of Texas harshly criticizes the department's actions and is planning to file a report with the United Nations Human Rights Committee. And a federal lawsuit was filed in May, alleging that sheriff's deputies illegally stopped a public bus and detained several Hispanics who lacked identification. Withering under the attacks of the ACLU and "immigrant rights" groups, El Paso County Sheriff Leo Samaniego temporarily suspended operation of the checkpoints during June and announced that his deputies would no longer hold illegal aliens for the Border Patrol basely solely on immigration status.

Midwest and Northeast Lawmen Respond to Invasion

Richard Jones, the sheriff of Butler County, Ohio, has demonstrated more backbone. Although he does not expect reimbursement, he has billed the federal government for costs incurred by the illegal aliens he jails. He has also erected a sign in front of the county jail, saying "Illegal Aliens Here" with an arrow pointing to the lockup, and has plastered six billboards in his southwestern Ohio county with the message, "Hire an Illegal—Break the Law!" On his Web site he warns businesses, "You know who you are, and we're coming. If you engage in an underground economy and you think that we don't know about it, we'll be visiting you."

In May 2006, Jones's deputies detained 18 illegal aliens at a construction site, but when he called Immigration and Customs Enforcement, no one responded. Sheriff Jones claimed such inaction is typical of ICE. Greg Palmore, a spokesman for the agency, responded with mind-numbing doublespeak on National Public Radio's *All Things Considered*: "If you're going to hold anybody, you've got to have the charges." Being an illegal alien is evidently not enough of an infraction to prompt ICE to action. Palmore further explained, "If two simultaneous calls come in—one that was national security, and the other being an undocumented immigrant that poses no significant public safety threat—you can surmise exactly where we'll put our resources." NPR's reporter failed to ask Palmore if there was, in fact, another call at the very moment that Sheriff Jones called and, if so, whether that call concerned national security.

On Ohio's eastern border, Belmont County Sheriff Fred Thompson is also making news. In June 2006, his deputies apprehended 20 illegal aliens when the lawmen stopped a van for a traffic violation. "There were bodies packed in everywhere," said Thompson. "Everywhere you looked, there was a body." His deputies contacted an ICE duty agent in Columbus and were told to release the detainees. Greg Palmore, again speaking for the agency, claimed that the ICE agent asked to speak with the suspected illegal aliens to ascertain their status but was told that was impossible. At that point, the agent is said to have ordered the deputies to release the illegals. But Sheriff Thompson claims the ICE agent never asked to talk with the suspects. Thompson says further that a dispatcher contacted ICE several times the next day and was "treated rather rudely." His deputies often stop vehicles loaded with suspected illegal aliens on their way through Belmont County, notes Thompson, and his department always contacts ICE. Routinely, ICE fails to take action. In the future, Thompson says he will deal with illegal aliens on his own. "What we're going to do is start seizing their vehicles and send them on their merry way."

Another local lawman who has made national news in his fight against the illegal alien invasion is Garrett Chamberlain, the police chief of New Ipswich, New Hampshire. In July 2004 he detained nine illegal immigrants who worked for a roofing company after he and one of his officers stopped the van into which they were packed. Although the men admitted that they had been smuggled across the border from Mexico, ICE refused to take custody of them. Chief Chamberlain had no choice but to release the prisoners. He did, however, contact New Hampshire's attorney general and ask for his opinion on the applicability of the criminal trespass statute that declares, "A person is guilty of criminal trespass if, knowing that he is not licensed or privileged to do so, he enters or remains in any place." The attorney general assured Chamberlain that he could arrest illegal aliens under the statute.

Early in May 2005, one of Chamberlain's officers stopped to aid Jorge Mora Ramirez, whose car had broken down. Ramirez was found to have a fake Massachusetts driver's license and a real Mexican one. He admitted to being in the country illegally. Chamberlain contacted ICE, whereupon the agency, as it had done in the past with other suspects, refused to take Ramirez into custody. Chamberlain then charged Ramirez with criminal trespass. Ramirez pleaded guilty to the charge, which carries a fine but no jail time, but changed his plea after the Mexican Consulate and the ACLU retained an attorney, Mona Movafaghi, to defend him. Movafaghi said Chamberlain had violated the Vienna Convention for not immediately putting Ramirez in contact with the Mexican Consulate.

Following Chamberlain's example, Richard Gendron, the police chief of Hudson, New Hampshire, arrested two illegal Mexican aliens, Sergio Robles Ruiz and Margarito Jaramillo Escobar, for criminal trespass after one of his officers stopped the car Ruiz was driving with a broken headlight at night. Meanwhile, Chamberlain's officers were making more arrests of illegal aliens for criminal trespass. It all came to an end in August 2005, however, when Jaffrey District Court Judge L. Phillips Runyon ruled, "The criminal trespass charges against the defendants are unconstitutional attempts to regulate in the area of enforcement of immigration violations, an area where Congress must be deemed to have regulated with civil sanctions and criminal penalties as it feels are sufficient." Applauding Runyon's decision, Movafaghi exclaimed, "Today is a great day for immigrants in New Hampshire." Although she specializes in immigration law, she, like so many others, conflates, most likely deliberately, the terms *immigrant* and *illegal alien.*

Chief Chamberlain, who looks as if he should be playing linebacker in the NFL, pledged to continue the battle against illegals, saying he would review a state law that prohibits employing illegal alien workers and ask New Hampshire's Attorney General Kelly Ayotte to organize a task force on the illegal alien problem. In 2005, at New Hampshire's annual celebration commemorating the signing of the Constitution, which occurs on September 25, Chamberlain was one of the principal speakers. Others included Jim Gilchrist, co-founder of the Minuteman Project, and Rep. Tom Tancredo from Colorado, who emerged several years ago as the most active and outspoken Congressional critic of President Bush's refusal to enforce immigration law.

The individual efforts of police chiefs Garrett Chamberlain and Richard Gendron have evidently inspired others in New Hampshire. A member of the state house of representatives, David Buhlman of Hudson, has organized a "House Immigration Caucus" and helped introduce several state measures aimed at illegal aliens. None of the bills has yet been passed into legislation. Buhlman notes that many legislators fear being branded "racist" should they support the bills. Nonetheless, he says, "Some people will support action on the state level, given that the feds are still not acting properly." Meanwhile, a New Hampshire chapter of the Minuteman Civil Defense Corps has been established by Ron Oplinus of Exeter. "We're tired of the government not doing its job, so we are stepping to the line in a totally legal manner and assisting the government," he said.

The Towns That Said "Enough"

Early in May 2006, a Hazleton, Pennsylvania, man was shot to death by two illegal aliens. The murder would not have been newsworthy in Los Angeles, where such killings have become commonplace. In Hazleton, however, the result was an eruption of anti-illegal alien sentiment that has caused the town's mayor, Lou Barletta, to propose a city ordinance, based on and named after Joseph Turner's Illegal Immigration Relief Act, against renting to or hiring illegal aliens. The ordinance would also make English the official language of Hazleton govern- ment. "We're hoping we would be lighting one candle in a dark room. If this is duplicated by other cities in the nation, it would have a real impact on busi- nesses who might think of hiring illegal immigrants," said Barletta.

Located in an old coal mining district 80 miles northwest of Philadelphia, Hazleton has undergone a demographic change during the last five years that is typical of what California towns experienced during the 1980s and 1990s. When Barletta took office in 2000, Hazleton had a population of a little more than 23,000, with Hispanics accounting for five percent. Now the town's population is pushing 31,000 and Hispanics comprise nearly 30 percent of the total. Violent crime, drug trafficking, gangs, and graffiti are common. "Illegal immigrants are destroying the city," said the mayor. "This is crazy. People are afraid to walk the streets. There's going to be law and order back in Hazleton, and I'm going to use every tool I possibly can." Whites in Hazleton, who as recently as the 1990s, rep- resented 95 percent of the town's population, are ardent supporters of Barletta. When he walked into a restaurant for lunch after having proposed the Illegal Immigration Relief Act, he was welcomed by a standing ovation. Hispanics are mostly of another mind. Jose Lechuga, who came from Mexico to the United States illegally, then was granted amnesty in 1986, says the mayor is "confusing illegal people with criminals."

Illegal aliens who commit no further criminal acts after illegally entering the country are still a major problem in Hazleton. Mayor Barletta claims that classrooms are overcrowded and the schools are failing, English has become a second language, hospitals are teetering on bankruptcy, and neighborhoods have been turned into slums. Francis Tucci, a 57-year-old lifelong resident of Hazleton and owner of a hair salon, echoes the mayor's sentiments. "We were a nice com- munity. You find bad everywhere. I understand that. But we're talking about here and now." The Hazleton town council agrees. In mid-June, the council voted four to one to approve the Illegal Immigration Relief Act. As required by the city charter a second vote was taken a month later and again the act was approved, four to one. The ACLU immediately sued to block the ordinance, arguing it violates the supremacy clause of the Constitution and would harass legal immigrants. In response, the city has retained the services of the former head of Immigration in the Department of Justice. Barletta says that the ordinance has nothing to do with legal immigrants, but "to illegal immigrants and those who would hire or abet them in any way, I say your time is up. You are no longer welcome."

The Virginia town of Herndon shares one thing in common with Hazleton. Its Hispanic population—most of it illegal—has grown dramatically over the last decade and is now approaching 27 percent of the total. Unlike Hazleton, whites account for less than 55 percent of the population, with blacks and Asians comprising another 20 percent. Attention in Herndon was focused on a day-labor center that was built with Herndon taxpayers' dollars and operated by a charity, Project Hope and Harmony, with funding from Fairfax County—against the wishes of many in Herndon. The center opened in December 2005. Most of those congregating at the center were illegal aliens from south of the border, often a hundred or more a day. Herndon citizens complained to their city council to no avail. Early in 2006, they formed the Help Save Herndon organization and a Herndon chapter of the Minutemen.

In May, elections were held for mayor and for four seats on the city council. The issue of the day-labor center dwarfed all others. The incumbent mayor and two councilmen who had supported the day-labor center were swept out of office. One incumbent councilman who had opposed the center, and one who had supported it, were reelected. "Politicians across the country should take note of the results of this election," proclaimed Chris Simcox of the Minuteman Civil Defense Corps in a written statement. "The central issue of this referendum vote was illegal immigration and elitist politicians ignoring the will of the American people for their own special interests. The voters of Herndon, Virginia, sent a clear message to their city officials: 'You're fired.'" Help Save Herndon also issued a written statement, saying the election was a "devastating defeat" for "those who believe in the aiding and abetting of illegal aliens." Reelected councilman Dennis Husch, who had opposed the day-labor center from the beginning, hoped that the election in Herndon would inspire similar efforts elsewhere. "I would like to think we've given hope to all those who are not satisfied with the situation. The federal government has let us down," he said.

Georgia Leads the South

Despite Virginians turning out the rascals in Herndon, the shining example of a crackdown on illegal aliens in the South is found in the state of Georgia. In mid-April 2006, Governor Sonny Perdue signed into law the Georgia Security and Immigration Compliance Act, which requires employers to access a federal database to verify the legal residency of their workers, recipients of state benefits to prove they are in the country legally, and jails to inform ICE if anyone incarcerated is an illegal alien. The act also creates a new criminal offense, human trafficking, and authorizes the training of local lawmen in enforcement of immigration law. Introduced in March by state senator Chip Rogers, the bill sailed through both the Georgia senate and house with little opposition. "I wish the federal government had protected our borders, but they have failed," Rogers said.

Georgia Senate President Pro Tem Eric Johnson noted that the state now has the seventh largest illegal alien population in the United States. Conservative estimates put the number of illegal aliens in Georgia at a quarter million. Many argue the real number is closer to 800,000. Johnson claims that Medicaid expenditures for emergency care for illegal aliens in Georgia during 2005 surpassed $100 million, and that the burden on the state's schools and prisons was even greater. "America wants to export a higher standard of living to other people, not import a lower standard of living to ours," he declared when the Security and Immigration Compliance bill became law. "Our heart has no limit, but our pocketbook does." Senator Sam Zamarripa, chairman of the Georgia Association of Latino Elected Officials, argued that the act "criminalizes workers and businesses" and "creates a class of people who are separate and unequal." Like so many Latino advocates, Zamarripa seemingly does not recognize that illegal aliens are criminals by virtue of their presence in the United States and should be kept separate and unequal—by deporting them.

The Georgia Security and Immigration Compliance Act does have its flaws. It went into effect in July 2007 and, even then, certain provisions were postponed until still later dates. Opponents of the act are hoping that by then the law will have been superseded by weaker federal law, especially an amnesty. Nonetheless, the passage of the act has already sent a message to illegal aliens, if home buying by Mexicans is any indication. "We're seeing a drastic drop," said Re/Max agent Alina Arguello. Agents like Arguello, who cater to Spanish-speakers, say that the once strong Latino home-buying market has declined precipitously since Governor Perdue signed the act into law. Diego Castaneda, a real estate agent in Norcross, had two clients, both illegal aliens from Mexico who were a week away from closing escrow, back out. "They were just scared," said Castaneda, who has seen his client base disappear. He says that the costly advertisement that he has run in *Mundo Hispanico*, a Norcross Spanish-language newspaper, no longer generates calls to his office. "If someone is here illegally," responds Senator Rogers, "buying a house would probably not be a wise investment."

Legislation similar to that passed in Georgia is pending in the state legislatures of both South Carolina and North Carolina. For the time being, Mecklenburg County in North Carolina is having its sheriff's deputies trained by ICE agents to interview suspected illegal aliens in the county jail. Sheriff Jim Pendergraph estimates that some 15 percent of the jail's inmates are illegal aliens.

Three years ago, no more than two percent of the inmates fell into that category. Pendergraph says he has been forced to take action because the federal government is not doing its job. Identifying illegal aliens is one thing. Deporting them is another. The latter action depends on the nature of the crime — in addition to the crime of illegally entering the country — that they have committed. Many illegal aliens, says Deborah McColgan, an ICE agent temporarily assigned to the Mecklenburg County Sheriff's Office, are arrested on charges, such as driving under the influence of alcohol, that are not deportable offenses.

What, then, does it take to get deported? Paulo Sergio Delacruz, an illegal alien from Mexico, was arrested in Mecklenburg County in March 2006 on drug and robbery charges. Taking advantage of a new computer database for fingerprints and photographs, the police identified Delacruz as the same person who, in 2001, was taken into custody twice for illegally entering Arizona from Mexico and, in 2005, arrested for possession of cocaine and violating open-container laws. Delacruz now faces deportation proceedings. If he is deported, that will leave, according to estimates, only 400,000 other illegal aliens in North Carolina — and Carolinians thought the Yankees were bad.

Americans Awaking From Their Slumber

Whether in the South, the Northeast, the Midwest, the Southwest, or the West, the vacuum created by the lack of federal enforcement of immigration laws is now being filled by ordinances, legislation, and lawmen at the town, county, and state levels. It appears that American citizens have finally been roused from their slumber by the magnitude and the deleterious effects of the illegal alien invasion.

When I began speaking to audiences outside of California on the topic of illegal aliens during the 1990s, I quickly learned that most people considered the invasion a problem peculiar to the state of California — a land foreign to Middle America. I assured them that what was occurring in California today would be occurring in their state tomorrow. For the most part, I was politely humored. I regret that my prediction has come true, and take no perverse delight in the fact. The war has already been lost in California as a whole, although a few individual communities are continuing to fight battles. In the 1950s, the Hispanic population of the state was in the low single digits; now it is approaching 40 percent. Accounting for much of that percentage are illegal aliens and their children — and grandchildren.

It is not too late for most other states, however, and we should be encouraged and invigorated by the rigorous legislation that has passed into law in such disparate states as Arizona, Colorado, and Georgia, and by the county sheriffs, police chiefs, and concerned citizens who are standing tall. Dereliction of duty by President Bush and other federal authorities does not mean that the rest of us have to strike the colors and surrender. It does mean, though, that we American citizens will have to abandon fears of suffering *ad hominem* attacks and fight for what is rightfully ours—before our country is overwhelmed by what is nothing less than a foreign invasion.

9

GREETINGS FROM GROUND ZERO

by Steven Greenhut

In Southern California, with its massive and diverse population, there are rare instances when almost everyone is talking about the same thing. The large and unruly immigration rallies in early 2006, where at least a half million legal and illegal immigrants clogged freeways and downtown Los Angeles streets to wave Mexican flags and protest Congress' proposed immigration bill, was one of those events.

Another one took place later in the year. At first glance, it might strike observers as a rather odd and minor event to spark widespread discussion: One of the radio stations on the crowded FM dial had suddenly flipped formats. The Southern California media market is intensely competitive, and radio stations flip formats all the time. Hardly anyone outside the media world ever notices.

The Day the Music Died

But in August, 25-year-old KZLA—known as "America's most listened-to country station"—changed its format to rhythm and blues. That left the nation's second-largest media market without an FM country and Western station. Los Angeles joined New York City, San Francisco, and some other Blue State metropolises in being country-free. As one AM talk-show host jokingly pointed out, Los Angeles is big enough to support Hungarian clogging music, yet it cannot support one of the most mainstream and popular forms of music in America today. Long-time KZLA DJ Peter Tilden was doing the talk-radio circuit to explain what it means when a region of about 17 million people can no longer sustain a C&W station, talking mostly about advertising dollars and competition. He didn't offer any real answers, but most folks understand what the format change reflects: The reality of ceaseless mass immigration and its impact on this populous region, which we all know is Ground Zero for Third World immigration.

The Los Angeles region, even more so than other major urban areas, has undergone a drastic and rapid demographic change. "The shift [in radio formats] demonstrates how America's changing ethnicity is remaking media, especially in big cities," reported the *Los Angeles Times*. Officials with KZLA's parent company told the newspaper that "The Los Angeles radio market is basically 40 percent

Hispanic, 11 percent Asian, and 8 percent black, and country fans are about 98 percent Caucasian."[1] "Ironically, KZLA's change comes at a time when country music is flourishing," reported the *Times*. "While album sales of most genres have declined, country music has experienced one of its best years." The article points out that country album sales are up 17.7 percent in the first half of 2006 and that country music radio audience share has been stable nationwide for a decade.[2]

There's much to criticize in the pop-influenced schlock that passes for country music today. But a good, old-fashioned country song could be written about the day the music died in Los Angeles. Country music, for better or worse, is an icon for the mainstream American culture. The loss of this format in the two largest metropolitan areas speaks not only of demographic changes but also of cultural attitudes, and accentuates the Blue State/Red State divide—a divide driven by an exodus of poor people from Third-World countries. Even in the big eastern cities where I was raised, country music was relatively popular. I recall, in the days that I lived in Washington, DC, the cab driver who was dressed in Indian garb and wearing a Sikh turban, pounding his left foot to the beat of some blaring country song. A friend, from Indonesia, was a country music aficionado, who knew much about Merle Haggard and Johnny Cash. To him, listening to country music was a badge of his American-ness—the mark of an immigrant who had embraced the mainstream culture.

Those examples don't occur often these days, where this region's immigrants often view assimilation as a sell-out to the white man, where learning English is optional, and where Anglos—the all-purpose term for non-Latino whites—are repeatedly warned that they need to adapt their culture and language to the increasingly dominant Mexican culture. This is a region where immigrants from Asia and Europe find themselves more interested in learning Spanish than in learning English, given that so much of the customer base here speaks only Spanish. So in this world, it's no surprise that one can find any number of Mariachi radio stations on the dial but not a single station that plays the ballads popular in America's heartland. And while those of us who live here understand the cultural changes, it took a seemingly minor event such as the format swap to spark a renewed discussion about where California is going and how we got where we are.

Mayhem in Maywood

Around the same time as the KZLA switch was provoking discussion and chuckles, a far more serious event took place—one that was covered only in the most oblique manner in the media. In the city of Maywood, just outside Los Angeles, a small group of Americans from around the Southland marched down this city's main drag with signs reading, "Save Our State: Stop the Alien Invasion."[3] Maywood, which is almost entirely Latino, has an official population of 28,000, but most locals estimate its actual population at double the number, given that so many illegal immigrants live there.

The protesters chose Maywood because it is a sanctuary city—officials there refuse not only to enforce immigration laws, but also to enforce many traffic laws, lest they ensnare the unlicensed illegal immigrants who live there. The August 26 protest drew about 200 counter-demonstrators, who held a large banner declaring an increasingly common sentiment around these parts: "We are indigenous! The only owners of this continent."[4] Libertarian gubernatorial candidate Art Olivier (yes, the Libertarian was on the side of the Save Our State protesters) told me that one of his campaign aides was beaten by the counter-protesters while a policeman from Maywood stood and watched without doing anything to help her. Olivier said that the counter-protesters pelted the anti-illegal immigration protesters with bottles and pulled down the American flag from the city's post office and hoisted the Mexican flag in its place.

Yet the only official news coverage of the event was banal and made no reference to the outrageous signs or the violence or the flag incident. This event, as with so many others like it that have taken place, was treated as a peaceful face-off between anti-immigrant protesters and Latino residents of the city. The *Los Angeles Times* article mostly quoted the city's mayor, explaining why it would be ridiculous for his city to try to enforce the nation's immigration laws.[5] Yet the Maywood incident provided insight into what the Southland's future might be-beyond slight cultural changes and switches in musical taste to the potential for angry ethnic communities battling each other, for ongoing violence and strife. If Maywood were a tiny anomaly, there would be no reason to worry. But throughout Southern California are many cities such as Maywood—predominantly Latino, heavily illegal, poor, and infested with gang violence.

Dramatic Changes

The KZLA story is indicative of what those of us who live in Southern California see everywhere. But it's worth looking at some of the numbers to confirm our experiences. On August 25, 2006, the *Los Angeles Times* printed a large color map of Los Angeles County, showing concentrations of people of different racial and ethnic groups. One city after another showed large non-white majorities.[6] Of course, many of those non-white communities are middle class and decent places, but a disturbingly large number are similar to Maywood. Here is the overall picture of the 10.2-million population county, as of the 2000 census:

45 percent Latino, 31 percent white, 12 percent Asian, and 9.5 percent African-American. Based on 2003 estimates, the *Times* reports that supposedly lily-white Orange County—the supposed home of TV shows *The OC* and *Laguna Beach*, and known as a hotbed of conservatism—is a majority-minority county, where 49.5 percent of the population is white. In Riverside County the white population is 48.5 percent and in San Bernardino County the white population is 40 percent, and falling. The changes have happened quickly.[7]

The *Times* reported two other prescient facts: First, the Latino population is far younger than the Anglo population, with whites averaging 40 years of age and Latinos averaging 25. Second, Latino fertility rates are far higher than the fertility rates for whites. "The future of California, according to Census 2000, will not look like a scene from *Gidget* or the cover of a Beach Boys album," wrote state librarian Kevin Starr, following the release of the 2000 Census data. "Rather, it will look like a Benetton commercial or a clip from the music video *We Are the World*. It will, in cultural terms, be predominantly Latino and Asian. In chronological terms, it will be the Millennial Generation. All this could change should there be a surge in immigration from one part of the world or another. But there is little chance that this surge would come from Ireland, Norway, or Sweden. If it comes, the likely source would be Mexico, Central America, or Asia and would thus intensify the Latino-Asian dominance in the emerging culture of the Golden State."[8]

Starr, like most observers, offers a calm, academic analysis of the demographic transformation. But some Latino leaders are engaging in what I call ethnic triumphalism. They are crowing about their ethnic group's takeover of the state, oftentimes in crude terms. The former chairman of the California Democratic Party, Art Torres, memorably called Proposition 187, which would have denied welfare benefits to illegal immigrants, the last gasp of white America in California.[9] This raises the important question in the subhead of Starr's piece: Will California have a common culture?

A Cultural Tsunami

I'm not suggesting that modern American culture is particularly good, but the nation—if we are going to remain a nation, and not become a world of tussling ethnic communities—needs common ideals, a common language, a common culture, a common history.

I'm always careful not to be overly critical of the immigrants themselves, especially the legal ones. The last thing we need, given the already unchangeable demographic tsunami, is for immigrants and their children to believe that they must automatically line up with the new culture because they buy the lies from the self-interested Latino activists that the old culture is inexorably hostile to them. Many immigrants, especially those from places such as Korea, China, India, Romania, Russia, and even Central America, are also disturbed by Balkanization, by ethnic activism, by the left-wing politics and militancy of illegal immigrants on display at those nationally televised rallies. Most of these immigrants came here legally, played by the rules, and waited in line. They don't have any desire to go back to their home countries. Many Mexican-Americans arrived in an earlier time, when assimilation was valued, and are disturbed by the newfound emphasis on being Mexican and speaking Spanish rather than being American and relying on English. But even though assimilation does work for many people, it isn't working in general, given that the number of new immigrants is so high that it swamps whatever process of assimilation previously existed. One can easily survive not only in Los Angeles but also throughout the whole region without speaking a word of English.

No matter how hard the many illegal immigrants work, no matter how good and decent most of them are, and no matter how understandable it is that they would leave rural Mexican hovels to earn a decent living in the United States, their migration here at rates of one-half million or more a year is causing many disturbing problems. We all know that different peoples have different cultures. A reasonable number of immigrants from any place coming to America adds cultural spice and interest, and is generally a good thing. Who would mind if, say, 500 or even 5,000 Ethiopians or Greeks or Russians came, say, to an American city of one million? But what about 50,000 or 500,000? At a certain stage, we reach a tipping point where the new supplants the old.

Even relatively large numbers of immigrants are acceptable to me if they cut their ties to the old country and want to be Americans. But this is not necessarily the case with newer Mexican immigrants. A Guatemalan-born teacher I know told me: "I'm not like the average Mexican immigrant. I want to be in America and make this my home. Their dream is to make enough money here and move back home." Many Mexicans here don't want to speak English and assimilate because they don't plan on staying. But time goes by quickly, and they do stay and their children don't necessarily learn the fundamentals of American society. The new waves of Mexican immigrants differ from the old waves of Italian and Polish immigrants owing to the proximity of the home country, and the endless sea of immigration that halts the need to assimilate.

What would Mexico look like if hundreds of thousands of Americans moved there every year without ceasing? You know the answer. English would be spoken everywhere, hamburgers would edge out burritos in most restaurants, American-style politicians would get elected to the Mexican Congress, and parts of Mexico, especially those along the coast, would be indistinguishable from the United States. The Americans in Mexico would take whatever benefits the Mexican government made available to them. Many of the Mexicans who lived there might not have anything against the United States or Americans, in particular, but it wouldn't make them racists to want to cling to their culture and not watch Sonora turn into Texas or Baja California turn into San Diego. Likewise, it's not racist not to want most of California to turn into a northern outpost of Mexico.

Strains on the Welfare System

It's not easy to make cultural arguments in a society that seems to have fully embraced multiculturalism, but financial ones should be easier to understand. Because the Mexican people who come here come mostly from the poorest segments of that society, America is importing Mexico's poverty. Because California has such a generous welfare state, similar to the sort of welfare states that exist in sclerotic Europe, the costs are enormous. Supporters of open borders insist that the illegal immigrants pay taxes. They pay some, of course, mostly in the form of sales taxes. But so much of their earnings comes in the underground economy, that they pay hardly any taxes. And even if illegal immigrants were paying income taxes (say, if they were using a phony Social Security number and getting a regular paycheck from a legitimate company), the amounts paid would be nominal. California has such a steeply progressive income-tax system that few working class people pay much of anything in taxes.

"Because so much of our legal and illegal immigrant labor is concentrated in such fringe, low-wage employment, its overall impact on our economy is extremely small," wrote Steven Malanga in the summer 2006 issue of the Manhattan Institute's *City Journal*. "If the benefits of the current generation of migrants are small, the costs are large and growing because of America's vast range of social programs and the wide advocacy network that strives to hook low-earning legal and illegal immigrants into these programs. A 1998 National Academy of Sciences study found that more than 30 percent of California's foreign-born were on Medicaid—including 37 percent of all Hispanic households—compared with 14 percent of native-born households. The foreign-born were more than twice as likely as the native-born to be on welfare, and their children were nearly five times as likely to be in means-tested government lunch programs. . . . The study's conclusion: immigrant families cost each native-born household in California an additional $1,200 a year in taxes."[10] Nearly a decade later, those costs are no doubt far higher. In the same issue of *City Journal*, Heather Mac Donald points to the violent gang culture that has taken root in predominantly immigrant neighborhoods not only in Los Angeles but also in Orange County communities such as Anaheim and Santa Ana. Calling California the bellwether for unbridled Hispanic immigration, Mac Donald writes that, "A whopping 28 percent of

Mexican-American males between the ages of 18 and 24 reported having been arrested since 1995, and 20 percent reported having been incarcerated—a rate twice that of other immigrant groups."[11] All this is costly, not just in societal terms but in actual dollars and cents. The Southern California jails, which are perpetually overcrowded, are filled to the brim with immigrant gang members. Yet it is controversial when the Orange County sheriff proposes something as reasonable as checking the immigration status of anyone arrested for a serious felony.

On August 28, 2006, the *Los Angeles Times* ran this headline: "Los Angeles County May Lose Another ER." According to the report, "Centinela Freeman Health-System is considering closing the emergency room at its Memorial campus in Inglewood, a step health experts and patient advocates say could further destabilize Los Angeles County's fragile emergency care network." The head of the county's emergency health agency sounded the alarm: "I want the public to know that their healthcare system is in jeopardy."[12]

If one had landed in Los Angeles from Mars or Peoria, one might have no idea why this emergency room was closing and why the county's health system was at a crisis level. Not until the last paragraph of the *Times* article does the reader even get a hint: "Emergency rooms can be a financial drain on hospitals because, by law, they are required to screen and stabilize any patient who comes to them, regardless of insurance status."[13] That's still not so clear. Let's try again: Southern California's hospitals are being inundated by illegal immigrants who use them for all their health care needs, from immunizations to check-ups to true emergency services. They do not pay anything for any of this. The times I've been to the emergency room in California, I've been told that I am not even allowed to show the hospital my insurance card until after the care is provided. I wouldn't turn anyone away from a hospital for a dire emergency, but this is borderline crazy. I pay my co-payment and my insurance company pays the rest, but illegal immigrants get whatever they want and then walk away without paying a dime. How many businesses can afford to give away their services and products for free and still stay in business? Not many. Yet the Inglewood situation is typical.

In August 2005, Northridge Hospital Medical Center's Sherman Way Campus, the oldest hospital in the San Fernando Valley, closed its doors for good. Earlier that month Elastar Community Hospital in East Los Angeles, which had filed Chapter 11 in 2003, closed its emergency room. "Six emergency rooms have closed in the last 14 months," reported the *Los Angeles Times* in a 2004 article. "Hospital and health care officials predict a further ten percent to 15 percent reduction in the county's emergency room capacity, with three large ERs at private hospitals thought to be at risk of closure. All this is taking place as the number of Californians without health insurance continues to surge. Since 1988, the number of emergency rooms in the county has fallen from 97 to 79. Trauma centers have fallen from 16 to 13. Though some remaining hospitals have expanded their services to make up for those closures, the Los Angeles County population has grown by more than 1 million and the portion of uninsured residents has climbed from 20 percent to 27 percent during that period."[14]

And then there is the public school situation. Thirty years ago, California public schools were renowned, among the best in the nation. Now they are atrociously bad. Test scores are horrific. Liberals like to blame property-tax-limiting Proposition 13, which was passed in 1978, for the problem. But as the Howard Jarvis Taxpayers Association points out, "K–12 school districts' revenues per student, adjusted for inflation, increased over 30 percent between FY 1977–78 and FY 2002–03."[15] The reason for the change is immigration. Many schools serve a largely non-English-speaking and poor population. A large percentage of students in the schools are the children of illegal immigrants.

The Los Angeles basin is one of the few places in the country where pressure is increasing on the infrastructure of roads, bridges, water systems, and sewers in older, built-out areas. Usually, new infrastructure must be built in newer areas, but immigrant families are doubling-up and tripling-up in old urban cores, which has the advantage of reviving some decrepit urban areas, but also puts enormous strain on public services when ten people live in a house that was formerly home to four people.

Illegal immigration has sparked a wave of identity theft. And time and again, Southern Californians must deal with the unlicensed drivers in their uninsured cars. Get hit by one and it's your insurance that pays. They leave the scene, usually without penalty. The result is a two-tier system, where those who play by the rules pay the bills, and those who don't live in the shadows and can do just about anything they please. This is most pronounced in the business world. In California's highly regulated, costly business environment, those companies that pay workers' compensation and the minimum wage and follow labyrinthine regulations must offer prices for services that are several times the prices paid by illegal labor operating without any rules. One can pay a mover $100 an hour or head down to the day-work center and hire a couple of illegal immigrants for $12 an hour. Same goes with painters, lawn services, and construction firms. Each new wave of new cheap labor depresses the price of the old labor, which exacerbates the hardship of those who immigrated here in earlier years. This is a high price to pay for low-cost lettuce and maid service.

Political Earthquakes

Politically speaking, the changes have been dramatic. Throughout the region, the most heavily immigrant areas have switched rapidly from conservative

Republican to liberal Democrat. The San Gabriel Valley was once solid GOP turf and Republican activists recall how throughout the 1980s one seat after another changed hands. In central Orange County, which is the most heavily immigrant area in that county, the same political tsunami took place. Many of the Asian areas have remained Republican. But most of the immigration here is from Mexico, and the emerging Mexican majority votes not just for Democrats but for the ones furthest to the left, such as Senator Richard Alarcon from the San Fernando Valley, who, when chided for supporting anti-business legislation, said, "If a few companies want to go and rip off some other state, that's fine with me."[16]

The one saving grace for Republicans has been that the new legal immigrants tend not to vote in high numbers. "Orange County's 1st and 5th supervisor districts have roughly the same populations, with the 1st including Santa Ana, Westminster, and parts of Garden Grove, and the 5th including much of the south county," reported the *Los Angeles Times*. "But turnout in the heavily minority—and Democratic—1st District runs about 40,000 compared with 130,000 in the mostly white and Republican 5th District."[17]

No wonder Democratic activists are concentrating their efforts on improving turnout among Latino voters. Republicans can still hang on in Orange County, anyway, by wooing the same voters. Meanwhile, in much of Los Angeles County, the Republican Party basically doesn't exist. California has a long tradition of successful Republican office-holders, but the Republican presidential candidate can no longer get within 1 million votes of the Democratic, and Democrats control almost every statewide office. This won't change. The Republican Governor Arnold Schwarzenegger was a fluke, elected after an unusual recall, and has governed of late in a way indistinguishable from any liberal Democrat. His chief of staff used to work in the previous Democratic administration and is former president of an abortion rights group.

Why the change? Immigration, of course. Conventional media wisdom holds that Republicans lost the Latino vote in 1994 when Governor Pete Wilson campaigned on behalf of Proposition 187, which would have denied welfare benefits to illegal immigrants. But Steve Sailer, writing in *The American Conservative*, successfully debunks this myth:

> The conventional wisdom is actually a bizarrely demonological distortion of the history of America's largest, most visible state. Instead of one man somehow permanently warping the political destiny of 37 million people, California's shift from the Republican to the Democratic column reflects tectonic demographic shifts, largely driven

by immigration, that are spreading nationwide, and thus demand honest study.

> The truth is close to the opposite. California voted for Republican presidential candidates in nine of the ten elections from 1952 through 1988. The collapse of the California GOP first became evident in 1992, two years before Prop. 187, when Republicans got skunked in California in the presidential election and two U.S. Senate races. In the last dozen major contests for president, governor or senator there, Republicans have won only the two times they appealed to voter anger over illegal immigration. The ten times they meekly avoided the topic, they quietly went down to defeat.[18]

The more immigration, the more Democratic the state, and the more Democratic the state, the more California builds a welfare state that is a magnet for new immigrants. And the more new immigrants, the more poverty in California and the United States. In 2004, the county seat of Orange County, Santa Ana, topped a national "urban hardship" list, beating out even such traditionally wretched cities as Gary, Detroit, and Cleveland. The reason is mass immigration of poor people. "This is not the story of black urban areas of the 60s and 70s," University of California-Irvine assistant dean Caesar Sereseres told the *Los Angeles Times.* "What's happened in Santa Ana may represent a new model of urbanization. It raises issues of what constitutes poverty."[19]

Libertarian Insanity

So immigration leads to more socialism. It leads to pressure for higher taxes and bonds to build more schools and roads. It leads the health care community to call for socialized medicine, because at least in a state-run system doctors and hospitals might have a chance of getting reimbursed for the costs of uninsured patients. It leads to divided communities, crime, violence, and to a backlash. No doubt, some of the folks protesting the "alien invasion" are mean-spirited and racist. I wouldn't defend them, but this backlash is to be expected when nothing is being done about a legitimate problem. Mass immigration, legal and illegal, is causing businesses and the middle class to flee the state, taking the tax base with them. It leads to ethnic and generational tensions, as young immigrants and children of immigrants will be forced to support an aging Anglo population living off California's overly generous pensions.

Yet many of my libertarian colleagues still cling to the idea of open borders. They argue that freedom demands that anyone from anywhere be allowed to come to the United States. That's a nice idea. But it's trouble when a wealthy welfare state borders a poor, Third World country. These open-borders libertarians refuse to grapple with the real-world results of their policy. One libertarian I talked to recently made dismissive comments about Americans upset about the border situation. I said that they raise some important points. His immediate retort: "They just don't like brown-skinned people." Another libertarian I talked to about the border called me a "nationalist." How do you argue with name-calling?

Open immigration leads to policies opposite those libertarians claim to want. It creates bigger government, fosters higher taxes, and destroys private property rights. Fortunately, not all libertarians support it. I have already mentioned the 2006 Libertarian Party gubernatorial candidate, Art Olivier, who believes that we need to build a wall on the border and to limit immigration. A number of others, including Nobel-winning economist Milton Friedman, agree that open immigration cannot coexist with a massive welfare state—to which open-borders libertarians reply that the problem is the welfare state, not immigration. Rather than shut the border, they would have us shut down the welfare state.

I would shut down the welfare state in a heartbeat, but we've already hit critical mass in California and elsewhere: Those who benefit from bigger government out-vote those who pay for it. Efforts to retard even the growth of government, at the state or national level, rarely succeed. We can't ignore immigration until we shut down the welfare state. The immigrants are coming too fast, and all the pressure is exerted on behalf of expanding government. Consequently, the libertarian argument is an infantile one, designed to change the subject. Why not try the reverse and slow immigration until we halt the welfare state?

Writing in *Liberty Haven*, Thomas E. Woods, Jr. pointed to Murray Rothbard's rethinking of the immigration question: "Imagine the pure private-property, or 'anarcho-capitalist' model, in which all property, from streets to parks, is privately owned. There is no such thing as a 'public space' under such an agreement, and therefore no 'immigration problem.' Individual property owners or contractual communities would be able to set their own immigration policy, and determine for themselves who would or would not be allowed to enter their private property."[20] Woods points up the error of many of these modern libertarians who embrace open borders: They believe that if something is public, then there should be no restrictions on it. That's why they oppose, say, speed limits and laws to ban the use of cell phones while driving, or efforts to drive the homeless out of public parks. I argue that the libertarian position should be neutral on such matters. Whoever owns the property should decide the rules. A specific road or park proposal might be good or bad for various reasons, but it is silly to suggest that because something is publicly owned that there should be no rules governing its use. If a private company owned the parks or roads, you could be sure that there would be many rules—probably more than exist now—governing behavior on that property. The libertarian position should be to argue for private ownership, not against public management of public property.

That brings us back to immigration, where the abundance of public property and public benefits makes it unsustainable to accept an endless amount of immigration from Third World countries. Woods correctly argues that, "It is puzzling why so many libertarians have so enthusiastically and uncritically accepted the 'open borders' position. It leads, in fact, to an infringement on the property rights of millions of homeowners, and a tremendous increase in state power."

Making Distinctions

No doubt, America can afford to have a relatively open border with Canada. Even if large numbers of people from Manitoba suddenly had the desire to move to Minnesota, there would be no major upheaval. Middle class and wealthy people from a similar culture do not cause major problems when they immigrate. My city in Southern California has one of the highest populations of Korean and Chinese people in the state. It is surrounded by several cities that are similar, demographically. The demographics have changed rather rapidly, over a course of maybe 15 years. Yet not much has changed. The area is still affluent, quiet, Republican. My neighbors work hard to learn English. They fly American flags and assimilate.

As I stated earlier, many immigrants are on the right side in this debate. They complain about the border situation. In California, especially, where such a large proportion of the population was born somewhere else, I would hate to embrace policies that force these folks into the "pro-immigrant" side of the debate. Endorsing a "no immigration" policy that makes no distinctions would do this. It would also harm the American psyche. Almost everyone I know embraces the "nation of immigrants" viewpoint. Most Americans would view it as an assault on something fundamentally American if we advanced policies completely to shut down immigration. Also this would be a losing and unnecessarily divisive battle, as it would give the open-borders supporters the ammunition they need to depict their opponents as "anti-immigrant." You can imagine how the media would treat a "stop all immigration" movement.

Those who argue for no immigration whatsoever are the mirror image of those who argue for open borders—both treat all immigrants the same, making no distinctions. Yet there's a huge difference in my mind between a well-educated immigrant who has jumped through hoops to become an American, speaks English, values his citizenship, and is well on the way to full assimilation, and a poor immigrant who broke the laws to come here, doesn't view the country as anything more than a place to earn a living, takes inordinate advantage of public services, and wants nothing more than to make some money and head back to his home country with it.

The best strategy for now is to build the broadest possible consensus to reject President Bush's comprehensive immigration solution. Any scheme that pretends to fix the whole problem in one bill would be a disaster. The United States should build a wall along the southern border, step up patrols there, and gain control of that situation. Thus, we should focus on stopping illegal immigration at the source, while remaining wary of proposals for a national ID card and of overly aggressive internal enforcement that would give government too much power.

Once the border situation is under control, we can let the broader immigration debate unfold from there, by determining the appropriate level of immigration and focusing on the fundamental concept of assimilation. Once the main problem has been fixed, much of the anger should subside and some reasonable, or at least tolerable, solutions might have an opportunity to emerge. There's no easy fix for a problem caused by years of foolish government policy, but our leaders need to stop pretending that there's no real problem. If they think all is well, then they should spend some time in Southern California learning what it's like to live at Ground Zero. In early March, a new country-and-western station appeared on LA's FM dial. Perhaps it's a small reminder that not all immigration-driven changes need to be permanent.

Endnotes

[1] Charles Duhigg, and Geoff Boucher. "The Reason KZLA Up and Left for Another Fan," *Los Angeles Times*, August 20, 2006, A1.

[2] Ibid.

[3] Art Olivier, interview with author, August 2006.

[4] Diggers Realm Web site, www.diggersrealm.com/mt/archives/001807html. Accessed September 1, 2006.

[5] Ted Rohrlich, "Protest Targets Maywood's Stance; Both sides shout it out in the tiny city that is known as a 'sanctuary' for illegal immigrants." *Los Angeles Times*, August 27, 2006, B3.

[6] Lorena Iniguez, "A Visual History of Los Angeles; The Southland's Ethnic Transition." *Los Angeles Times*, August 25, 2006, B2.

[7] Joel Rubin, "O.C. Whites a Majority No Longer; Rapid Asian and Latino Growth Has Changed the County's Look, Census Data Show. Experts Call It a Watershed." *Los Angeles Times*, September 30, 2004, B1.

[8] Kevin Starr, "California Resettled; The Future Golden State Will Be the Home of Ever-Increasing Bipolar, Even Tripolar, Identities and Styles. Will it Have a Common Culture?" *Los Angeles Times*, April 22, 2001, M1.

[9] Patrick McDonnell, "Brash Evangelist," *Los Angeles Times Magazine*, July 15, 2001, p. 14.

[10] Steven Malanga, "How Unskilled Immigrants Hurt Our Economy." *City Journal*, Summer 2006, p. 14.

[11] Heather Mac Donald, "Seeing Today's Immigrants Straight," *City Journal*, Summer 2006, p. 28.

[12] Charles Ornstein, "Los Angeles County May Lose Another ER," *Los Angeles Times*, August 28, 2006, B3.

[13] Ibid.

[14] Jason Felch, "County Feels Symptoms of Health Crisis Relapse," *Los Angeles Times*, August 29, 2004, B1.

[15] "The truth about government revenue since the passage of Proposition 13," statement from the Howard Jarvis Taxpayers Association, n.d.

[16] Editorial, *Orange County Register*, July 1, 2003.

[17] Scott Martelle, and Jean O. Pasco, "New Faces, Same Politics in O.C.; The county has more and more Democratic-leaning Latinos, but many recent arrivals aren't voting, so it remains firmly Republican. Will that last?" *Los Angeles Times*, October 3, 2004, B1.

[18] Steve Sailer, "New Republican Majority?" *The American Conservative*, May 8, 2006.

[19] Mike Anton, and Jennifer Mena. "The Hard Life—Santa Ana Style; The O.C. city tops a new urban-hardship index with a brand of poverty characterized not by blight, but by bustling employment and very crowded living quarters," *Los Angeles Times*, September 5, 2004, B1.

[20] Thomas E. Woods, Jr. "Liberty and Immigration." Available at www.libertyhaven.com. Accessed August 26, 2006.

10

UP MEXICO WAY: THE CULTURAL TRANSFORMATION OF AMERICA

by Thomas Fleming

"Poor Mexico," sighed Porfirio Diaz, "so far from God, so close to the United States." Though a hero in the Battle of Puebla (May 5, 1862), in which the Mexicans defeated French troops supporting the Emperor Maximilian,[1] Diaz is one of the least appreciated of Mexican dictators. He did his best to live in peace with God (or at least with the church) and with his powerful northern neighbor, but since his ouster, the Mexican state has been defined by its opposition to the Catholic Church, the United States, and Diaz himself.

Mexico is not an easy country to understand. Though, like the official United States, official Mexico has defined itself by political and social revolutions, no one in his right mind would try to sum up Mexico as a nation "dedicated to the proposition that all men are created equal" or speak of exporting the Mexican way of life to the rest of the world. If America is an idea, Mexico is a palpable fact—dense and impenetrable as a jungle teeming with life and fraught with lurking dangers. From the point of view of most educated Americans, Mexican culture is far stranger than, say, the culture of Italy or Poland, and, though Mexico is, in some senses, far more European than the United States, a few days spent in the real Mexico present a challenge to the point of view of not just North America but of the West itself.

Everything about Mexico seems paradoxical to the Anglo-Saxon—a fiesta of life punctuated by the dance of death. Human nature being what it is, a common response to the unfamiliar and the paradoxical is fear and loathing. Mexico's greatest poet, Octavio Paz, thought Americans instinctively feared the zoot-suited Pachucos who prowled the streets of California cities in the 1940s, but it is just as likely that many middle-class Americans felt the same amused contempt for the Pachucos as they did for the "low riders" of the 1960s and 1970s.[2]

When people in America think about Mexicans, the first thought is probably not, alas, of bandits like the Californian Joaquin Murrieta, who (at least in ballads) avenged the wrongs done his people, or of writers like Octavio Paz, who have made Mexico the cultural equal or superior of the United States. More typically, the image of the Mexican comes from such Hollywood icons as Leo Carillo, who pioneered the role of the silly but, occasionally, dangerous *bandido*,[3] or, for a more recent generation, Cheech Marin: "Mexican Americans don't like to get up early in the morning, but they have to, so they do. Mexican Americans love education, so they go to night school, and they take Spanish and get a B."

Every Mexican rights group complains about the racism and bigotry of Anglo-Americans, and their complaints are not without justification.[4] Americans, however, are hardly unique in this respect. There has probably never been a time in human history when members of different ethnic groups respected each other. Greeks despised Romans as crude; Romans despised Greeks as effeminate, and the French and English shared a similar set of prejudices against each other.

A people defines itself, in part, by rejecting the bad qualities it attributes to foreigners. Anglo-Americans demonstrate their respect for cleanliness, diligence, self-restraint, and lawfulness by deriding Mexicans as dirty, lazy (until recently), and violent. When Americans decide to set a novel or action film in Mexico, chances are there will be rivers of blood.[5] Mexicans return the compliment, making fun of gringos as stiff, unemotional, unspiritual, and sexless. The gringo stereotype is not restricted to illiterate campesinos who have never met educated Americans. Carlos Fuentes, Mexico's most important novelist, has, since childhood, spent a great deal of time in America, teaching at Princeton, Harvard, Columbia, and Brown. He speaks flawless English and knows the United States better than most of its citizens. And yet, despite Fuentes's deep experience and many American friends, his fiction still plays upon the gringo stereotypes. In *The Old Gringo*, the aging Ambrose Bierce is a joyless writer who comes to Mexico seeking a passionate death, while the beautiful Yankee schoolmarm can only find erotic fulfillment in the embrace of one of Pancho Villa's peasant officers who feels he can tell her important things because:

> [He] could tell it only to someone from a land as far away and strange as the United States, the Other World, the world that is not Mexico, the foreign and distant and curious, eccentric, and marginal world of the Yankees who did not enjoy good food or violent revolution or women in bondage, or beautiful churches, and broke with all traditions just for the sake of it, as if there were good things only in the future and in novelty. . . .

What, I wonder, would be the fate of an American writer who attributed to Mexicans a love of violent revolution and women in bondage?

Prejudice is rarely one-sided, but the relationship between the two bigotries, American and Mexican, is not symmetrical, or, at least, has not been up till now. For two centuries, Mexico has seen itself in the mirror of the United States, while people in the United States (with a few interesting exceptions) have hardly given a second thought to Mexico.

No one knows how many Mexicans and Mexican-Americans reside in the United States. There are perhaps 15 million Mexican immigrants (a conservative estimate), a third of them illegal and perhaps 15 million U.S. citizens of Mexican origin or descent, making a total of some 30 million. There are at least ten million more people from other parts of Latin America. As a percentage of the American population, Mexicans and Mexican-Americans have overtaken African Americans as the dominant minority group. If current high rates of immigration are permitted to continue, this figure could double in a decade. Given the differential in birth rates between non-Mexican and Mexican-Americans, the United States may be rapidly headed toward a situation resembling that of Canada, which is bilingual, bicultural, and binational. In the worst case, this would produce an armed struggle between the two groups. More optimistically, one might imagine a future United States in which Americans of Mexican descent have been peacefully assimilated.

Conflict or Assimilation?

The term "assimilation" has distorted many a discussion of immigration. Mexican immigrants are not a blank slate on which pop culture and public schools can engrave some predetermined "American" message. They are a distinct people, who bring with them their own language, culture, and history. In sufficiently large numbers, such a people is as likely to influence as to be influenced.

When two cultures come into a long-lasting contact, whether through conquest or migration, several results are possible. The range of possibilities can be broadly characterized as conflict or amalgamation, though the two are not mutually exclusive: In border areas, the people of one culture may imitate much of the other's folkways without necessarily growing to love the people across the frontier. Texans on the border have learned to eat Mexican food and pepper their language with mispronounced Spanish phrases, but they may still express hostility to Mexicans, both individually and collectively. Similarly, Mexicans in Juárez may watch American television, eat at McDonald's, and spend a good deal of the year on the American side of the border, without abandoning their resentments against their wealthy neighbors to the North.[6]

The most dangerous meeting of cultures is the sort of warfare that was conducted by the Indians of the American Southwest and Northern Mexico with European settlers. For generations the Apache fought with Mexicans and Americans to maintain their existence. They lost and became marginal players in a country they once possessed, much as Mexicans, after two wars, became marginal players in the northern parts of Mexico that are now American states.

One result of immigration, then, is that the dominant group (as measured in terms of force, numbers, or cultural vitality) may annihilate the identity of the other group, either by practicing a literal genocide or by the no less effective method of cultural genocide, which robs a people of its national symbols, history, and identity. This is not to say that such methods are mutually exclusive or 100 percent effective. The Roman occupation of southern Britain established the Latin language and Roman civilization throughout the territory they occupied, but the Celtic language never disappeared until Anglo-Saxons virtually eliminated, apart from a few place names and stray words, most significant traces of Celtic culture. On the other hand, the invaders might be eventually subjugated by the original inhabitants, as Turks, for example, were eventually dispossessed and expelled from Serbia and Greece in the 19th century.

Even in the most violent conflicts, the conquerors will take women from their conquered subjects and absorb at least some of their culture. To describe this process of mixing, I prefer the word amalgamation rather than assimilation, which assumes that cultural transformation is a one-way process. The classic definition of assimilation was offered by Robert Park and Ernest Burgess: "a process of interpenetration and fusion in which persons and groups acquire the memories, sentiments, and attitudes of other persons and groups, and by sharing their experience and history are incorporated with them in a common cultural life."[7] This definition was a valuable (if implicit) contribution to the immigration debate that erupted after World War I.

Since the 1920s, however, little of the vast, largely unreadable sociological "literature" on assimilation that has overflowed the study of immigration is helpful to any discussion of real world issues. For one thing, few of the social scientists appear to have any idea of what, historically, the American identity (or rather identities) is or are. For one recent neoconservative pundit, America is defined in such simplistic terms as the public use of the English language, liberal egalitarian political ideas, and the Protestant work ethic.[8] Such an ahistorical definition conveniently leaves out large groups, including Catholics, Southern "Crackers," and traditional conservatives. Fond of graphs and choking on a speciously technical vocabulary of invented terms, political sociologists display little knowledge of

American history and still less of traditional American culture. They write glibly of immigrants assimilating, without ever considering what it is they are assimilating to, and, when confronted by irredentist natives who do not welcome a massive influx of foreigners, they take no interest in their point of view, which even in the mildest form is typically condemned as racism.[9]

This abstract approach to assimilation derives, ultimately, from the conviction—as naïve as it is chauvinistic—that America is an exceptional country, one not rooted in blood, soil, and kinship, but a nation "dedicated to the proposition that all men are created equal." Proponents of this view are quick to label the more old-fashioned view, that the nation is a metaphorical extended family, as bigotry, but no amount of repetition or rhetorical extravagance can disguise the dangerous logic that is at work. If I love my country because it is mine, I must be loyal to it, even when I disagree with its policies, but I do not necessarily regard it as superior to everyone else's country, and I may have no inclination to say that all other countries, to the extent they are legitimate and worthy of respect, must approximate my own.

But that is exactly what the advocates of the "propositional nation" do insist upon. The United States is not only the best nation in the history of the world, but also it is a beacon to all mankind, the natural home of all the good and decent people in the world and the enemy to all regimes that deny their subjects equal rights. Thus, by the same argument, a propositional nation is obliged to open its borders to strangers "yearning to breathe free," but it is also justified in engaging in endless crusades to impose its propositions on the rest of the world.

The old fashioned patriotism of European nations could and did encourage violent conflicts, but ideological nationalisms of the Communist, National Socialist, and Democratic-globalist types produce a crusading mentality that is ever on the lookout for new threats to eliminate. Since democratic-globalists are always eager to throw the name of Hitler at those who advocate restrictions on immigration, it is worth noting that the Third Reich, eager to fill jobs that had been abandoned by conscripted soldiers, encouraged immigration into Germany.[10]

Violent immigrants may destroy a native culture and identity, as British settlers did in North America. On the other hand, it may be the immigrants who are absorbed, peacefully or not, by their hosts. France, in the 19th and early 20th centuries, received a steady stream of immigrants from Italy, Spain, and even Poland, but the comparatively slow rate of immigration and the power of French cultural institutions (army, schools, church) did a thorough job of assimilating the newcomers.

More often, however, a small but dominant immigrant group, while establishing effective power, gradually adopts the language and culture of its subjects, particularly when the preceding culture is older and on a higher level. This is, to one degree or another, what happened after the barbarian occupation of France, Italy, and Spain, but not until the standard of living had collapsed and with it much of the cultural proficiency of the Roman world.[11] Medieval Italy and France were not simply revivals, much less continuations of, the old Roman order. The everyday language was less complex and contaminated with Germanic words; personal vengeance and dueling were acknowledged forms of justice; sanitation, hygiene, and health had collapsed to a primitive level.

There are infinite possibilities to the process of amalgamation. For all the Germanic influence on Italy, Renaissance Italians, in language and literature, were far more like the ancient Romans than like their German contemporaries. English language and culture, by contrast, became a vibrant mixture of Anglo-Saxon and Norman elements. The basic roots of the language are typically Germanic—words like pig and calf, earth and food—while the language of the higher culture (law, politics, the pleasures of the table) are typically expressed in French and Latin—pork and veal, estate and cuisine.[12]

Finally, in some instances, different ethnic groups may live side by side as the French and English have done in Canada, Flemish and French in Belgium, and French, Italians, and Germans in Switzerland, to say nothing of the ethnic patchworks of the Austro-Hungarian Empire or post-colonial states in Africa. Sometimes the coexistence is peaceful, as in Switzerland; at other times one or the other group may long for separation, as in Quebec, Belgium, and Yugoslavia. Sometimes the frictions are sufficient to lead to violence as among Serbs, Croats, and Muslims in Bosnia, Basques in Spain, Hutus and Tutsis in central Africa.

Which scenario will be played out in the event that the Hispanic population becomes a significant minority, say, one-fourth or one-third of the population? The answer we are likely to give to this question will be determined partly by the outlook of those giving the answer. Certainly, most non-Hispanic Americans, whatever their views on immigration, expect Spanish-speaking immigrants to abandon their language and accept the mainstream "values" of American culture. On the other hand, there are leftists, as well as Chicano nationalists, who oppose assimilation. Some might welcome a reconquest of the territory taken from Mexico, while others speak of the multicultural society that will include many cultural alternatives to the white bread Anglo-American tradition.

Assuming, for the moment, that the preferred model is assimilation of immigrants to the "American way of life" and that the least desirable would be a *Reconquista* that turns the Southwest into something like a more violent, Spanish-speaking version of Quebec: What are the most favorable conditions under which a sizeable minority can be integrated into the mainstream? There are two sides to this question, defined, roughly, by the border between the United States and Mexico. Indeed, the border may well define the emerging identity of the United States.

Greater Juárez, the American Future?

Relations between our two countries are most acute in the regions where the two peoples live in close proximity. If Mexicans and Americans are to amalgamate, we might expect to see that process already in operation on the U.S.-Mexican border, which is flanked on both sides by a series of border towns that seem to reflect each other as much as they represent the cultures of their respective cultures. From the West, where San Diego—epitome of American opulence and consumerism—is faced by tacky and squalid Tijuana, which every year launches tens of thousands of illegal immigrants into California's underground labor markets; to El Paso and Juárez, a common city divided by historical conflicts and a border that is more irritating than relevant, to Del Rio and Acuña, Laredo and Nuevo Laredo, McAllen and Reynosa, Brownsville and Matamoras—America and Mexico are redefining themselves and each other in a cultural equivalent of *Spanglish*.

El Paso–Juárez may be the most emblematic. The two cities, originally one, are roughly of the same size; both have suffered seriously from urban decay and to a more grotesque degree from the "urban renewal" planned by shortsighted and greedy developers and politicians. There are pleasant neighborhoods in both cities, and, while El Paso has a more interesting historic core with one good hotel and one good restaurant and while Juárez exhibits signs of a growing economy, it is Juárez that attracts the tourists (and not simply for cheap booze) and El Paso that draws the workers.

El Paso, with its barrios comprising most of the sprawl, is scarcely an American city. A majority of the inhabitants speak Spanish at home, and a surprising number of billboards, even on I–10 coming from the airport, are in Spanish. The American border guards hardly speak any more English than their Mexican counterparts, but there is this difference: Mexican immigration officials and guards on the Juárez side tend to be polite and friendly—though some of their cops maintain a ferocious grimace reminiscent of group photographs of Pancho Villa's lieutenants—while our Mexican immigration officials on the U.S. side combine the ferocity of the Federales with the manners of a sullen teenager rampaging through a shopping mall.

Ciudad Juárez is emblematic not merely of the border, but of modern Mexico. Rafael Loret de Mola (a prominent Mexican journalist) has put it simply: *"Juárez es Mexico. La ciudad y el héroe, cuya epopea le encumbró . . ."* ("Juárez is Mexico, the city and the hero, whose epic story has exalted it").[13]

It was in this city, then the southern part of El Paso del Norte, that President Benito Juárez took refuge from the French troops, and it was Juárez that Gen. Francisco Villa took and retook, to the delight and shock of the American spectators across the Rio Bravo.

With over two million inhabitants, Juárez is one of the larger cities in Mexico. Although the sense of Mexican identity has been intensified by proximity to the United States, the city fathers appear to be doing their best to ape suburbanized America. For Loret de Mola, this would only confirm his view that Mexico is virtually a captive nation imprisoned by an expanding American Empire. The *Paseo del Triunfo de la Revolución* (a major commercial street) has been ravaged by Americanization. The bullring has been torn down to make way for a shopping development, and the widened street is now adorned with chain restaurants and chain motels. Juárez and the other border towns show the worst side of Mexico. Is this the American future?

Border towns are always dangerous places, if only because criminals can cross the border, commit a crime, then slip back into their own country. While El Paso has been one of the least violent cities in the United States, Ciudad Juárez, though peaceful compared with the capital, has among the highest murder rates in Mexico. That is saying a great deal. In 1999, the U.S. homicide rate, overall, was 5.7 per 100,000. This is a high rate compared with most countries in Western Europe, Italy (2.25), Belgium and England/Wales (1.41), and Ireland (0.62), but America seems safe when compared with Mexico, which, despite very strict gun laws, has a homicide rate of 17.58 — over three times the U.S. rate. Just as significant, perhaps, is the Mexican celebration of violence and death, which Mexican writers trace back, correctly or not, to the Aztecs. This is a source not of shame but of pride. As one song about the Mexican Revolution puts it: "They say there's death in Mexico, that every day they kill each other there."[14]

It is difficult to make comparative generalizations, but, according to the Overseas Security Advisory Council (a federal advisory committee whose mission is to advise Americans on security issues in foreign countries): "In the categories of murder, rape, and robbery, Mexico's Distrito Federal (Mexico City and the surrounding region) posts three to four times the incidence of these crimes than does New York City, greater Los Angeles, or Washington, DC."[15] What this means when Mexicans enter the United States can be measured by the fact that in 2003, while about 27 percent of prisoners in federal prisons were aliens, 67 percent of that figure were Mexican — or 18 percent of the total. When other Latin Americans were added in, the percentage reached 23 percent.

While some of the murders in Juárez can be attributed to the drug wars, a more puzzling question is the high number of women who have been murdered, both in Juárez and in other parts of Chihuahua state. Juárez officials naturally like to blame outsiders for the violence, but there is some truth to the story that poor men and women in Southern Mexico come to border towns hoping to take advantage of the opportunity to work in the Maquiladora factories. About half of them are women, who (according to reports from Human Rights Watch and the AFL-CIO) are subject to sexual harassment, violence, and discrimination. The women, once they find work, begin to imitate what they have seen and heard of the North American lifestyle: They try to control the money they earn, and they think they have a right to go out with their friends on the weekends. This liberation leads to conflicts with husbands and boyfriends, who take revenge by beating and killing the women.[16] There is also suspicion in Juárez that soldiers from Ft. Bliss routinely cross the bridge into Mexico in order to commit crimes. The story, though absurd on the face of it, may be not entirely fantastic: The FBI reports significant gang activity among Ft. Bliss soldiers.

The usual tensions and conflicts that have always marked the U.S.-Mexican border have become acute in recent decades. As in Sicily, the huge profits to be made by importing drugs into the United States have produced a fierce competition between rival drug lords and between the gangs and the police. The Mexican police and military play an ambiguous role. In some cases, their conflicts with the drug smugglers result from their attempts to enforce the law; in others they are more interested in extorting bribes; in still others they are merely criminals. One of the most effective death squads hired by the drug cartels, "Los Zetas," consists of former Mexican soldiers. Mexicans complain, with some justice, that a large number of the hired killers—a majority, according to some Mexican officials— are U.S. citizens, though it is not hard to guess their ethnicity.

There are plenty of dishonest policemen in the United States and even entire police forces that have been corrupted. In Mexico, however, corruption and criminality are more the rule than the exception; border cities like Tijuana, Nuevo Laredo, and Juárez resemble battlegrounds. Caught in the middle are Mexican journalists, whose courage in reporting on the drug wars has made them targets of violence.

Juárez and the other border cities are an ugly hybrid of the worst of American and Mexican cultures. But they are hardly much different or much worse than the barrios of Los Angeles and Chicago. They are also, if immigration is not controlled (unlikely) and American education reformed (impossible), the American future.

Poor America

Any country that expects to absorb or "assimilate" a large population of aliens must have a coherent sense of itself. Such a sense of identity is the product of many elements, such as a single language, a unified culture based on shared moral values and common faith, and a sense of history. To shape and transmit this identity, strong institutions and traditions are required: a national literature and an accepted set of classics, effective schools that reflect and reinforce the moral and social outlook of the nation, a self-confident church or, failing that, a set of cooperating churches, some form of adolescent initiation such as universal military training. France had all of these in the period before World War II, but with the abandonment of compulsory military service and the collapse of education and decay of Christianity, French institutions were simply unable to cope with the flood of North African Muslims.[17]

The United States today has lost or destroyed most of the institutions of its common life. American and English literature is seldom read and scarcely taught, and the Greek and Latin classics, which used to bind Americans with the cultures of Europe, have vanished. Public schools are a demonstrable failure from every point of view, and even the most widely held moral rules—regarding theft or adultery—are not or cannot be taught. American churches are beset by scandals and are, in any event, too weak to undertake the necessary process of moral formation; the all-volunteer army eliminates whatever good effects a common military experience might have.

Just as significant as the weakness of American institutions is the fact that America has always been a divided country. Even before the Revolution, the different sections had been settled from different parts of Britain with different dialects, customs, and ways of life.[18] These differences did not disappear but became more acute in the 85 years between the Declaration of Independence and the secession of South Carolina. South and North, nearly 150 years after the outbreak of the Civil War, are still distinctive regions. The growing interest in southern history and the southern identity is proof, if any proof were needed, that the differences between Florence, South Carolina, and Stockbridge, Massachusetts, are at least as great as the differences between Dublin and London or even between Quebec and Cincinnati.

Religion might be expected to bind together a diverse country, and, indeed, most Americans tell pollsters they are Christians. Although most Americans belong to one or another Protestant church, the largest Christian denomination is Roman Catholic, comprising more than a fourth of the population. There are dozens of Protestant denominations, and, although Protestant churches show some signs of coalescence, there is still a great divide between mainline liberal churches and mostly conservative Evangelicals; neither group has much in common with Catholic and Orthodox Christians, who, despite their strong similarities, have little use for one another. And, as the religious mix has been enriched to include Muslims and Hindus, religious disputes become more acute. Far from being a unifying force, religion divides Americans as much as at any time in our history.

Despite the pieties of multiculturalism, racial and ethnic conflict is a fact of everyday life. There is an endless variety of conflicts—black v. white, Anglo v. Hispanic, black v. Asian. But even in the white Christian population, not all is sweetness and light. Descendants of North European immigrants do not always like people whose ancestry is from Southern Europe, and neither necessarily feels much sympathy for East Europeans. Not long ago, it was a sociological fashion to speak of "unmeltable ethnics," but the phenomenon is scarcely new. Irish and Sicilian Americans still nurse resentments over the treatment their grandparents and great-grandparents received upon arrival. Although they are officially banned from polite conversation, racial and ethnic jokes are as common as sexual jokes, and they are increasingly brutal.[19]

Quite apart from this regional, religious, and ethnic diversity, there is per- haps an even greater gulf between ordinary "Main Street" Americans and the elite and professional classes who control the universities, media, and federal government. There is hardly a major political issue on which self-described conservatives and self-described liberals or leftists can agree upon.

The only cement holding Americans together is the mass culture that is destroy- ing the American character, the national government that has turned a nation of citizens into a mass of taxpayers and tax-consumers, and, since the collapse of the Soviet Empire, a series of threats (many of them largely imaginary) to American security—Libya, Serbia, Iraq, Iran, North Korea. As one prominent neoconserva- tive has said on a number of occasions, if Communism did not exist, it would have to be invented, because only the threat of Communism kept Americans united. With the loss of the Communist enemy, it has been necessary to discover—or invent—an endless parade of Hitler-imitators bent on global domination.

Poor Mexico

For "assimilation" to succeed, the host country's cultural institutions must be vig- orous, but what of the guests? Ideally, there should be enough shared values and compatible folkways to smooth the way. In the 19th century, British Protestants had the easiest time, followed by other North-European Protestants. German Protestants, although they did attempt to retain German as a second language, fit in more easily and more quickly Americanized than Italian and Polish Catholics.

Mexican culture is not only alien but, compared with the culture of the United States, vibrant, with a literature and musical traditions as distinctive as its cuisine. Americans are prone to lump all the countries south of the border into a generic category of "Latin America," submerging the obvious differences between Portuguese-speaking Brazil and its neighbors, between Chile and Argentina, which are more European than the United States, and Guatemala (45 percent Indian, 45 percent Mestizo, five percent white) and Peru (45 percent Indian, 37 percent Mestizo, 15 percent white, five percent Asian). But it would be a serious mistake even to conflate Mexico (60 percent Mestizo, 30 percent Indian, nine percent white) with its neighbor Guatemala. Guatemala, in the pre-Conquest period, was dominated by Mayan Indians, while in Mexico, though ethnically quite diverse, the most powerful state on the eve of Conquest was the Aztec empire in the Valley of Mexico.

Books can tell a great deal about the Indian civilizations that rose and fell in Mexico before the arrival of the Spanish, but books are no substitute for a trip to Mexico City. Both the Aztec Templo Mayor, with its excellent small museum, and the magnificent Archeological Museum in Bosque de Chapultepec make an indelible impression upon visitors. All the displays have been crafted to teach one message: the Aztecs, with their glorification of human sacrifice and cannibalism, represent the apex of Mesoamerican culture, a civilization that can stand comparison with ancient Greece and Rome, and modern Mexico, far from being the creation of the conquistadors who destroyed Tenochtitlan, is the continuation of the Aztec empire. Neither of these dogmas is quite true, but they are an integral part of the Mexican state and the Mexican Identity.

Octavio Paz, who has brilliantly explained the political dimensions of the Aztec myth, spent some time studying Mexican-Americans in California after World War II, particularly the so-called *Pachucos*, who combined social rebellion with a dandified costume. "The *pachuco* does not want to become a Mexican again; at the same time he does not want to blend into the life of North America."[20] The *Pachuco* phenomenon is not restricted to Mexican Americans. In losing their ancestral identity, Swedes, Italians, and Poles did not necessarily become Americans in a sense that Thomas Jefferson or Mark Twain would have understood.

Paz was writing about the 1940s, but revisiting the themes of the *Labyrinth of Solitude* in 1979, he did not paint a picture of compatible cultures: "Our countries are neighbors, condemned to live alongside each other; they are separated, however, more by social, economic, and psychic differences than by physical frontiers."

While the more obvious differences in wealth and power might be overcome, he added:

> The really fundamental difference is an invisible one, and
> in addition it is probably insuperable. To prove that it has

nothing to do with economics or political power, we have only to imagine a Mexico suddenly turned into a prosperous, mighty country, a superpower like the United States. Far from disappearing, the differences would become more acute and clear cut.[21]

In his various writings on the question, Paz has analyzed several differences between the two countries. Mexico, he argues, exults in the body and lives to celebrate the festival, while the United States, until recent decades, seems ashamed of the body, and, even now, is capable only of a joyless hedonism. While Americans shrink from the reality of death, Mexicans revel in death and horror.[22]

National Myths: Mexico

North American culture was formed by the Reformation and the Enlightenment, while the Spanish culture brought to Latin America the product of the Catholic Counter-Reformation that tried with all its might to suppress the Enlightenment. While the Spanish Catholics, in approaching native cultures, were inclusive, English Protestants were exclusive, marginalizing and segregating the Indians in reservations. One result is the prevalence of the Indian element in the Mexican gene pool. Unlike the United States, whose identity is the product of mostly European immigration, Mexico, despite the obvious fact that its political and economic elite have a great deal of European blood, defines itself as an indigenous nation. The exploits of Cortez, far from being regarded as the founding of a Spanish-American civilization, are condemned as a brutal conquest of a high civilization.

Mexican independence was not achieved by Indians and mestizos, though both groups played a part, but by the criollos, that is, descendants of Spanish settlers who resented their second-class social and political status.[23] Even after gaining their independence, Mexicans continued their hostility to Spanish landowners, but their cry of "Down with the Spanish" could be interpreted as a less than veiled threat against the criollos, who maintained their preeminence down to 1858, when a civil war between liberals and conservatives led, first, to the defeat of the conservatives, then to the disastrous French intervention that put Maximilian on a very shaky throne, and finally to the execution of Maximilian, the triumph of Benito Juárez, who plays the part of the George Washington of Mexico, and the triumph of the Mestizos.

An important part of the Mexican national story is the country's long-standing conflict with the United States. This conflict found its most dramatic expression in the secession of Texas and the Mexican War, neither of which are forgotten in Mexico, but many Mexicans have also resented U.S. investments in their agriculture and oil. President Cárdenas's nationalization of foreign oil reserves and property in 1938 was a popular move. The establishment of Maquiladora factories, on both sides of the border, combining the advantages of cheap Mexican labor and American technology, was supposed to help the Mexican economy, but the advantages have been reduced or eliminated by the North American Free Trade Agreement, which has tended to put small farmers out of business and yet permitted the drain of U.S. jobs from Mexico (as well as from the United States) to Asia.

Investments in Mexico were seen in the United States as nothing more than good business, but to many Mexicans—and not all of them Marxists, but even some conservatives—they were simply "war by other means." Diego Rivera's famous murals in the Palacio Nacional in Mexico City powerfully portray a set of cynical American tycoons exploiting Mexican resources and collaborating with a corrupt Mexican political (and religious!) leadership to subjugate the people.

The Mexican mythic imagination has been conveyed by revolutionary murals, novels and poems, and by a series of lively shoot-'em-up films that commemorate revolutionaries and bandits alike. The subjects of these films are often derived from the popular ballads known as corridos. Classic corridos celebrate the heroic life—and more often death—of bold men who cannot be intimidated. Significantly, many are entitled "Fusilamiento de so-and-so."[24] A good example is "Fusilamiento de General Argumedo." Typical of popular ballads, the song exists in several forms, but in most, Argumedo asks General Murguía for a public shooting:

> Listen, my General
> I am also a brave man,
> I want you to execute me
> Publicly before the people.

Denied this consolation, Argumedo, who had fought for a series of revolutionary leaders—Madero, Pablo Orozco, Huerta, and Carranza—showed no fear but smiled:

> Farewell mountains,
> Sierras, cities, and towns,
> Where I confronted bullets
> That resembled raging fires.

Some corridos are nationalistic, like one that takes up Cárdenas's nationalization of foreign oil interests, and there is a major cycle of songs about Francisco Villa, the bandit-turned-revolutionary-turned bandit who slaughtered unarmed gringos for the fun of it. A grateful state of New Mexico has commemorated Villa's attack on the American village of Columbus, New Mexico, by dedicating a state park to the memory of his raid. More recently the heroes of corridos are the brave drug lords who, in the course of pursuing their profession, outwit or kill the US authorities. These "narco-corridos" are deservedly popular, and there are entire radio stations (for example, in LA) devoted to them. Monoglot Americans would probably be disturbed, if they could translate the words of such popular ballads as "El Gringo y el Mexicano,"[25] but "where ignorance is bliss, 'tis folly to be wise."[26]

National Myths: America

Uncontrolled Mexican immigration is exerting great pressure on the brittle American identity. The United States has not been a nation for well over a century. It is more like an Indian stew: Never taken off the fire, the mess of wild carrots and fish is gradually transformed by the daily addition of squirrels and squash, birds and deer—none of them skinned or gutted—and the odd bit of human body. By the end of a month, the burgoo has gone through so many transformations as to be unrecognizable. In the same way, a largely Anglo-American Protestant country was transformed first by North-European, then by South-and-East European Catholics and Jews, and, in the latest phase, by Latinos, principally Cubans, Puerto Ricans, Central Americans, and—above all—Mexicans.

In the 19th century, America, though crude and ill-formed, possessed a certain exuberant self-confidence that impressed all but the most civilized visitors. Immigrants had only two choices: either retreat to an ethnic ghetto or rural community, where their language and folkways were maintained, or assimilate. Their children (unless they lived in San Francisco's Chinatown) would have no choice. Few immigrants could return home, and, once an influx trickled out (as after 1921), direct contact with the mother-country ceased. Foreign language newspapers began to die on the vine, and the various ethnic organizations formed to preserve an Old World culture were gradually transformed into social clubs.

Latino immigrants can, and do, return frequently to Mexico or Guatemala, and even if they do not, their language and culture are being constantly reinforced by a steady stream of new arrivals. And what indoctrination they and their children receive from schools and television teaches only the politics of historical resentment and ethnic privilege. Enrolled in a bilingual program, carefully instructed to hate the United States as an oppressor, and exposed to no cultural influences that do not encourage recklessness and indolence, Latin-American immigrants have few incentives and fewer opportunities to embrace whatever is left of traditional American civilization.

Ultimately, assimilation can only work when there is a vigorous culture that can shape the children of immigrants in its own image. In a healthy society, history and myth reinforce the sense of group identity and common purpose, but, in the United States, there is hardly a national hero or symbol that has not come under attack. Students of English literature no longer need to read Shakespeare and Milton; George Washington and Thomas Jefferson have been replaced in the national pantheon by minority representatives such as Rosa Parks and Cesar Chavez; and for the old heroic story of the pioneers carving their future out of the wilderness we have substituted a story of white male patriarchal oppressors who beat slaves, massacred Indians and Mexicans, exploited women and children, and subjugated homosexuals.

Mexican immigrants arriving in the United States today are greeted by a shoddy mass culture—food chains, mass music, and reality TV—that offers few incentives except to the lowest characters. The choice of most immigrants is either to assimilate, jettisoning language and cultural identity in favor of mass culture, or remain Mexican. Ironically, the latter may be the better choice, since the longer immigrant children remain in the United States and "the more 'Americanized' they become, the more likely they [are] to engage in risky behaviors such as substance abuse, unprotected sex, and delinquency."[27]

Immigrants who arrived 100 or even 50 years ago were confronted by an American myth that emphasized the courage, generosity, and rugged independence of the American spirit. That patriotic myth, however, has been displaced by a new myth that demonizes Americans. The American ideal today lies not in the past but in the future, at the end of a long road, signposted by the liberation of slaves, women, children, homosexuals, and immigrant minorities. Lincoln, though a man flawed by the prejudices of his day, took the first big step forward toward a just world; he was followed by labor agitators, the leaders of the NAACP, feminists, and the various movements advocating the rights of immigrants, especially Latin American immigrants, Cesar Chavez's United Farm Workers, LULAC, and so on.

The New Myth also offers a new version of U.S. relations with Mexico. For earlier generations, the defenders of the Alamo were heroes who were ruthlessly slaughtered by Santa Anna, the archetypal Mexican leader: corrupt, violent, and incompetent. The Mexican War was a just response to Mexican aggression, and the vast territory[28] acquired by treaty after the war deprived Mexico of an unsettled land they could never exploit.

The American Left, by contrast, has applied their universal paradigm of American oppressor/minority victims to Mexican-American relations. Although only the tiniest fraction of Mexican-Americans today are descended from Mexicans who once lived in the American Southwest, all Mexican immigrants have automatic entrance to the privileged class of victimized minorities. Of course, this privilege is not translated into bank accounts or good jobs—those are reserved for immigrants who learn to speak English and to play by American rules. But students in public schools are encouraged to cling to their native tongue and taught the litany of complaints against the Anglo ruling class.[29]

Peter Skerry, over a decade ago, argued that Mexican-American leaders, in deliberately playing the race card on all occasions, were beginning to influence even third-generation Hispanics to think of themselves as a persecuted minority. His evidence was persuasive: Fewer and fewer Chicanos described themselves as white, and increasing numbers were now claiming to be victims of discrimination.[30] Victimology, certainly, plays a major role in the multicultural educational programs that are perpetuating, and, in some cases, creating a Chicano identity.

The Culture of Revolution

At heart, the celebration of the Mexican identity in American schools is an attack on Euro-America. It is not hard to find the evidence for this. In a *Cinco de Mayo* celebration at Michigan Tech, Native American storyteller, lecturer, and poet Bobby Gonzalez speaks on "The Legacy of Columbus: 500 Years of Racism and Resistance." In Racine, Wisconsin, *Cinco de Mayo* is the occasion to teach students about immigration rights by showing a PBS video series, *Matters of Race*, that enrages the students by its depictions of open racism on the part of white townspeople in the film.

Through such programs young Latinos and Latinas are taught to discover their true identity as victims. One graduating senior (class of 2006) from the University of Minnesota had been adopted from Colombia by a loving Anglo family who valued her culture, but she felt bad about not speaking Spanish. Through multicultural studies in high school and college, however, she learned to see things from a Latin American perspective and decided to major in Chicano Studies.

As I continued to study Chicano Studies I realized just
how ignorant I was and I felt betrayed by our education system because there is so much they do not teach us in high
school. We learn about how bad African American people
were treated and how they were slaves and they were hung
but we never learn that so were the Chicanos right beside
them. I remember the day that one of my professors told
us that Chicanos were hung and he showed us pictures. I
was shocked because my whole life before then I thought it
was only African Americans who were treated that brutally.
It was as if he turned a light on inside my brain because
I then realized that I was going to use the knowledge I
was learning in Chicano/a Studies to teach our youth. . . .
I know that my job in life is to work with youth and to
continue to educate myself, continue to research our history and teach it to the students I work with. I now work at
Academia Cesar Chavez Charter School and I am part of
a school whose mission is to teach Latino culture, value,
and history.[31]

Similar stories are told in a variety of Chicano studies programs. Chicano radi-
cals may have little influence today, but they are funded and encouraged by public schools and public universities whose job is the education of future citizens.
Watered down, the same attitude of alienation is projected by Spanish-language
story books and textbooks aimed at elementary school children. If the children
of Mexican immigrants are reluctant to integrate into the American mainstream,
the problem lies as much with American governmental institutions as with the
mental attitudes of the immigrants themselves.

Conclusions

Some years ago, when I began speaking and writing on the immigration question, I ran into trouble very quickly. So long as I was content to quote George
Borjas's and Donald Huddle's statistics on the economic impact of immigration,
my arguments were treated politely by advocates on both sides, but when I made
the mistake of raising the question of culture, of the kind of country that America
would be turned into by mass immigration, I was informed by opponents of
unrestricted immigration that anyone who raised the cultural question would be
accused of bigotry. *How convenient,* I thought. Anyone who goes to the root of the

immigration question is a bigot, just as anyone who points out the shaky moral and legal foundations of affirmative action is a racist, and anyone who argues for moral order is a fascist, and anyone who criticizes a reckless decision to go to war is unpatriotic or even a traitor.

The future of American culture is the heart of the immigration question, and if the cultural question remains taboo, the doom of America is fixed, even if the means and the will were found to seal the border and repatriate large numbers of illegal Mexican immigrants. Economic analysis of the immigration crisis, important as it is, does not touch this most fundamental issue, which is the kind of country we are leaving our children and grandchildren. Economics is a blind science that cannot tell the difference between citizens and foreigners, friends and enemies. We are told, for example, that the soundest criterion for legal immigrants is their educational level and potential earnings. This may be, but if 400 million hard-working and intelligent Chinese immigrants were admitted, our economy would boom, but our grandchildren would be Chinese, not American. Chicano activists understand this reality, which is why they talk about *Reconquista* and dream of rebuilding the Aztec world of Aztlan. Professional critics of immigration policy who pretend this question does not exist are like the coward who hears burglars invading his home and pulls the covers up over his head.

America's weakness and self-hatred were not forced upon the American people at the point of a bayonet. We accepted the propaganda and paid for the soft-core Marxists who shoved it down the throats of our schoolchildren. In the decades following World War II, American culture was transformed. Our historical and cultural roots were torn up, and, to the extent we have an histori-cal imagination, it is of ourselves as the descendants of oppressors, exploiters, and murderers. Now in our weakness and self-contempt, we fear high Mexican birth rates, because Anglo-Americans refuse to have children, and we cannot stanch the hemorrhaging border for precisely the same reason that we insist on teaching our children to hate the people and habits that made their country. The fault, my dear American Brutuses, is not in the stars — nor in demographic forces or tectonic shifts of geopolitical power — but in ourselves that we are underlings.

The first step toward addressing and resolving the cultural problems pre-sented by mass immigration is to quit denying their existence. The second is to give up the glib and futile language of assimilation and recognize the fact that immigrants will affect us as much as we affect them. The third is to recog-nize that the larger part of the problem is of our own devising: American mass culture, including the schools that purvey mass education, are breeding grounds for anti-American resentment and American self-hatred.

To halt and reverse this process, Americans must be willing to take several boldly conservative steps. Quite apart from whatever is done to control legal and illegal immigration, we have to transform the teaching of humanities, in elementary and high schools as much as in universities. The conservative defense of the "traditional" curriculum has been, up till now, predicated on liberal and leftist concepts like "freedom of expression" and "respect for diversity." Western culture is not valued as something good in itself or as our precious heritage but only as the foundation for an "open society" that encourages toleration of opposing points of view. It is time to dispense with such fantasies, which have little to do with the flesh and blood people who created and defended the West, and to revive the older understanding, that the purpose of a nation's educational system is to form the character and historical imagination of the nation's citizens. In our case, this would mean that European and American history must be taught from a Western and American point of view; that, beginning in the lower grades, the classics of English and American literature must be made required reading, and that the Greek and Latin classics, which, along with the teaching of Latin, were the foundation of our civilization for over two thousand years, are given once again their honored place in the curriculum.

The celebration of American history and the revival of our civilization should not be made at the expense of the rich cultural heritage that Mexicans and other Latinos bring with them. Although many, if not most, recent immigrants have been poorly educated, there is no reason why they and their children cannot be encouraged to learn pure Spanish and to imbibe the literary and cultural traditions of Spain and Latin America. Study of their authentic history and culture would replace the narcissistic and inflammatory Chicano Studies programs that indoctrinate Latinos into a culture of victimology that can only retard their social and economic progress.

The theory of assimilation encouraged educationists to think they could impose a uniform culture on this vast continental empire of diverse regions and states. The result was the sterile ideology taught in civics classes and expounded every four years at the two parties' national conventions. Instinctively, students turned away from the lies and embraced either the culture of revolution or the mass commercial culture of self-gratification. True diversity would mean a revival of regional and ethnic identities within the context of a broad Anglo-American paradigm. Just as individual states and counties are beginning to control illegal immigration, they might be allowed to develop their own variations on the European American civilization that is our heritage so long as the traditional core is strengthened. Yankees and Southerners alike respect Thomas Jefferson; Polish and Italian Americans love Shakespeare. We all, as American citizens, revere the rule of law and the British liberties preserved in our Constitution and the Bill of Rights.

If American citizens prove themselves incapable of taking control of their future, by controlling immigration and restoring the institutions of their civilization, they will not so much be losing their country as acknowledging that it is already lost. In 476, when a German immigrant soldier sent the last Western Emperor into early retirement, he only made the fall of Rome official. Roman Italy had collapsed even before the Gothic sack of Rome in 410 that inspired St. Augustine to write *City of God*. In failing to solve its immigration problem, Italy became the battleground for alien invaders for nearly 1,500 years.[32] The Eastern Empire was more fortunate: The emperors wrested control from the barbarian immigrants and embarked upon a cultural revival that made Constantinople the most glorious city in the world. Their empire, which endured the shock of Islamic terrorism and barbarian invasions, was far from perfect, but it lasted for a millennium. Which course America will follow is in the hands of the American people.

Endnotes

[1] This is the victory commemorated in the celebration of the holiday (more in the United States than in Mexico) of *Cinco de Mayo*.

[2] Low riding eventually became a respectable hobby for suburbanized middle-aged Chicanos, more kitsch than ethnic assertion.

[3] As the progressive bandit chieftain in Rouben Mamoulian's *The Gay Desperado* or as Pancho, the usually affable sidekick of the Cisco Kid.

[4] Arturo Rosales, for example, writes casually of the "dynamics of Anglo-American racism toward Mexicans," *Chicano*, p. xiv.

[5] Cinematic examples of the violent Mexico stereotype abound: notably, *The Wild Bunch* and *The Magnificent Seven*, though the even more violent *El Mariachi* is a Mexican film set in the border town of Acuña. Perhaps the fictional archetypal is Malcom Lowry's *Under the Volcano*, a serious modernist novel that seems to doom the hero to a violent death by the very fact of locating him in Mexico.

[6] For a fictional portrayal of the cultural conflict on the border, see Carlos Fuentes's brilliant novel, *The Crystal Frontier*.

[7] *Introduction to the Science of Sociology*, 1921, p. 735.

[8] Peter D. Salins, *Assimilation American Style* (New York: Basic Books, 1997).

[9] See, for example, Michael S. Teitelbaum and Jay Winter, *A Question of Numbers: High Migration, Low Fertility, and the Politics of National Identity*. New York: Hill and Wang, 1998.

[10] For a discussion of nationalism, see Fleming, *The Morality of Everyday Life*, pp. 53–64.

[11] Bryan Ward-Perkins, *The Fall of Rome and the End of Civilization*. Oxford: Oxford University Press, 2005; documents the collapse of industry, art and architecture, sanitation and hygiene, and law and order that Europe suffered as a result of barbarian immigration.

[12] Noted long ago by Walter Scott, who puts the argument into the mouth of Wamba the Witless in *Ivanhoe*.

[13] Rafael Loret de Mola, p. 15.

[14] *"Porque dicen que en Mexico se muere/y que diario se matan por allá."*

[15] Overseas Security Advisory Council Mexico City, Mexico: 2006 Crime and Safety Report, March 15, 2006.

[16] Loret de Mola, *Ciudad Juárez*, pp. 201–208. Carlos Fuentes has memorably portrayed the life of these young women in one of the stories of *The Crystal Frontier*.

[17] I owe this insight to the late Jean Cau, whom I interviewed not many years before his death in 1993. Cau, in addition to being a distinguished dramatist and journalist, was one of the editors of *Paris Match*.

[18] Hackett-Fisher, *Albion's Seed*.

[19] There is no scientific way of measuring this, but a quick Google search for *sex jokes* turns up about 21,500,000 results, while *race jokes* and *ethnic jokes* add up to more than 15,000,000.

[20] *Labyrinth of Solitude*, p. 14.

[21] "Mexico and the United States," *Labyrinth of Solitude and Other Writings*, p. 357.

[22] *Labyrinth of Solitude*, p. 23.

[23] The reforms of the Spanish Bourbon state, in centralizing government authority, exacerbated Creole resentments in the New World.

[24] An excellent four-disk set with libretto, *The Mexican Revolution: Corridos about the Heroes and Events, 1910–1920 and Beyond!* is available from Arhoolie Records.

[25] Recorded by Los Tigres del Norte, a "Norteño" group from Sinaloa, now living in San Jose, CA.

[26] Though perhaps safety.

[27] Carola Suárez-Orozco and Marcelo Suárez-Orozco, *Children of Immigration*, p. 5.

[28] Extending to southern Wyoming and Oregon.

[29] Steven H. Wilson, "Brown over Other White: Mexican Americans' Legal Arguments and Litigation Strategy in School Desegregation Lawsuits," *Law and History Review*, Spring 2003; also available on historycooperative.org.

[30] Peter Skerry, *Mexican Americans: The Ambivalent Minority*. Cambridge, MA: Harvard University Press, 1993; especially Chapters 10 and 11.

[31] See Katie Groh Aviña's essay on www.chicano.umn.edu.

[32] Cf. Girolamo Arnaldi, *Italy and Its Invaders*. Transl. by Antony Shugaar. Cambridge: Harvard University Press, 2005.

11

IMMIGRATION, THE BORDER, AND THE FATE OF THE LAND: NOTES ON A CRISIS

by Gregory McNamee

The tracker kneels in the middle of a dry desert wash, looking intently at the sandy, rock-strewn floor. The earth bears faint impresses of many kinds. Here are small crumbling mounds of sand that look like miniature volcanic craters, their sides slowly collapsing. Over there are larger, deeper wedge-shaped ruts that sink an inch or so into the sun-baked ground. Here are narrow, two-foot-long tracks that sweep sinuously along the wash. Over there are smallish pockmarks that look as if tiny meteors had struck the earth.

He looks up and studies the mesquite and paloverde trees that line the wash. It is early morning in late autumn, but the sun still glints fiercely along the edges of his mirrored sunglasses, bearing the promise of heat to come. It does not glint at all from his matte-finish automatic rifle, slung in ready position over his camouflaged shoulder, or from the insignia that he bears, all carefully designed to blend in with the surrounding country.

Finally, he stands, and as he relates what he has found, the dry wash begins to fill up with phantom actors on a busy stage set. A man on horseback passed by three or four days ago. The horse wasn't carrying a burden apart from its rider. A little snake crossed its trail soon after. It rained after that. In the night, coyotes ambled across the scene. Some birds hopped around. A few hours ago, before dawn, two men came this way, heading south. More men passed, heading north. Many more.

A full-blood member of the Tohono O'odham Nation, the tracker serves in an elite unit of the U.S. Customs and Border Protection Service called the Shadow Wolves. The unit is made up of Native American officers who blend modern techniques of police investigation with ancient skills of tracking, or "cutting for sign," passed down over the generations.

Founded in 1972, the Shadow Wolves originally had two major responsibilities. One was to interdict the traffic in narcotics passing north from Mexico across the 2.5-million-acre Tohono O'odham Reservation and then to consumers across the United States. The other, fittingly for a customs unit, was to track merchandise coming south from the United States across the reservation and then into Mexico, all of which was crossing over duty-free. Until recently, the Shadow Wolves, numbering fewer than 40 men, accounted for 40 percent of the contraband seizures along the U.S.-Mexico border. Though incidental to their main task, they were also responsible for turning back tens of thousands of illegal immigrants.

We find ourselves in a sea of trampled backpacks, electrolyte-drink bottles, underpants, toothbrushes, and cigarette butts that stretches south toward the international line. "UDAs. Undocumented aliens," the tracker says. "The coyotes"—the human smugglers who guide border crossers through the remote desert and take them to places such as Tucson and Los Angeles, or, just as commonly, abandon them in the desert once the money has been collected—"make them leave their backpacks and other things behind so that they can fit more of them into the trucks."

Now that the unit has fallen under the dominion of the Department of Homeland Security, the Shadow Wolves have a different priority. A Border Patrol press officer jumps in to speak for the unit. "Our first job is to find terrorists," he says. I look at the tracker, who looks at me. I ask the press officer, "How many terrorists have you found?"

I think I see the trace of a smile in the tracker's face.[1]

Cabeza Prieta

One hundred and fifty miles to the west, hard by the Mexico line, stands a weathered mountain range called the Cabeza Prieta. It is a place of weird landforms and scarce but formidable vegetation, a graduate school for desert rats that only the best prepared dare enter. The geography of the place says, *Stay away.* To emphasize the point, the sky rains metal as military aircraft drop payloads of bombs and spray rivers of bullets onto the vast proving ground in which the Cabeza Prieta stands.

And yet that same sea laps at the mountains' flank. A small city's worth of shoeprints punctuates every wash and pass: cowboy boots, tennis shoes, huarache sandals, even high-heels. They are all pointed north, leaving a broad avenue through a desert that, absent the occasional bomb crater, was until recently as pristine as any in North America—so much so that environmental activists in Arizona have long pressed for it to be given national monument status and its attendant protections[2]

That will not happen, not while the Cabeza Prieta is a war zone. The sea rises and rises.

Frontier or Battleground?

It is the same in San Diego, in Marfa, in Laredo, in Columbus. The southern frontier of the United States, from the Pacific to the Gulf of Mexico, is a battleground, its territory contested by a vast army of would-be immigrants facing a much smaller, but still numerous, host of soldiers, police officers, and other defenders. To call the land a battleground is by no means metaphorical, as it once would have been, for ever larger portions of the border are being fortified and armored. The flanks of the Ajo Mountains, not far from the Cabeza Prieta by southwestern standards, bear concrete and steel *chevaux-de-frise* that wouldn't be out of place on the Normandy beaches in 1944,[3] while the steep canyons of the Coastal Range north of Tecate, Mexico, bear rank after rank of concertina wire.

Where the fortifications are not so sturdy, the sea has broken through. The case of the Buenos Aires National Wildlife Refuge, in south-central Arizona, is representative. Comprising 118,000 acres of high-desert grassland, the refuge harbors several rare plant types such as the Pima pineapple cactus, along with many species of animal, including pronghorn antelope, bighorn sheep, masked bobwhite, and other creatures not often seen elsewhere. Yet the refuge's officers have few resources to protect these animals and plants; instead, a full third of its annual budget of about $1.5 million goes to law enforcement, while much of the rest is eaten up by such mundane details as removing trash—500 tons of it in 2005—and carting away abandoned vehicles, dozens of which lie scattered across a no-man's-land of dry washes and sandy hills.[4] Add to them the foot traffic of as many as 3,000 *alambristas*, or "wire-hoppers," a day and an endless stream of Border Patrol vehicles, ranging from all-terrain buggies to massive Humvees, and the land, once far from the center of anything in particular, once pristine, looks as if it has been chewed up by a wood chipper and spat out along the flanks of the rocky Baboquivari Range.

Three thousand may be a low estimate. Indeed, no one knows how many men, women, and children cross the international frontier illegally each year.[5] However it is measured, the number is massive. We can extrapolate to some extent from federal statistics, which reveal that, in 2005, Arizona's two Border Patrol sectors apprehended 577,500 undocumented aliens, nearly half of the nationwide total. If a million are being caught each year, then it stands to reason that many more are slipping through, eventually making their way to Phoenix, Los Angeles, San Antonio—and from there to Virginia, North Dakota, Vermont, wherever there is work to be found. Indeed, according to some estimates, there are now 11 million illegal immigrants in the United States, most Hispanic, most concentrated along the southern border—but with perhaps a million apiece in North Carolina, Illinois, and New York.

Why should so many people cross over such difficult terrain each year? Never mind the motivations—and never mind the value judgments—about why they come in the first place. The chief reason that illegal crossers enter the United States through seemingly forbidding yet environmentally sensitive portals is that it is a matter of federal policy that they do so. In the 1990s, the Border Patrol seems to have determined that immigrant traffic through the normal ports of entry—that is, places such as Nogales, El Paso, and National City—was too vast and visible for comfort; it made for bad press when TV crews showed up and had to wait no time at all to film a wave of alambristas hopping walls and rivers to enter the United States, usually uncontested. The Border Patrol therefore massed agents in those cities, driving would-be migrants out into the remote, unpatrolled desert along the length of the border. Gone are the days of cross-border tunnels from one urban house to another; gone are the days of convenient television footage. Now the bulk of seizures of contrabands and arrests of illegal entrants takes place in the wild country far from the restaurants, bars, and other amenities that, uncharitable though it may be to say, make a frontier law-enforcement officer's life a little more bearable.

Whether morale boosting and staff retention—or mere convenience—underlay the federal government's decision is arguable, but the effects have been marked. One is the destruction of great tracts of land, public and private, along the international frontier. Another, better noted in the media, is the appalling number of deaths each year in the desert, as naive crossers from better-watered climes take their coyotes on faith that the big city lies just across the line. Women make up a large percentage of the dead—and women wearing high heels, trusting in just those assurances, make up a large percentage of that number.

The Border Patrol's decision—memorialized as the Southwest Border Strategy in 1994—to restrict illegal immigration to the remotest and most difficult areas had a logic, of course. Seven years later, the General Accounting Office summarized the strategy as making it "so difficult and costly for aliens to attempt illegal entry that fewer individuals would try." As anyone who watched the numbers of crossers climb in the 1990s in response to sweeping economic changes in Mexico knows, that goal was never met.[6] Quite the reverse: Despite expense and hardship, more and more individuals are trying, and more and more are succeeding. The land bears witness, as remote places such as Organ Pipe Cactus National Monument are overrun by agency decree.

Environmental Impact

There are remote places, and there are *remote* places. Nogales is a supremely busy border port, but it is far enough away from the center of things that it takes a walker 10 days to arrive in Phoenix, where a large job market exists for unskilled workers. That does not stop walkers from making the trek. Only a few miles west of Nogales, the sheer rock walls of the Atascosa Mountains make a formidable barrier to travel; the lowlands farther west are laced with river and stream channels that make for far easier passage, even though it is through an unforgiving desert. Neither geographical fact deters crossers. Charge an overburdened Border Patrol with watching all that territory, and you are already set for failure—for alambristas, it seems, will take any risk to cross just about anywhere. All of the technology at the agency's disposal—motion sensors and motion-activated lights, trip wires, closed-circuit televisions, aerial drones—has not lessened their numbers, any more than technology slowed progress on the Ho Chi Minh Trail. Yet, at least until very recently, the agency seems to have preferred technology to boots on the ground, with the result that for many years the border has been essentially open.

It is a first principle of ecology that everything is connected to everything else, so I want to formulate a few hypotheses to help make what I think are some needed connections.

First, a hungry, needful army in motion will go where it will. Read Sun Tzu, and you will learn that only an army that is equally matched—or very much better informed—has a chance of winning.

Second, concertina wire and steel walls do not seem to have the desired deterrent effect in keeping people out.[7] Strangely, however, they do keep people in. When crossing becomes as challenging as it is now, involving not border cities but vast tracts of desert and mountains, then undocumented aliens who successfully enter simply do not leave, as they once did, working for a few months, then returning to their towns and villages to live until the money ran out, then crossing over again. Having won the alambrista lottery, few take the risk of going home only to find themselves shut out, and so they stay.

A postulate: The only thing that will keep crossers from the fragile open desert is to restore border cities as the natural point of passage. Either that, or build a wall too high to jump, an immodest proposal that has been making the rounds.

Third, in absolute terms, it doesn't matter who does the crossing. Ten thousand Vikings, 10,000 Tibetan monks, 10,000 environmentally attuned Cheyenne, 10,000 Boy Scouts are going to have a deleterious effect on a given landscape if they all pass over it at once. As far as the land is concerned, the question of immigration is value-free and color-blind. From the perspective of a blade of grass, we all look like elephants.

Fourth, and that said, the crushing environmental problems of immigration are most keenly felt on the southern border, and there is a cultural dimension to them that is inarguably related to ethnic and national mores. Hispanic American cultures have no formalized tradition of environmental caretaking, very few works of literature or art that present respect for the land as a desideratum, no shared sense of the value of clean air, water, and wilderness. This is not to say that there are no passionate individuals working to change all that, such as Homero Aridjis of Mexico City; yet, from what I have seen in my residency and travels in Mexico and points south, there seem to be no culturally imposed disincentives, no shame attached to tossing a bottle or a sack of garbage out the nearest window, the idea being, perhaps, that someone poorer than you will find it and make use of what can be made use of, which after all is a kind of recycling. None of this is an insurmountable problem; people can be taught not to destroy their nests.[8] But it does have immediate effects—as witness the sea of garbage that marks the border.

More closely related, though, is the question of Third World poverty, which Americans have tended not to notice or to understand, much as they have tended not to notice or understand much of what happens beyond the nation's immediate confines. Claude Lévi-Strauss, the French anthropologist, observed on arriving in the Amazon, "What travel discloses to us first of all is our own garbage, flung in the face of humanity,"[9] and the things left behind in that sea of trash are the things of the poor, poorly made, disposable—and sold by American firms, if made by Mexican (or, more usually these days, Chinese) suppliers. Hispanic people have no cultural imperative to make of the earth a wasteland, but poor people everywhere tend to place environmental matters on a low order of priority. It is so on the border, but not so long ago it was true throughout our own country; I well remember the Virginia Appalachians of my youth, a time when rivers caught fire, as a region where no creek bed was complete without a rusting box springs, a few hundred burned-out tin cans, and a decaying truck chassis or two. In this regard, I think of two of the most effective environmentalists I know, a young Brazilian woman and a middle-aged Mexican man who, working together, have made a productive organic garden in a poor district of a multiethnic city—namely, Chicago, to which they emigrated, one legally, the other not. Both are educated, both now comfortable, having worked hard, all of which leads to a point: If you want to lessen the heavy footprint of humankind on a place, nurture its people's intelligence, give them something to do, and afford them some reason to enjoy life on earth.

However (and here is the fifth postulate), after their arrival here, most of the unskilled immigrant poor remain poor. They drive the substandard vehicles available to them through the secondhand market, vehicles that are minimally maintained and, in the immediate future, are likely to be gas-guzzling behemoths ditched by panicked suburbanites in favor of hybrids and motorbikes. (Watch, soon, for an appalling increase in the number of traffic fatalities nationwide as these vehicles swell the roads.) They live in substandard housing whose owners have not found it convenient to install energy-efficient appliances. That housing lies far from city centers, which are now being reclaimed by two groups of middle-class people: young professionals, who find city life congenial; and older "empty nesters" who find that being able to walk to grocery stores, pharmacies, and cultural events outweighs home ownership in the distant suburbs. Many cities are already experiencing white flight in reverse: in Atlanta, in New York, in Washington, in San Francisco, downtown is increasingly a place of wealth—safe and clean—while the distant suburbs are filling with the poor.

Travel to a construction job site nearly anywhere in the country, and the language you hear spoken will be Spanish. The widespread immigration of unskilled workers is to the disadvantage of the American underclass, who wind up paying for the privilege in the form of increased taxes, and it benefits only the well-to-do who employ them.[10] It is for this reason that you can find organs for the rich, including, at times, *The Wall Street Journal,* calling for both unrestricted immigration and the abolition of minimum-wage laws, the result of which would be a huge pool of cheap workers, a Third World of epic proportions right here at home. It is for this reason that Antonia Hernandez, former president of the Mexican American Legal Defense Fund, once remarked that "immigration has an impact on our economy . . . and most of the competition is to the [existing] Latino community. We compete with one another for those low-paying jobs."

California, America's most populous and once highly prosperous state, has, by at least some economic indexes, become the third poorest state in the nation.[11] As of 2004, a full 28 percent of Californians were immigrants, most unskilled, as compared to less than ten percent in 1969. In the latter year, real household income for the poor was 12 percent higher than it was in 2004, even as a far higher percentage of poor families worked full-time. Poverty endures, then, and so do its ecological effects. If a housecleaner traveling by bus for hours from Riverside to work in Santa Monica contributes little to the overall environmental problems of the state, a truckload of construction workers driving an old, particulate-spitting vehicle across a gridlocked landscape surely does great damage.

The Mexican scholar Jorge Castañeda once suggested that illegal immigration is really California's problem,[12] and as recently as a decade ago that argument would have been mostly right. Now, as undocumented aliens scatter across the country by the hundreds of thousands, even millions, the problem has grown to embrace every region. Still, California speaks to us: One look at the sprawl and ruin that is greater Los Angeles, from the San Gorgonio Pass to the Pacific Ocean 150 miles west, suggests the future of an urbanized nation, a blade runner state in which the Darwinian struggle holds center stage.

The Great Wall

The last set of environmental effects caused by illegal immigration along the border is the product of the government's response to it. Faced with the problem of a very long border and too few people to guard it, government agencies of various sorts are busily building a high-tech, multiple-cordoned Great Wall along the border—at least at points where access is convenient. Plans are being made to extend it from ocean to ocean. One scenario for western Arizona envisions a concertina-wire topped fence at the international line, followed by a moat, followed by a steel wall, followed by a no-man's-land of loose gravel and low-strung wires, followed by another fence, followed by a control road patrolled by robotic vehicles. (If that sounds to you like the creepiest science fiction, then you are not alone.) Farther to the west, near San Diego, the Department of Homeland Security has proposed terraforming large tracts of land along the California-Mexico border, filling in canyons, shaving off ridgelines, and raising a triple fence of concrete and barb wire. The California Coastal Commission rejected that plan, but it is being revised, even as ostensibly conservative U.S. representatives from southern California have taken the side of DHS against state authorities on the matter of sovereignty.

Certain state agencies in Arizona and New Mexico have called for a less fearsome fence, low but electrified, that would certainly be less expensive to build if no less difficult to maintain. Their sense of fiscal responsibility is laudable, but as would any barrier, this fence would disrupt another kind of migration: that of wildlife, which knows no international boundaries. Pronghorn, jaguars, wolves, coatimundi, bighorns, and many other species require large areas in which to move freely. Before border policy pushed aspirant migrants into the deserts and mountains, the animals had just that room to roam. Now their habitat is vanishing. Any sensible discussion of what to do about the immigration problem will include recognition of their plight, for a homeland of empty ranges and silent trees hardly seems worth defending.

Population Shock

On or about October 15, 2006, the population of the United States of America reached 300 million.

When the population reached 200 million, in 1967, Hispanics numbered less than five percent of the population. In 2006, the figure was close to 14 percent, larger than the African American population. In 2046, when the population is expected to be 400 million, the figure will reach 25 percent—that is, if current trends continue and the nation's population grows by 2.8 million immigrants a year, as well as by natural increase.[13]

One hundred million new inhabitants is a strain on any human community. One hundred million new Americans, living in a society organized not on consuming—such a nicely neutral word—but devouring, will be a planetary catastrophe.

Is there any way to keep that flood of newcomers from crashing on these shores?

Short of a militarized, environmentally neutral border, perhaps not. That is, not unless one of the environmental causes of immigration over the southern border is remedied: the collapse of private agriculture in Mexico as a result of the spectacularly ill-advised North American Free Trade Agreement. That treaty, signed under Clinton and endorsed by both former and current Presidents Bush, had the effect of making official Mexico's newfound role as America's southerly breadbasket, as the provider of fresh produce to New England in the dead of winter, of cheap foods to the rest of the continent at all times of the year. (The long distance from Mexican fields to Alaskan supermarkets is one reason, of course, that it takes 65 calories of fossil fuel to produce one calorie of food energy for the American market.) The treaty also helped complete the thoroughgoing industrialization of Mexican agriculture, introducing laborsaving, profit-maximizing machinery while removing people from the land—a sure cause of economic and social catastrophe in any farming community, as development economists such as Charles Hall, Gregoire Leclerc, and Hernando de Soto will tell you.[14]

In the last decade, those displaced farmers have tended to move in two directions. Some have gone to the conurbation of Mexico City, the population of which is now unofficially estimated to be 30 million, a great part of which lives in oceanic wildcat slums that stretch from the capital for scores of miles. Others have gone to el Norte, where, if nothing else, the slums tend to be a touch more congenial, the prospects a little better, and the cities less vast, at least for the time being. I was reminded of this recently when I complained about the size of Phoenix, which has a population of about three million. A friend who lives in Los Angeles retorted, "Three million? That's fewer than the number of illegals here alone."

Getting that crop of farmers back to the farm is likely an impossibility, but developing the economic structures that would make it possible to feed a family in the abundantly fertile nation of Mexico is not. This is a problem to which, I very much hope, American agricultural economists will turn in earnest, for the result can only be beneficial to all concerned on many different levels.

Even with such sweeping changes, illegal immigrants will come. They will come from the south, for, as Jorge Castañeda writes in *The Mexican Shock*, mass migration is unlikely to end so long as radical inequalities exist between the United States and Mexico; inequalities that NAFTA, as it is now constructed, does nothing to solve.[15]

If immigration laws are to acquire the sense of fair play on which we as a nation pride ourselves, then we are going to have to look beyond our southern frontier and onto the larger world and declare our intentions. There is either room, or there is not, or there is some: The fundamental question is whether the American lifeboat is overcrowded and will sink if it takes on more passengers. By many measures, not least of them American patterns of consumption, it is and it will.

On all this my friend Edward Abbey had much to say. Abbey fired his opening shot in a long debate in a letter to the *New York Review* of Books of December 17, 1981, in which, arguing from just that "overcrowded lifeboat" theory, he called for an immediate halt to all immigration into America. A harsh formula, but especially when Abbey added that we be especially vigilant about immigration from Mexico and Central America. Abbey proposed that the Border Patrol be expanded to a force of at least 20,000 heavily armed guards, so that the American way of life might be made safe from threats "to degrade and cheapen [it] downward to the Hispanic standard."

In a series of letters to southern Arizona newspapers, Abbey later suggested that what he really wanted was for the Border Patrol to issue rifles and ammunition, gratis, to would-be immigrants at the border and to point them southward to Mexico City, where they might complete the aborted revolution begun 75 years earlier. Until his death in 1989, Abbey further elaborated this argument,[16] happily urging that the tide of immigrants from Latin America be turned away at the American frontier, while leftists, liberals, businesspeople, Mexican American groups, and so-called conservatives alike joined battle against him, each for their own reasons.

That was in a more innocent time, of course. Things are different now. Abbey is buried in the Cabeza Prieta, and I imagine that he is busily turning over in his grave even as thousands of footsteps erode it away.

In an overcrowded lifeboat, it does not necessarily matter who is drawing the rations. If we agree that there is no room at the inn, immigration must halt or at least be radically curtailed from everywhere. And, quite apart from deciding whether our immigration laws will be made fair and rational, it is in the national interest to reduce pressures to emigrate, no matter from where, and particularly by those who have no skills. In the case of Mexico, as I have said, this means agitating for a thorough program of land reform so that smallholders are not displaced and forced into the cities or across the border, as is now occurring in record numbers. In the case of other countries, it similarly involves encouraging agricultural and industrial self-sufficiency. At a time when huge numbers of the world's too-abundant people live in poverty—by some estimates, there are perhaps 3.5 billion poor on the planet today—we should be encouraging population controls and the broader distribution of resources within the limits of carrying capacity.

Another postulate: Happy people do not emigrate. Leaving family and homeland to enter a strange country and speak a strange language is among the most unsettling of experiences a human can undergo. My ancestors came from Ireland and Sweden to escape grinding poverty and hunger, not on a lark. Yours probably came here for similar reasons. Americans who have not traveled or lived abroad can scarcely imagine how difficult this is, but most can understand the economic desires that prompt people to make that difficult decision in the first place: In a world of haves and have-nots, the have-nots will naturally want to go where the haves live. Call me a raving socialist for saying so, but if we can do something to attend to those economic desires where they arise, then we may do much to reduce the impulse to leave home.

One thing everyone agrees on is that it is exceedingly difficult to conduct a rational discussion on the whole issue of immigration, let alone legislate it fairly. By raising that issue, the conservative senator Alan Simpson of Wyoming once remarked, "You'll trod on every segment of American society and be called everything from xenophobe to racist." He was right, and things are worse today. And so we have the politics Abbey described thus: "The conservatives love their cheap labor; the liberals love their cheap cause." (But, he added, "neither group, you will notice, ever invites the immigrants to move into their homes.")

Faced with such conundrums, many environmentalists have chosen to remain altogether silent on the question of immigration, perhaps hoping that it will go away on its own. Immigration is, after all, a cyclical issue in American politics, one that rises and falls every ten or 20 years. I have the feeling, though, that this time it will not disappear: There are too many ruined canyons, tracts of desert land, and streambeds for that. So raise it environmentalists must. At a time when our society seems to be tapped dry, with 60 million poor and unemployed and a national debt in the trillions, the lifeboat may well have sprung one too many leaks to allow more passengers, regardless of where they board. If it is to take on more, determining just how it will require informed, dispassionate debate on many fronts: social, economic, cultural, and environmental. If it is not, then the question remains how to become a fortress without walling itself off in the manner of a Chinese dynasty or Stalinist state, and without our becoming prisoners within. There are no easy answers.

In the meanwhile, what remains is to protect our garden.

Endnotes

[1] In August 2006, following complaints by retired agents about the denaturing and uselessness of their work, Arizona congressmen introduced a bill to reassign the Shadow Wolves to the Department of Immigration and Customs Enforcement, effectively relieving them of supposedly anti-terrorist duty. The legislation is pending as of this writing. For more on the organization, see Gregory McNamee, "Shadow Wolves: Cutting Sign," Native Peoples, March 2006.

[2] For visual documentation, see the alarming photographs by Michael Berman that accompany Charles Bowden's *Inferno* (University of Texas Press, 2006) and Bill Broyles's *Sunshot* (University of Arizona Press, 2006).

[3] Jennifer Talhelm, "At Organ Pipe, park rangers confront damaging reality of illegal immigration," *Associated Press*, June 19, 2006.

[4] U.S. Bureau of Land Management, Southern Arizona Project to Mitigate Environmental Damages Resulting from Illegal Immigration, Annual Report 2005 (U.S. Government Printing Office, 2006); Tony Davis, "Crossers Burying Border in Garbage," *Arizona Daily Star*, July 30, 2006.

[5] "Immigration by the Numbers," *Washington Post*, May 26, 2006.

[6] U.S. General Accounting Office, "Border Patrol: Available Data on Interior Checkpoints Suggest Differences in Sector Performance," a report released on July 22, 2005.

[7] Indeed, nothing does. See William Langewiesche, *Cutting for Sign* (Random House, 1996), in which one Border Patrol tells Langewiesche, "We could link hands out here and still not stop them."

[8] Or so one hopes. See Joel Simon, *Endangered Mexico: An Environment on the Edge* (Sierra Club Books, 1997).

[9] Claude Lévi-Strauss, *Tristes Tropiques*, Atheneum, 1961, p. 135.

[10] Roger Lowenstein, "The Immigration Equation," *New York Times Magazine*, July 9, 2006.

[11] "The Not-so-Golden State," *The Economist*, May 25, 2006. See also Kevin Starr, *Coast of Dreams: California on the Edge, 1990–2003* (Knopf, 2004).

[12] Jorge G Castañeda, *The Mexican Shock: Its Meaning for the United States* (New Press, 1995), p. 25.

[13] On the occasion of the publication of his book, *An Empire Wilderness* (Random House, 1998), journalist Robert Kaplan told me, "It won't be the old America, and this will be dislocating and upsetting for some people. But it won't happen overnight. Historians will wonder, in a hundred

years, just when it was that the United States as we know it disappeared. The answer will be that it happened so gradually that no one really noticed." This is gradualism as mithradatism.

[14] See the essays collected in Hall and Leclerc's edited volume, *Making Development Work* (University of New Mexico Press, 2007); de Soto, *The Mystery of Capital: Why Capitalism Triumphs in the West and Fails Everywhere Else* (Basic Books, 2003); and David S Landes, *The Wealth and Poverty of Nations* (Norton, 1998).

[15] Castañeda, *The Mexican Shock*, p. 13. See also Carlos Fuentes, *A New Time for Mexico* (Farrar, Straus & Giroux, 19 96); Andres Oppenheimer, *Bordering on Chaos: Guerrillas, Stockbrokers, Politicians, and Mexico's Road to Prosperity* (Little, Brown, 2003); Joseph Stiglitz, *The Roaring Nineties: A New History of the World's Most Prosperous Decade* (Norton, 2003).

[16] See, for example, Abbey's essay, "Immigration and Liberal Taboos," collected in *One Life at a Time, Please* (Henry Holt, 1988).

12

FROM INVASION TO CONQUEST: ILLEGAL IMMIGRATION INTO EUROPE AND THE UNITED STATES

by Alberto Carosa

The United States is in the fortunate position of being able to avoid the mistakes made by those European nations, which in recent decades have had to deal with thorny issues relating to their immigration crisis, by drawing lessons from them. Is the United States prepared to learn these lessons? Recent events do not suggest as much, judging from the problems Congress has had in working out, let alone passing, legislation to curb illegal immigration and mass demonstrations by undocumented immigrants across the country to assert their "right" to legalization.[1]

Unlimited Right to Immigration?

Common sense tells us that something is wrong when demonstrations by illegal immigrants are viewed as justifiable reactions to unjust treatment. But, of course, common sense is precisely what is lacking in the debate on the immigration issue—all the more so, in fact, in Europe and, most notably, Italy, where such demonstrations have been the order of the day for many years. At the outset of this chapter, however, I need to make a preliminary point very clear: My criticism is of uncontrolled and illegal immigration, not immigration per se. However well-intentioned, any advocacy of uncontrolled immigration for the sake of its presumed benefits is a contradiction in terms: How can an uncontrolled process produce beneficial results, which are, normally and precisely, the fruits of careful forethought and planning? Rather, the likely result of any such uncontrolled process is chaos. Every state has a sovereign right to protect its borders and enforce its laws, which must be respected, and to allow entry only to foreigners of its own choice. There is no such thing as an unlimited right to immigration. Whenever immigrants illegally enter another country, they show a fundamentally disrespectful and antidemocratic attitude by imposing their unrequested presence on its inhabitants, in much the same way as does a stranger who breaks into a private house. There are surely exceptions, for example, immediately imperiled refugees, but we must not forget that "the abuse does not remove the use." If legal or illegal immigrants are therefore guests in their host country, at least, until they obtain their full citizenship status, is it acceptable for them to stage demonstrations claiming their "rights?" This is the result of what we may describe as the erosion of state sovereignty, whose ultimate outcome can only be the state's total surrender.

In this regard, few precedents in Italy are enlightening. In Bologna on September 22, 1990, 3,000 North African street hawkers (normally referred to as *extra-comunitari*, namely non-EU citizens, or *"vu cumprà?"* a slightly pejorative term, literally meaning "wanna buy?") marched through the city center to declare war on bourgeois, middle-class society by shouting slogans like "Occupation is necessary!" "Occupation is right!" and claiming, "We are immigrants, we have rights, we have many of them. We want to live here, we want to live here comfortably. We want also the right to vote, we are nothing without the vote. We don't want to obtain rights as a concession, but we want to seize them also by force."[2] On June 3, 2000, a similar demonstration was held in Brescia; it featured signs and posters labeling as "traitors" their colleagues who had condemned the use of violence to press one's rights.[3]

Immigrants of Islamic descent, as their numbers grow, have become conspicuous for their increasing arrogance and aggressiveness. In the wake of the uproar caused by the Danish cartoons of Mohammed in 2005, the spokesman (probably self-appointed) of the Muslim community in Como, Italy, lashed out at those Italian papers that had reprinted the irreverent sketches. He demanded that Italy, if it desired pardon, make public apology, impose jail terms on the responsible editors and journalists, and ensure that full-page ads be run at least twice a week by Italy's main dailies for four months, explaining the figure and vision of Mohammad to the Italian people, and create legislation to protect Muslims and the appropriate worship of their prophet.[4]

Immigration or Immigrationism?

If Islamic immigrants have come to epitomize such arrogance and bullying, one rightly wonders whether it is possible to speak of immigrationism, rather than of simple immigration. If immigration is the phenomenon, *immigrationism* is the underlying ideology. A clue as to the ultimate aim of immigrationism was provided by the late Oriana Fallaci, who, in one of her later books, referred to a project called "Eurabia," symbolizing Europe under Arab (therefore, Islamic) domination. The first known use of this term, Fallaci contended, was traceable to the mid–1970s, when a journal of that name was printed in Paris, written in French, and edited by one Lucien Bitterlin, then president of the Association of Franco-Arab Solidarity and currently the chairman of the French-Syrian Friendship Association. *Eurabia* (price: five francs) was jointly published by Middle East International (London), France-Pays Arabes (Paris), the Groupe d'Etudes sur le Moyen-Orient (Geneva), and the European Coordinating Committee of the Associations for Friendship with the Arab World, which Fallaci described as an arm of what was then the European Economic Community (EEC), now the European Union. These entities, Fallaci said, not mincing her words, were the official perpetrators "of the biggest conspiracy that modern history has created," and *Eurabia* was their house organ.[5]

The second issue of *Eurabia*, Fallaci reported, clearly outlined the projected strategy: An arrangement between European and Arab governments by which the Europeans, following the 1973 OPEC oil crisis and the first acts of PLO terrorism, agreed to accept Arab immigrants along with Arab oil. They also agreed to disseminate propaganda regarding the glories of Islamic civilization, to provide Arab states with weaponry, to side with them against Israel, and generally to toe the Arab line on all matters political and cultural. Hundreds of meetings and seminars were held as part of this "Euro-Arab Dialogue" (or rather, Arab monologue, which always carefully avoided such words as "Islam," "Islamic," "Muslim," "Koran," "Mohammad," "Allah"), all, according to Fallaci, marked by European acquiescence in Arab requests. These meetings included a seminar in Venice in 1977, attended by delegates from ten Arab nations and eight European ones and concluding with a unanimous resolution calling for "the diffusion of the Arabic language" and affirming "the superiority of Arab culture." (Interestingly, whereas nobody batted an eyelid at the time, 24 years later Italian prime minister Silvio Berlusconi sparked a worldwide furor merely by hinting at the notion of Western superiority over Islam.)[6] In particular, the resolution demanded that the fundamental rights of Arab workers be fully respected. These rights, which had to be identical with those of European nationals, included also the "inalienable right to practice their own religion" and the right to export to Europe their culture—therefore, additionally, the right to disseminate and spread it. (When will the same rights apply also to Westerners in Arab countries?)

Step-by-Step Strategy

Algerian President Houari Boumedienne, the man who ousted Ben Bella three years after Algerian independence, bluntly declared before the General Assembly of the United Nations in 1974: "One day millions of men will leave the southern hemisphere of this planet to burst into the northern one. But not as friends.

Because they will burst in to conquer, and they will conquer by populating it with their children. Victory will come to us from the wombs of our women."[7]

In 1972, Oriana Fallaci interviewed the Palestinian terrorist George Habash, who told her that the Palestinian problem was about far more than Israel. The Arab goal, Habash declared, was to wage war "against Europe and America" and to ensure that henceforth "there would be no peace for the West." The Arabs would "advance step-by-step. Millimeter by millimeter. Year after year. Decade after decade. Determined, stubborn, patient. This is our strategy. A strategy that we shall expand throughout the whole planet." Only later did Fallaci realize that Habash "also meant the cultural war, the demographic war, the religious war waged by stealing a country from its citizens. In short, the war waged through immigration, fertility, presumed pluriculturalism."[8] In a book by British journalist Adam LeBor, *A Heart Turned East* (1997), a London-based mullah is quoted as saying, "We cannot conquer these people with tanks and troops, so we have got to overcome them by force of numbers."[9]

There is nothing new in all this, as the history of northern Africa (a thriving Christian land in the first centuries A.D.) and, more recently, of Lebanon show. In fact, a gun and a knife, if not a tank, were sufficient for an Islamist militant, the Dutch and Moroccan national Mohammed Bouyeri, to "execute" in Amsterdam a perpetrator of the offense of "Islamophobia"—the flamboyant and irreverent Dutch filmmaker, Theo van Gogh, who had produced a film critical of the treatment of women under Islam. Bouyeri first opened fire at van Gogh, repeatedly stabbed him, slit his throat, and finally pinned a five-page document on to the victim's chest with a knife. This letter, filled with such threats as "Islam will be victorious through the blood of martyrs" and "only the death will separate the truth from the lies" in both Dutch and Arabic, envisaged the downfall of the "infidel enemies of Islam" in Europe, including the Netherlands and the United States.[10]

Whereas the United States appears to be too big a mouthful to swallow, at least for the time being, with regard to the Netherlands, radical Islamists may have a point: According to the latest available data, Muslim immigrants number almost one million, including 300,000 Moroccans, and account for six percent of a population of 16 million. A recent government paper indicated that by 2010 large cities such as Rotterdam, Amsterdam, the Hague, and Utrecht will have Muslim majorities. The Dutch Muslim community is already an increasingly large and visible presence; Amsterdam alone is home to more than 100,000 Muslims—13 percent of the city's entire population.[11]

One of the points commonly made in these fanatical war declarations is that the fates of Europe and the United States are inextricably intertwined, the seeming assumption being that these are the two pillars of Christendom needing to be broken down if the rest of the West is to follow suit. If so, then the striking similarities between the immigration crisis on both sides of the Atlantic Ocean shed light on one of the central enigmas of our time: the fact that in a mere three decades Europe became home to an estimated 20 million Muslims, accounting for more than 70 percent of all its immigrants.[12] Also, the dates somehow tally: If the whole process started in earnest in the early 1970s in Europe, Ted Kennedy's revised immigration bill was passed only a few years earlier in 1965, favoring unskilled immigrants from the Third World whose quota was increased to 85 percent of the annual total. Not surprisingly, post–1965 immigrants to the United States have sharply been distinguished by a higher incidence of poverty and welfare dependence.[13]

The number of illegal aliens in the United States is estimated between 12 million and 20 million people,[14] of which the overwhelming majority comes from Mexico. Thus, *Eurabia* stands in relation to the European Union as Mexico does to the United States. Commenting on the *Schadenfreude* that marked much of American reportage on the French urban riots in late 2005, *Le Figaro* editorialized that France is paying the price for its arrogance. "Vengeance is a dish best served cold," the paper went on noting. "America will never forget the criticisms of its society during the Iraq war and after the hurricane in Louisiana. But their criticism is not entirely unjustified. It underlines 40 years of political failure." Yet the United States has little cause to celebrate France's plight, considering the threat posed by massive illegal immigration across its own borders.[15]

Failed Integration

The French paper was referring to France's failure to integrate its millions of North African Muslims. Common sense argues that for integration to be successful in any degree, the immigrant population should be relatively small. To admit endless waves of illegal immigrants is a recipe for national disaster. Yet, today, the number of immigrants living in France is a disproportionately large and growing one. Indeed, it may be said that Boumedienne's prophecy was starting to be realized as early as 1975, when France decided to allow immigrants to be joined by their families arriving from their country of origin. Before that date, immigrant workers often married French women who then brought up the children and integrated the family into French society, aided by the compulsory secular school system. However, since the principle of *régroupement familial* (family reunion) became law, extended families from abroad have been raising their children in accordance with their native culture. Owing to unemployment, many of these families, who often do not speak French, live solely on state aid, completely cut off from society. In addition to unemployment, Muslim polygamy has been identified as a root cause in the French riots. Though prohibited officially, unofficially it is tolerated, despite the protests of politicians—including the then-Minister of the Interior Nicolas Sarkozy (since elected president of France on a "zero tolerance" platform against illegal immigration) and Gerard Larcher, Minister of Labor—and academics, such as the world renowned historian and member of the prestigious Académie Française Hèléne Carrère d'Encausse.[16] In an interview in *L'Express*, Sarkozy decried polygamy as "one of the cultural differences which makes integration more difficult for a French youth of African origin than of another descent."[17] According to recent estimates, polygamous families in France number at least 20,000, each of them including 25 sons.[18] No surprise that legal and/or illegal immigrants from Francophone West or North Africa end up living (or trying to survive) in marginalized slums, run-down hotels, or fire-hazard buildings that burn from time to time, fueling the rage of the rioters.

For any immigration policy to be successful, a sense of reality is critical. No country in the world, including the United States, has unlimited resources that can accommodate a limitless number of immigrants, legal or illegal, especially as most of them come from an Islamic cultural background whose Shari'a is viewed as incompatible with Western law and the West's way of life.[19] Yet reality is exactly what the policy makers ignore. To those who object that the invasion of Europe by Muslim immigrants is not comparable to the invasion of the United States by its Latino neighbors, one may reply that invasion is invasion and bound to produce the same results, if not in the short term, certainly in a longer one, as the Mexicanization of the United States paves the way for its Islamization as well. The major difference between the United States and Europe in regard to the immigration crisis is that the process of disruption is much more advanced in the Old Continent, owing to its rampant secularization. By diluting or erasing its Christian identity, Europe is depriving itself of the only effective means to integrate its Muslim immigrant population.

We often hear and read erudite disquisitions on the various models of integration: the difference, for example, between the "multiculturalist" and "assimilationist" approaches and the reasons why one was more, or less, successful in one country than in another. The fact is, however, that all these models have proved in one degree or another a flop, as terrorist attacks and related crises throughout the western European countries, instigated by homegrown militants, indicate. Indeed, 40 percent of Muslims living in Great Britain want Islamic Shari'a introduced into parts of that country, according to a poll reported by the *London Sunday Telegraph*.[20]

But how could Europeans have sown the seeds of their own destruction by ensuring the perfectly predictable consequences of, as one author has aptly put it, "the folly of mass immigration?"[21]

Fifth Columns

One explanation is that none of this would have been possible without effective "fifth columns" nested in, and virtually dominating, the nerve centers of the European nations, taken both separately and collectively as members of the European Union: These include especially the courts, government bureaucracies, politicians, schools, the media, charities, NGOs, and so on. Here we find another striking parallel with the situation that exists in the United States, where the Supreme Court is increasingly accused of striking down laws and imposing new ones on its purely arbitrary whims, for which the Constitution offers no justification. In his *Men in Black: How the Supreme Court Is Destroying America*), Mark R. Levin points out how the allegedly "conservative" black-robed justices of the Supreme Court are subverting democracy in favor of their liberal agenda by endorsing terrorists' rights, condoning flag burning, importing foreign law, and granting illegal immigrants rights equal with those of citizens.

A similar phenomenon is observable in Europe, and especially in Italy, which has come to play a pivotal role as a sort of bridgehead in the influx of illegal immigrants into Europe. In certain sectors of the Italian judiciary, members clearly pursue their own immigrationist agenda by thwarting restrictionist measures and making virtually impossible the enforcement of sound immigration laws. What happened with the so-called Bossi-Fini Law is a case in point. This law was passed by the Berlusconi-led executive after the President's center-right coalition was elected to office in 2001, as part of a political platform endorsed by the Italian voters. One of its (avowed, at least) aims was to curb illegal immigration by making it possible for the government to return undocumented and unemployed immigrants in Italy to their country of origin. This, in theory, would have been an improvement, since the previous law, which had been passed by a center-left executive, provided for an expulsion mechanism so twisted and clumsy as to make deportation virtually impossible. But sectors of the judiciary have placed so many hurdles in the way of the Bossi-Fini law that assaults on Italian shores, especially those of Sicily and the Isle of Lampedusa, by decrepit boats teeming with illegal immigrants mostly from Africa and the Middle East continued more or less unabated throughout the five-year mandate of the center-right government. Now, with the accession of Romano Prodi's center-left government, the situation may revert to the status quo ante, one of the new government's stated objectives being the complete repeal of the Bossi-Fini law.

Alas, ordinary citizens bear the brunt of the situation. The newspapers are filled with reports of serious crimes committed by illegal and undocumented immigrants who have been served time and again with expulsion orders, to which they paid no attention at all. To add insult to injury, Italy's Supreme Court of Cassation has recently handed down a verdict to the effect that a recidivist illegal immigrant who systematically ignores his expulsion order may not be arrested, on grounds that such an action would be "illegitimate."[22] The illegal immigrant may only be escorted to the border and then expelled, the judges decreed, cost and logistics notwithstanding.

Dick Lamm, a former governor of Colorado, at a recent immigration-overpopulation conference in Washington, DC, filled to capacity by many of American's finest minds and leaders, spoke of an eight-point plan to destroy America, which according to him includes the following: "Make it impossible to enforce our immigration laws." The planned destruction of the United States as described by Lamm bears an impressive similarity with the situation in the other side of the Atlantic Ocean, the obvious and inescapable implication being that the same strategy has been adopted to assure the surrender of the two main pillars of the Western world.[23]

The Italian Case

In Italy, the pressure on opponents of illegal immigration is furthered by international agencies, which have targeted Italy by questioning the validity of its *centri di pemanenza temporanea* (CPT, Centers of Provisional Residency), citing alleged abuses of the illegal immigrants' human rights. After landing illegally, undocumented would-be immigrants are taken into custody in the CPTs and scattered along the shores of southern Italy for identification and immediate repatriation by air to the country from which they initiated their sea crossing (usually Libya). As a result, international commissions have arrived in Italy to investigate the conditions in which these illegal immigrants are kept and to question whether repatriations are being carried out too hastily so as to impinge on the immigrants' human rights. Though the commissions ruffled a lot of feathers, in the end nothing serious came of their investigations, beyond the implication that Italy must henceforth receive these uninvited guests with open arms, providing them with five-star hotel accommodation, caviar, and champagne.

But what about the right of native Italians to the territorial integrity of their country? Apparently, the underlying assumption common to the immigrationist lobbies in Europe and the United States is that responsibility for illegal immigrants lies not solely with the immigrants themselves, but also with the makers of policy designed to curb their influx. By the same logic, a rape victim might be said to be responsible on the grounds that, had she not attempted to resist, the crime would not have taken place. Worse, Europe appears to have embraced this perverse logic, as Marcello Pera, Italy's former Senate speaker, pointed out in observing that Europe appeared to have developed "a cultural attitude, a bizarre 'guilty syndrome' according to which everything that is happening to us, including the attacks by Islamic fundamentalism and terrorism, assuming that we are allowed to call it 'Islamic,' is justified by our (American) iniquities and errors."[24]

An example of this logic at work was the reaction, widespread in Europe, to the Danish cartoons crisis, characterized by apologies delivered on behalf of those who had dared to offend Islam accompanied by deafening silences in response to the burning of churches and the killing of Christians. (In Italy a Northern League minister in the Berlusconi government, Roberto Calderoli, had to resign after appearing in public wearing a T-shirt with the controversial Danish cartoons of Islam's prophet; he was promptly subjected to judicial probe for having offended Islamic religious sentiments.) This state of psychological subservience, perhaps a harbinger of total subjugation in future, was effectively described by British Life Peer and former deputy speaker of the House of Lords, Baroness Caroline Cox, in an interview in which she alleged that "In the UK much of our leadership is already more or less in dhimmi status, and nobody dares to speak out, for fear of intimidation, for fear of retribution, and because it's not politically correct." This situation of dhimmitude, according to the baroness, "describes the subordinate status of Jews and Christians under Muslim domination, which today, under the influence of global jihad, is becoming a worldwide reality." She went on to remark that "In *The Muslim Weekly* British energy minister Mike O'Brien describes the Labour government as the 'best friend' of Muslims and openly boasts that the government has introduced measures against religious discrimination and hatred after requests from the Muslim Council of Britain."[25]

Evidently, accommodationism was insufficient to exempt Britain from actual or planned terrorist attacks. "Our attitude must be moderate and not confrontational," Baroness Cox contended, but

> I think we do need to be seen to take militant Islam seriously, not to generate Islamophobia, but unless we do there will be an Islamophobic reaction, because Islamic terrorism does create fear, and terrorism creates fear by definition, and fear does not make distinctions, and so unless we are seen to be taking militant Islam seriously, there will be a backlash against Muslims. . . . There will be much more generalized Islamophobia. . . . We must, must, must take the agenda of militant Islam very, very seriously. Enough is enough, and much has already been conceded to those who abuse the freedoms of democracy to destroy that democracy.[26]

Does Baroness Cox exaggerate? Not really, if one credits a recent decision taken by the EU to appoint a commission charged with formulating a code of the "Islamically correct," or glossary of revised terms for politicians and officials wishing to eschew Islamophobia. Among those terms deemed ambiguous, misleading, or devoid of foundation are "Islamic terrorist," "Islamist" (as synonymous with *extremist*), and "jihad," in the sense of "holy war."[27] Among the reasons why Italy has played a significant role in the advancement of the immigrationist agenda is the de facto witting or unwitting support offered by some in the Roman hierarchy for uncontrolled and illegal immigration, including, in some instances, resort to civil disobedience initiatives, as in the debate over the allegedly restrictive Bossi-Fini law in 2002.[28] And this "good example" has spread not only to the rest of the EU, but also to the United States, where as recently as March 2006 Cardinal Roger Mahony, who leads the Archdiocese of Los Angeles, the largest Roman Catholic diocese in the country, attacked the House immigration bill during Ash Wednesday Mass and pledged a campaign of civil disobedience in the archdiocese's 288 parishes if it becomes law.[29]

As a faithful Catholic, I fully side, in principle, with the Church's efforts to relieve the plight of the poor, downtrodden, and marginalized—including immigrants—through her charitable agencies like Caritas and other religious-related NGOs. On the other hand, I cannot but question her embrace-all approach to immigration, irrespective of any prudential consideration whatsoever: Is there not a risk that the advertised assistance so promptly and generously offered by these charities will amount to a powerful incentive for continued mass immigration? And, from the church's perspective, are there no other causes or issues as worthy, or even worthier, of a similar mobilization of resources?

A New "Dogma"?

As charity starts at home with our most immediate neighbors, one is entitled to wonder whether it is just to spend enormous amounts of money and resources to cope with the effects of illegal immigrations. Consider, for instance, the costs involved in keeping vessels patrolling the sea, pulling decrepit boats overladen with illegals to the shore for a safe landing to Lampedusa or other Sicilian ports, arranging prompt airborne transfers to avoid overcrowding in the holding centers for migrants, providing the necessary health assistance to people exhausted by days at sea with scant food and water, admitting many of them to hospitals, and so forth. Ron Johnson, executive director of the Arizona Catholic Conference has aptly observed that, "While Catholics must adhere to Church teaching on the 'non-negotiable issues' concerning 'intrinsically evil' acts, there are other issues on which Catholics in good standing can differ, including immigration."[30] In other words, the reported claim to an unlimited right to immigration is not a new "dogma" or "revelation," at least so far as the Catholic Church is concerned. Be that as it may, there is no doubt that, as Archbishop Giovanni Lajolo, the former equivalent of the Holy See's foreign minister, has noted, the faith factor is becoming increasingly important in the debate over immigration.[31]

"In welcoming the stranger we should not distinguish between 'legal' and 'illegal' migrants. Illegal immigration is not something the Church can approve of or encourage," Cormac Cardinal Murphy-O'Connor of London has written in a message to his parishes. "But our Gospel mandate is to assist strangers, whoever they are, and meanwhile to urge that the rights of undocumented workers be respected." He added that the Church has long taught that to migrate is a right for families "when they are unable to achieve a life of dignity in their own land," as Pope Pius XII wrote in his classic 1952 document *Exsul Familia* (the title refers to the Holy Family's flight into Egypt). But Catholic teaching also recognizes the right of nations to control their own borders and to regulate immigration. *Exsul Familia* emphasizes that the needs of immigrants must be weighed against the needs of the receiving countries, and that the rights of these nations must not be exaggerated to the point of denying access to needy people from other countries.[32]

Italy's present minister of health, Livia Turco, a Catholic who started her political career as a member of the old Communist Party PCI and cannot therefore be suspected of an anti-immigration bias, says "International migrants do not come from poor and isolated lands, unconnected to the world markets. . . . In the short term, international migrations are the result of economic development, rather than the lack of it."[33] Indeed, illegal immigrants wishing to come to Italy can afford to pay many thousands of dollars to their smugglers, thus encouraging a vicious new trade—human smuggling—around the globe. These flesh cartels are run by the same crime syndicates—including those run by Colombian drug lords, the Chinese Triads, the Sri Lankan Tamil Tigers, and the Russian Mafia—that traffic in drugs and arms. But smuggling people has become more profitable than even the heroin trade, while carrying much lighter penalties.

On another front, a number of France's major church leaders, including Cardinal Jean-Pierre Ricard, President of the French Bishops Conference and Archbishop of Bordeaux, in a letter dated April 22, 2006 have expressed concern over the drafting of a bill to reform the country's immigration law, lamenting that it "will implement selective immigration, allowing only the well-qualified and educated" and that "this draft only contains measures that would have the effect of restraining the possibilities to regularize the situation of these aliens."

On April 24, 2006 another letter was sent to the government by the country's director of Catholic Charities, Jean-Pierre Richer, who, along with other associations, expressed concern over the issue. That letter was entitled, "We cannot compromise with immigrant's rights."[34]

Trampled Rights

But if no compromise is allowable in respect of immigrants rights, the rights of the invaded native population are ignored, if not trampled upon. How often has native opinion of mass immigration been solicited, via referenda, or other means? A basic contradiction needs to be clarified: Have those prelates of the church, who remind illegal immigrants that they must respect the law of their host country if they want their rights to be respected as well, considered that these immigrants owe their presence in Europe to their having committed a criminal offense in coming here in the first place? And since when do ends justify means in Catholic doctrine? One may argue, as a modest consolation, that at least those millions of Mexicans illegally entering the United States are not Muslim. But that is hardly the main point. Common sense suggests that the constant, massive, and unfettered influx of million immigrants, however well-intentioned they may be, disrupt sooner or later the native social fabric, and that, rather integrating within the host country, they will in the end disintegrate it. Moreover, there is reason for thinking that many Mexican immigrants are far from well-intentioned. "Because of the United States' contentious history with its southern neighbors, these extremist Mexican immigrant groups coming across the border couldn't care less about assimilating with American society, and, in fact, prefer not to," says Armstrong Williams. "For they believe that it's their land and that Americans better leave or get used to their presence."[35]

A similar tendency is exhibited by Muslims who long for the good old days of the caliphate in Spain, when the country was under Islamic domination, and make no secret of their intention to regain it, whether the Spanish like it or not. Meanwhile, Muslim immigrants have created in Europe Islamic enclaves that are already taking on the character of conquered provinces that no longer belong to the European countries around them, as described by the liberal American expatriate Bruce Bawer in his book *While Europe Slept: How Radical Islam Is Destroying the West From Within.*[36] In France, a public official has met with an imam at the edge of Roubaix's Muslim district, out of respect for his declaration of the neighborhood as being Islamic territory to which she had no right of access. In Britain, imams have pressed the government officially to designate certain areas of Bradford as being under Muslim, not British, law. In Denmark, Muslim leaders have sought the same kind of control over parts of Copenhagen. And, in Belgium, Muslims living in the Brussels neighborhood of Sint-Jans-Molenbeek already view it, not as part of Belgium, but as an area under Islamic jurisdiction in which Belgians are not welcome. Thus, in Europe's growing Islamic neighborhoods, where police are often afraid to venture, European law is being supplanted by Shari'a. European women venturing into or near such enclaves have been assaulted and, in some cases, raped by gangs of macho Islamic males as a penalty for violating Muslim dress codes and failing to exhibit the subservient status some Islamic subcultures require of females.

In Brussels, the most popular name for baby boys is now Mohammad. Sustaining the population of a nation requires that on average each couple gives birth to 2.1 children. The average European couple now has fewer than 1.4 babies, compared to 3.6 babies born to the average Muslim immigrant couple in Europe. Across Western Europe, 16 to 20 percent of babies are being born into Muslim families.

Wealth Transfer

Already the wealth of traditional Europeans is being bled away and transferred to new Muslim immigrants and their children. One mechanism for this is the European welfare state. In Denmark, Bawer has observed, only five percent of the population is Muslim, but this minority demands and receives 40 percent of the Danish government's total welfare payments and other taxpayer-subsidized social benefits. Even the liberal *New York Times* magazine in February 2006 reported on the social impact of this growing Islamic drain on the resources of European welfare states such as Sweden and Denmark.

Bawer further documents how Norwegian (Oslo) imams preach brazenly that Muslims should expect such welfare benefits — and feel justified in supplementing them by stealing from stores — as a way to make non-Muslims pay the discriminatory jizya tax[37] that is extracted from non-Muslim citizens in Muslim countries. In this case, *jizya* would be extracted from the infidel "host" societies — societies that have not yet accepted their subservience to Islamic Law! Such radical mullahs have told their European congregations that Islamic Shari'a law justifies also other forms of stealing from European merchants and companies in order to transfer wealth from Europeans to Eurabian Muslims.[38]

Muslim Supremacism

Among those Norway-based Islam religious leaders is the country's most controversial refugee, Mullah Krekar, a Muslim supremacist said to have established in 2001 *Ansar al-Islam* (Supporters of Islam), a group of Kurdish separatists and Islamic fundamentalists, with funding and logistical support from Al Qaeda and

Osama bin Laden. Mullah Krekar, also known as Faraj Ahmad Najmuddin, was reported in the Oslo daily *Aftenposten* as saying that "Islam will defeat the Western mindset." The women in the EU produce 1.4 children against the 3.5 produced by the Muslim women living there, he explains, so that "30 percent of the Europeans will be Muslim by 2050." What is more, he claims, the Western mind-set, having allowed itself be corrupted by "materialism, selfishness, and wildness," has destroyed Christianity. As an example, he cites the embracement of homosexuality, "which would have never been accepted by Jesus."[39]

While we may thank the mullah for reminding us of our Lord's teachings on homosexuality, we should also note that some Catholic prelates are prepared to open their churches to illegal immigrants seeking refuge there and proceed to convert them into mosques, as indeed has happened in Belgium.[40] Some senior Catholic emissaries, on the other hand, being far less "politically correct," have not minced their words. Years ago in a pastoral letter, Cardinal Biffi, then the archbishop of Bologna, warned that Muslim invasion threatened the values of Christian Europe and suggested that Italy's immigration policy should favor Catholics over Muslims. "Those who belong to other, non-Christian religions," he wrote, "are to be loved, and helped in their needs as much as possible." But clearly not all immigrants are to be loved in the same way at the same time. "It's necessary to be seriously concerned about saving the nation's own identity," the Cardinal wrote. "Italy is not a deserted or uninhabited land, without history, without living traditions and without an unmistakable cultural and spiritual shape." Biffi claims that most Muslims have come to Europe not to assimilate but with the hope of "making us all become essentially like them"; his conclusion was Europe must be either Christian or Muslim.[41] Needless to say, Biffi words sparked turmoil and drew harsh criticism from church and lay leaders alike.

A more recent example of a similarly energetic approach to the threat of Islam is an essay that appeared in *Studium*,[42] an authoritative Italian bimonthly journal on Catholic culture founded in 1906. The essay, entitled "The Islamic Question," occupies 30 pages of the journal. The really interesting thing about the article is the identity of its authors, Roberto A. M. Bertacchini and Piersandro Vanzan. Vanzan is a Jesuit, a professor of pastoral theology at the Pontifical Gregorian University, and a contributor to *La Civiltà Cattolica*, the publication of the Jesuits in Rome, subject to authorization by the Vatican. Readers familiar with *"La rabbia e l'orgoglio"* and other writings on Islam by Oriana Fallaci will find many points in common between her writings and Bertacchini's and Vanzan's article. Fallaci was a great admirer of Benedict XVI, while the Pope, in addition to having read a number of her books, received her in a private audience on August 1, 2006, at Castel Gandolfo. The only substantial point separating Oriana Fallaci's analysis from that of Bertacchini and Vanzan is that she considers Islam to be incapable of reform and incompatible with the Christian West, while the other two acknowledge that an integration of the two civilizations is possible, albeit extremely difficult (a possibility Benedict XVI himself is known to have acknowledged).

According to "The Islamic Question," Islamic terrorism is a complex response to the confrontation with the West, which Islam sees as a devastating, deadly threat. For the zealots, everything that comes from the outside is a poison to their traditional way of life, driving them to claim that only one way exists to avert cultural catastrophe: expel the invader and hermetically seal the borders of Islam. But this defensive strategy can never work against Western civilization, which, unlike all previous civilizations, is not localized or territorially circumscribed. The pervasiveness of the global village is such that there is only one way to escape its grasp, and that is to destroy it. For the formula of "modernizing Islam," Al-Zawahiri substitutes another: "Islamizing modernity" and therefore the West.

Within the Muslim world, Islamization means de-Westernizing everything: from political and cultural institutions to economic ones, even to the point of rethinking banking operations. Outside that world, it means spreading Islam through vigorous missionary activity, in both Europe and the United States: a program supported above all by Saudi Arabia. But according to the most radical interpretations, Islamizing the West means violently attacking its political and economic power, without sparing the civilian population.

Aisha Farina, an Italian woman from Milan who converted to Islam and has publicly expressed her veneration for bin Laden as a reliable guide, has this to say: "Maybe all the Italians will end up converting. In any case, we will conquer you peacefully, because our numbers double every generation, but you are at zero growth." But Islam is advancing in other ways, too. In Mazara del Vallo in Sicily, since the end of the 1970s, a Tunisian community has enjoyed permission to preserve its identity in all respects, through Tunisian schools, teachers sent from Tunisia, Tunisian laws, and so on. Polygamy, though illegal, is tolerated there. In other places, Muslims open unauthorized schools that are not closed down. Practitioners perform infibulation on women, but no one is charged with the crime. The situation fosters an asymmetry among citizens before the law, according to which minorities, at first protected, are later privileged—further proof of the incompatibility of radical multiculturalism and the rule of law.

Moderate Islam or Muslims?

Thus, Bertacchini and Vanzan insist the Islamization of the West is not a phantasm: It is an intention and a fact that emerges from an objective examination of the evidence. The phantasm is so-called Moderate Islam, there being no institutional and moderate form of Islamic theology. There are moderate Muslims, some of whom see clearly and with perspective. But Islam itself, or rather the institutional religious culture of the Muslims, has reacted in its encounter with modernity by entrenching itself in fundamentalist positions. This is why it would not only be prudent, as Giacomo Cardinal Biffi has suggested, to discourage Islamic immigration to Europe, but also it would be self-destructive to encourage it without demanding reciprocation in terms of integration. An open and liberal society becomes paralyzed when it encounters a closed and incompatible civilization. Tolerance was promoted within Christian civilization in order to defuse its internal conflicts. But its introduction made sense, because tolerance was a value recognized by all parties, which were able to discover a theological foundation for it.

But Islam has no foundation for tolerance in the broad sense that characterizes our secular societies. In Saudi Arabia, Islam protects itself by banning the visible wearing of a cross. But how can it protect itself in Europe? There is not just the offense of girls wearing jeans. There is the offense of schools, newspapers, labor unions, women in leadership roles, cinema, television, libraries: It is the West in the sum total of its institutions that is a threat to Islam, not by intention but by its existence. Dialogue with moderate Muslims should not only be pursued, but also it should be broadened and the moderates supported in every way possible, to a greater extent even than the West supported the anti-Soviet resistance. But these approaches must be combined with the politics of distrust and suspicion, which would utterly discourage the presence of the Islamizers in Europe. These are, in fact, the ideological column of terrorism: You cannot fight the one without opposing the other.

Today, Islam challenges Europe to recognize the civil identity of the immigrants' religion. The challenge is a serious one, which Christianity has not been able to oppose on its own behalf with the same forcefulness. Finding a solution on a basis of equity will not be easy, but it is unthinkable that a Muslim minority should be granted the civil protection of its identity and the cultural recognition that the secularism sprung from the French Enlightenment presumes to withhold from the Christian majority.[43]

"Islamically Correct"

The 57 countries belonging to the Organization of Islamic Conference have called for the United Nations to adopt a resolution to condemn Islamophobia, in terms so vague that the then U.S. Ambassador to the UN, John Bolton, spoke of "unacceptable demands."[44] These countries also called upon the EU to draft and enact special laws against Islamophobia, including an ethical code of conduct for the European media, with particular attention to the defamation of Islam and its prophet. But whereas the UN seems not to have bowed to the Arab pressures, the EU is reported to have created an ad-hoc commission to develop guidelines for a glossary of "Islamically correct" terms to be used by officials and politicians. As an example, *Avvenire*, the voice of the Italian Bishops Conference, protests the term "Islamic terrorist," which the bishops think should be replaced by the following: "terrorist which advocates Islam outrageously and illegitimately."[45]

And in a shocking verdict, the Court of Appeal in The Hague has decided to serve Ayaan Hirsi Ali, the Somali-born Dutch politician who is subject to constant death threats for her criticism of Islam, an eviction order from a safe house in The Hague after a court upheld protests from neighbors concerned by the potential security risk she poses. As a result, Ali was reported to have left the country and moved to the United States to take a job with the American Enterprise Institute in Washington.

Aspects of the crisis of European civilization have been addressed by Marcello Pera, an MP for Forza Italia who served as Senate speaker during the last five years of Berlusconi's center-right government. A liberal secularist turned conservative who is seeking to develop an effective relationship with traditional Catholics under the leadership of Benedict XVI and adheres "to the doctrine of liberals who side with tradition" (his own words), Pera has spared no effort for a year now to revive *"occidentalità"* or *"westerness"*—that is, a sense of pride in being a Westerner. Though not a believing Christian, he believes that one must live *velut si Deus daretur* or, more exactly, *velut si Christus daretur*. On February 23, 2006, this senior politician presented his "Manifesto for the West, bearer of civilization" in defense of the West and its Christian roots. By mid-March the manifesto had attracted some 7,000 signatures from Italy and abroad; additional ones are being appended by the day.[46] Yet Senator Pera has not minced words in his criticism of today's Europe, which he argues (taking a phrase from Benedict) "no longer loves herself."[47] "If your embassies are stormed, your churches burned down, your Christian faithful slain, and you claim that the satirical cartoons went beyond the licit line, than you mean that you, Europe, are feeling responsible for such violence and are about to apologize," Pera wrote. "If the clash does exist and is against us, then we must win it. Because either we win the war which has been declared on us, or our civilization is doomed."[48]

A Serious Crisis

Among the gravest signs pointing to the seriousness of Europe's moral and spiritual crisis has been, in Senator Pera's view, its response to the fall of communism: Instead of celebrating victory, western Europe reacted like an abandoned orphan. Having lost its Christian identity, it was faced now with the prospect of relinquishing its anticommunist one. And there is also Europe's reaction to the attacks of September 11. "Hours after the attack on the Twin Towers and the Pentagon we were all Americans. The second day we were Americans only in the obituaries. The third day there were no Americans left in Europe."[49]

Pera continues, among the many other telling symptoms of Europe's spiritual crisis are the efflorescence of national laws contradicting the fundamental values of Christianity: The adoption of secularization as an ideology, or as a kind of state religion; the refusal of a role for religion to play in the public sphere; and the embrace of multiculturalism and of relativism, according to which all cultures and civilizations have the same dignity and the same value.

But Pera is concerned especially with the immigration issue. "When dealing with domestic policies relating to the integration of immigrants it is necessary to safeguard our own identity," he contends. "To speak only of the rights of minorities and to ignore the rights of the majority is a serious mistake. Multiculturalism is a weak doctrine and a wrong policy, which has already produced ghettos and social tensions in Europe."[50] Echoing Benedict XVI, Pera calls for the concept of reciprocity to be honored. "While to practice the Islamic religion is a right in countries of Christian tradition, this same right should not be denied when it is a matter of practicing the Christian religion in Islamic countries," he maintains. "It is surprising and sad that the West calls for respect for individual rights and forgets to include among them one of the most significant of them." It must be borne in mind, he points out, that "tolerance," "dialogue," "equality," and similar words are empty ones; ultimately, if we abandon our identity, they are terms of surrender. "Terrorists say they are attacking us because we are 'Jews and Christians.' Indeed, we are, and we should not deny it, conceal it or be ashamed of it," Pera proclaims. "Quite the contrary. We should reject the blackmailing argument according to which affirming our own identity amounts to arrogance vis-à-vis other people's identity. The opposite is true: To assert our identity is the first step, the prerequisite, for acknowledging the identity of others and for engaging in a real dialogue with them."[51]

Christian Diaspora

Those who have remaining doubts about Islam's offensive against the non-Islamic world need only recall that the onslaught is by no means out of the blue but rather dates as far back as the early 1980s, at least. For example, the 1980 resolution by the Islamic Council in Lahore, which was made public in London by *Mashrek International*, a journal of Islamic culture, called for "the Middle East region to be fully Islamic by 2000. The population groups who do not belong to the Islamic creed must be destroyed."[52] As to whether or not this objective has been achieved, the relevant figures speak for themselves. Christians in Turkey under the Ottoman Empire accounted for some 30 percent of the population;[53] today they number 100,000 or 0.15 percent of the population.[54]

In a passionate interview headlined, "We Christians targeted by Islamic hatred in the Holy Land," the Franciscan custodian of the Holy Sites, Father Pierbattista Pizzaballa reveals that in 1948, when Israel was established, Christians in Israel and the West Bank accounted for 14 percent of the population; today, they are hardly two percent. In 1950 Christians in Bethlehem accounted for 75 percent of its citizens; now they are less than 12 percent. And, if the trend continues, there will be no more Christians in the Holy Land in 20 years. Pizzaballa cites 93 cases of injustices committed between 2000 and 2004, a very partial list of the crimes and abuses against Christians, including assaults, rapes, murders, abductions, insults, theft of property, and the illegal occupation of real estate. "The Palestinian authorities are hardly doing anything to punish the culprits," he claims. "And in some cases among them were the very policemen . . . who should be protecting us."[55] A paramount example of this Christian Diaspora is Lebanon, a primary target of the Lahore resolution: After 15 years of civil war, over two million Christians were forced to leave the country and settle in Europe and the United States.

From this perspective, the Islamic immigration to the West must be seen as the second arm of the pincers. During the Synod of Bishops in the Vatican in 1999, the Archbishop Emeritus of the minuscule Catholic community of Izmir (Smirne) in Turkey, Msgr. Giuseppe Bernardini, deeply impressed the audience by recounting how, during an official meeting on Islamic-Christian dialogue, an unnamed senior Muslim delegate calmly and seriously proclaimed the Islamic plans for Europe in the following terms: "Thanks to your democratic laws we will invade you, thanks to our religious laws, we will dominate you."[56]

First Europe, Then America

A more recent example of how Europe and the United States are alike in having being targeted by Islamic fundamentalism is a broadcast by Sheik Nasser bin Suleiman Al-Omar over the Arab satellite network Al-Jazeera on April 19, 2006, in which the sheik predicted that Islam will take over Europe first and then America. His remarks were a follow-up to a previous interview by Al-Majd television on June 13, 2004, in which he claimed that "America is collapsing from within." Islam is "advancing according to a steady plan," Al-Omar promised his listeners, "to the point that tens of thousands of Muslims have joined the American army and Islam is the second religion in America." America, he concluded, is defeated. "I have no doubt, not even for a minute, that America is on its way to destruction." But the United States "will be destroyed gradually," he cautioned, and called upon Muslims to be "patient."

Libyan leader Muammar Al-Qadhafi declared in a speech aired over Al-Jazeera on April 10, 2006, that Islam will take over Europe without violence within a few decades.

> We have 50 million Muslims in Europe. There are signs that Allah will grant Islam victory in Europe—without swords, without guns, without conquests. The 50 million Muslims of Europe will turn it into a Muslim continent within a few decades. . . . Europe is in a predicament, and so is America. They should agree to become Islamic in the course of time, or else declare war on the Muslims.[57]

Patrick Buchanan argues in his latest book, *State of Emergency: The Third World Invasion and Conquest of America,* that civilizations die by suicide, not murder. A case in point is modern Italy, whose borders, for all practical purposes, are kept open to any and all comers, whether legal or illegal.

Demographic Suicide, the "Italian Way"

One means by which Italy is destroying herself is her plummeting birth rates. Pope John Paul II is said aptly to have referred to what he called "Europe's demographic suicide." As Massimo Introvigne, director of the Center for Studies on New Religions, has observed, birth rates below replacement levels are typical of dying civilizations. "The fact that children are not born is not only an economic but a moral and religious problem, and it is the sign of a terrible crisis of hope. Without hope, a civilization dies," he contends. "The moral crisis is also confirmed with the practice and legislation on subjects such as marriage and adoption by homosexual couples, euthanasia in Holland and experimentation with embryos."[58]

According to Riccardo Cascioli, president of Italy's European Center of Studies on Population, Environment and Development, cultural change, rather than economic incentive, is needed to counteract the demographic decline in many developed countries by promoting the family and encouraging procreation. Undoubtedly, improvements in fertility rates have occurred in some European countries after decades of pro-birth policies, but they are not sufficient to reverse the trend toward demographic winter. Commenting on the message Benedict XVI sent April 28, 2006, to the 12th plenary assembly of the Pontifical Academy of Social Sciences, in which he spoke of "a disturbing deficit of faith, hope and, indeed, love," Cascioli claimed that the Pope touched an exposed nerve. "A nation without children is a nation that does not even have a desire to fight for its own values and freedom, so much so that it believes it is not worthwhile to transmit them. And, because of this, it prepares to be a land of conquest for emerging civilizations," he continued. "The real issue has to do with the meaning we give to life, because there is no financial incentive that could convince me to have children, if I live withdrawn in myself and am afraid of the future." As for immigration, "Though [it] is necessary to replace the labor force in decline, the rate of [immigration] tends to increase rapidly, especially [by] young people, making more difficult the integration and transmission of the culture of the host country. Often, xenophobia arises as an angry reaction to this situation."[59] It is a suicidal delusion, contrary to all evidence, that specific accords with the relevant Mediterranean African countries are the ideal solution to stem the increasing tide of illegal immigration. In the case of Italy, most of the illegal immigrants landing on its shores are known to have departed from Libya, where over one million illegals are reported to be camped, patiently waiting their turn to be ferried across the sea to the "promised land" of Italy. But whenever an accord with Qadhafi's country, regularly hailed as the "intelligent" solution to the problem, is struck, it proves a resounding failure even as the Libyan leader raises the stakes, having recently said no to joint cooperation with Italy and Malta in helping patrol its coastline unless the EU provides him with more money and more resources.[60]

The Muslim Arab-born commentator Magdi Allam has accused Qadhafi of being the real culprit behind the chaotic immigration situation in the Mediterranean that has resulted in the drowning deaths of countless people: The Libyan, he charges, is cynically using his country's status as a transit point for desperate immigrants in order to blackmail Italy's government.[61] A recent bill permitting immigrants to become Italian nationals after five years of permanent residence, instead of ten as at present, goes a long way to show how, for the Italian government, "integration" is actually a process of accession to as many demands as possible made by the powerful immigrationist lobby. (Meanwhile, next year, Riccione, one of Italy's most famous sea resorts on the Adriatic coast, is quietly planning to set aside sections of beach reserved exclusively for Arab women. Suppose Christians were to request beaches reserved for those attired in decent bathing suits!)[62]

Communist Threat Replaced by Islam?

The suicidal syndrome is not unprecedented, having influenced Western—especially Western European—policy during the Cold War period. Indeed,

Samuel P. Huntington has argued that, "This new war between militant Islam and America has many similarities to the Cold War."[63] If Huntington is fundamentally correct in his premise that the Communist threat has been replaced by the Islamist threat, he is unjustified in concluding that "Militant Islamist groups . . . do not expect to convert Europe and America into Islamic societies," in contrast to "communists [who] wanted . . . to fundamentally change the democratic political and capitalist economic systems of Western societies into communist systems,"[64] as it is a basic tenet of the Koran that every Muslim must work to extend the "*uhmma*," the community of Muslim faithful, to the entire world.

The Islamist revolutionaries and those Westerners who overtly or covertly side with them view massive illegal immigration as the means to "peacefully" expunge, once and for all, the European peoples, and their descendants beyond the boundaries of Europe from the face of the earth. When those who are determined to defend the West's Christian identity are accused by these same revolutionaries and their Western accomplices of racism, one may fairly ask: But who are the real racists here?

Endnotes

[1] This chapter is a follow up to a previous study I coauthored with Guido Vignelli, *L'invasione silenziosa*, Il Minotauro, Rome, 2002. For a review of *L'invasione silenziosa*, see E. Christian Kopff, "When Immigration Becomes Migration," in *Chronicles*, (August 2002) or http://chroniclesmagazine. org/Chronicles/August2002/0802Kopff.html.

[2] *l'Unità*, September 23, 1990.

[3] In *L'invasione silenziosa*, p. 138.

[4] *Il Giornale*, February 23, 2006.

[5] Oriana Fallaci, "The Force of Reason," Rizzoli International, pp. 143–152 (Italian edition).

[6] See the Daily Telegraph Online, September 29, 2001, http://www.telegraph.co.uk/news/main. jhtml?xml=/news/2001/09/29/wberl29.xml.

[7] Oriana Fallaci, "The Force of Reason," p. 53.

[8] Oriana Fallaci, "The Force of Reason," pp. 135–137.

[9] *Los Angeles Times*, April 10, 2006.

[10] Alberto Carosa, "Too Tolerant, Too Long," *Catholic World Report*, December 2004, p. 32.

[11] Alberto Carosa, "Letter from the Netherlands," *Chronicles*, January 2006, p. 42.

[12] *Chronicles*, op. cit.

[13] Ann Coulter, "Brown Is the New Black," Human Events online, April 12, 2006.

[14] Terence P. Jeffrey, "Outnumbered 40,000 to 1," Human Events online, April 12, 2006.

[15] *Le Figaro*, November 7, 2005.

[16] *Corriere della Sera*, November 16, 2005.

[17] *Catholic World Report*, January 2006.

[18] *Corriere della Sera*, op. cit.

[19] *Catholic World Report*, op. cit.

[20] *London Sunday Telegraph* online, February 19, 2006.

[21] Anthony Browne, "The Folly of Mass Immigration," at http://www.opendemocracy.net/debates/article.jsp?id=10&debateId=96&articleId=1193.

[22] *Il Giornale*, June 7, 2006.

[23] See http://theroadtoemmaus.org/RdLb/21PbAr/Hst/US/Mexifornia.htm.

[24] "A Growing Gap: Living and Forgotten Christian Roots in Europe and the U.S.," delivered at the symposium, "The Spiritual Crisis of European Civilization," Vienna, April 27, 2006, at http://www.marcellopera.it/redazione-20060427-02/.

[25] See http://www.catholicworldnews.com/news/viewstory.cfm?recnum=37839 or the *Catholic World Report*, March 2005, p. 48.

[26] *Catholic World Report*, op. cit.

[27] *Avvenire*, the voice of Italy's bishops conference, April 27, 2006.

[28] *Chronicles*, July 2004, p. 43.

[29] *Washington Times*, April 4, 2006.

[30] *The Wanderer*, May 25, 2006.

[31] In news agency ZENIT, May 28, 2006.

[32] *The Tablet*, April 29, 2006.

[33] Livia Turco, *I nuovi italiani*, pp. 263–264.

[34] See http://www.catholicnewsagency.com/new.php?n=6569, dispatch from Paris dated April 25, 2006 in *Catholic News Agency*.

[35] Human Events online, April 20, 2006.

[36] See http://www.frontpagemagazine.com/Articles/ReadArticle.asp?ID=21820.

[37] See http://www.frontpagemag.com/Articles/ReadArticle.asp?ID=21609.

[38] See also http://www.frontpagemag.com/Articles/ReadArticle.asp?ID=216091.

[39] See *Vesten er i krig med islam* (The West is at War on Islam), *Aftenposten*, March 13, 2006.

[40] "Muslim Refugees Desecrate Belgian Churches," *Catholic News Agency*, May 9, 2006, http://www.catholicnewsagency.com/new.php?n=6683

[41] Stefano Nitoglia, *L'Islam com'è, un confronto con il Cristianesimo*, pp. 133–139.

[42] Roberto A. M. Bertacchini and Piersandro Vanzan, "The Islamic Question," *Studium* (n.1/ January–February 2006.

[43] See also Sandro Magister in http://www.chiesa.espressonline.it/dettaglio.jsp?id=48741&eng=y.

[44] *Il Giornale*, February 19, 2006.

[45] *Avvenire*, April 27, 2006.

[46] "The Pope and Pera: An 'Axis of Good'?" *Inside the Vatican*, April 2006.

[47] Marcello Pera and Joseph Ratzinger, *Senza radici*, p. 78, in the *Lettera a Joseph Ratzinger*, 2005, pp. 73–95.

[48] "Apologia dell'Occidente," *Il Messaggero*, April 3, 2006.

[49] "The Spiritual Crisis of European Civilization," paper by Marcello Pera presented at the Symposium "A Growing Gap: Living and Forgotten Christian Roots in Europe and the U.S.," Vienna, April 27, 2006, http://www.marcellopera.it/diario/2006/04/27/redazione-20060427-01/.

[50] Op. cit.

[51] Op. cit.

[52] Stefano Nitoglia, *Islam, anatomia di una setta*, 1994, p. 56.

[53] Op. cit., p. 59.

[54] *La civiltà cattolica*, May 6, 2006, p. 209.

[55] *Il Corriere della Sera*, September 4, 2005.

[56] Stefano Nitoglia, *L'Islam com'è, un confronto con il Cristianesimo*, 2002, pp. 121–122.

[57] See also the Washington-based MEMRI (The Middle East Media Research Institute), Special Dispatch Series, No. 1152, May 2, 2006.

[58] See *Catholic News Agency* ZENIT, August 18, 2006.

[59] Zenit, May 5, 2006.

[60] *Il Giornale*, August 27, 2006.

[61] *Il Corriere della Sera*, August 21, 2006.

[62] ANSA wire news agency dispatch, August 9, 2006.

[63] "Who Are We? The Challenges to America's National Identity," 2004, p. 358.

[64] Op. cit., p. 359.

13

FALSE RIGHTS, REAL DUTIES, PRUDENT RULES: A CHRISTIAN VIEW OF IMMIGRATION

by Guido Vignelli

We live in the era of rights. The liberal mindset, common by now to the right as well as the left, prompts us to view the aim of politics not as the achievement of the common (national or international) good, but as a balanced settlement and satisfaction of conflicting rights. Generally, when any "human right" (from the right to life to that of amusement) is asserted or upheld, it is interpreted in a purely ideological and figurative sense, namely as if it were a primary, universal, and necessary commitment, similar to the Kantian categorical imperative; as such, it becomes an absolute. Alas, history shows that any right that does not flow from a concrete duty becomes a sort of idol. From this distorted perspective, progressives argue for a right of emigration/immigration, which implies the right of reception by the host country. For them, this right is an absolute right, neither qualified by limitations nor balanced by duties; while the host nation, having itself no rights in respect of immigration, is accorded only the duty, likewise absolute, to accept the arriving immigrants. Thus, the right of emigration (immigration) is elevated to the status of an idol to which all other considerations must be sacrificed, including the host country's identity, security, and prosperity. Those who are not prepared to accept such a biased and sectarian perspective stand accused of being antidemocratic, xenophobic, and even racist, subject to public abhorrence and possible referral to international courts.

Limits and Conditions

Actually, there is no absolute right to immigration. That it is licit to flee religious or political persecution, or environmental and economic disasters, does not imply the absolute right to enter and occupy a foreign territory, whether or not this is done in a "peaceful" manner. Just as, in the moral domain, it is impermissible to commit evil to achieve good, so in the juridical realm it is illicit to violate another's right for the purpose of securing one's own right.

It is true that, in the case of immigration, the occupier's right may be urgent and primary, as against that of the occupied, but rather we are concerned here with an issue of justice. Moreover, the matter is not one of individual rights but of the requirements of the common good, which encompass and transcend the individual good. The issue is not a question of reconciling or balancing the occupant's rights with those of the occupied, according to the liberal theoretical pattern, but of asserting the right of nations and civilizations to resist destruction by attempting to meet the irrational demands of hundreds of thousands, or millions, of immigrants. The right to emigrate is licit and feasible only if it is "relativized" and set in the context of moral reality.

To assert a right to immigration without taking into account the legitimate demands of the receiving country is tantamount to asserting the duty of a people to destroy itself in order to save another—indeed, to proclaiming a preposterous right to invasion, which would amount to an obvious violation of international law equivalent to arguing that, whereas immigrants have only rights, their hosts have only duties—a formulation contradicted by an Italian bishop, Msgr. Maggiolini, who has stated that "There is no right to invade, neither a duty to let oneself be invaded."[1]

If it is illicit to enter a private house and turn it upside down, it is equally so to invade a nation, in the process disrupting its social, juridical, cultural, and religious institutions. Moreover, just as the wronged householder is justified in calling the police, so would be the nation's government in resorting to the international police, as, for example, the government of Palestine is doing today. And if the Palestinian people are entitled to their own identity, why shouldn't the Italian people be as well? Threatened by immigrant invasion, the host nation is entitled to decide for itself if it wishes to accept any immigrants at all. Even if it decides to open its doors, the state has the right—the duty, in fact—to safeguard the common good by establishing filters, raising fences, setting entrance quotas and conditions of acceptance in respect of those immigrants it does agree to receive.

Prima sibi caritas

The proponents of unqualified welcome for immigrants are wont to cite the demands of Christian charity, or at least of natural law. But here again, ambiguity is introduced by the fact of a value having been transformed into an idol.

Actually, the relevant Christian doctrine is *prima sibi caritas*. By divine commandment, primary charity is that due to oneself, one's family, one's fatherland,

and most of all to one's Christian civilization. The primary and ordered love of oneself produces, by natural and necessary extension, love of others, the love of strangers. Christ's commandment is clear: "Thou shalt love thy neighbor as thy self." But "neighbor" means less he who is near to us physically or geographically than he to whom we are bound by obligations, family relationship, and affinities, especially of the supernatural kind. But most of all, our neighbor is that person whose natural or supernatural welfare depends on our action and on our witness. This understanding extends beyond the spiritual life to that of the social and civil realm, according to the dictates of natural law.

Normally, only those who preserve the fullness of their own good can aspire to contribute to the good of others, in the temporal as well as spiritual domain. Nobody can supply what he does not possess, nobody can pass on that legacy that he failed or refused to defend, but instead squandered as an irresponsible "prodigal son" no "good Samaritan" can assist a needy man with assets that he has dissipated. This rule applies in the case of "foreign aid." If Europe turns her back on the Christian civilization that was entrusted to her by Providence, thus betraying her historical mission, she will be unable as well to benefit the less civilized and fortunate peoples, while sliding with them into barbarity and chaos.

Etienne Gilson, following St. Thomas Aquinas, holds as follows:

> A man can render himself useful to his neighbor only insofar as he maintains himself in his own nature and accomplishes his own good. He may consecrate himself to a universal mission only if he fulfils his own specific mission in accordance with God's plan.[2]

If, on the contrary, on pretext of "making oneself the neighbor," that man repudiates his nature and loses his own identity, or if he performs a universal role at the cost of renouncing his personal mission, that man has dissipated himself and thus failed to promote the good of others. The rule applies not only to individuals, but also to families and peoples.

Xenomaniacal Solidarism

Modern solidarism has invented a new and subversive obligation to "love the stranger." Thus, humanitarianism asserts an ideological "love for the far away" to replace the evangelical "love of neighbor." Moreover, both "stranger" and "far away" are construed less in the geographical than in the cultural sense. Xenomaniacal solidarism expects Christian families and peoples to promote "world peace" and "brotherhood," paradoxically by repudiating the identity they should embrace and squandering the assets entrusted to their stewardship and charitable conscience.

Self-sacrifice and self-repudiation on the part of the West (naturally, nothing of the sort is demanded of the Third World) have nothing to do with asceticism, being instead unholy: the renunciation of a legacy not of sin but of civilization and of holiness, by which merits become faults and faults, merits, amounting to apostasy that promises to lead the apostates into a future of slavery. Europe's refusal of its identity is harbinger also of global conflict, since, as Augusto Del Noce has warned, "The demise of Europe would not be thus the beginning of a new universality, but would perhaps encompass the definitely denied hope of any future universality whatsoever; the downfall of European mediation would imply the mere unresolved contraposition between occidentalism and orientalism."[3]

The "National Preference"

The biblical injunction to love our neighbor permits us to declare a "national preference," or "preferential option for the nation," based not on a shabby national egoism but on the prudent primacy of the common good.

As Pope Pius XII said, "There exists an order established by God, which requires a more intense love and a preferential good done to those people that are joined to us by special ties. Even our Lord has given the example of this preference towards the country, when He cries on the destruction of Jerusalem."[4] And Pope John Paul II has described native traditions and national identities as goods worthy of defense and talents to yield:

> We have to do all we can to assume this spiritual heritage, to confirm, maintain and develop it. This is an important task for all the societies, but perhaps more in particular for those which must defend their own existence and essential identity of their nation from the risks of a destruction generated from outside or of a decomposition from inside.[5]

In fact, the migratory invasion of the West represents the concrete union of these two dangers: the destruction from outside, and the decomposition from inside.

Applied to the problem of immigration, national preference establishes the principle that the acceptance of immigrants must be subordinated to (and measured by) the defense of the common good—the spiritual good especially—of the receiving nation. It is necessary "to supervise in order that all that favors harmony has to be integrated and that, on the contrary, all that breaks the harmony has to be repulsed. We cannot risk inserting in a community heterogenic elements which expect to remain extraneous and which finish by ruining the community. We would commit a serious crime against the vital principle of the society."[6]

The Supremacy of the Common Good

Propagandists for immigrationism, both moderates and extremists, distort the basic formulation of the problem. The issue is not whether to suspend the rights of the host country in order to guarantee those of the guest, or even how to balance those of the one against those of the other. It is that the asserted rights of the immigrants, if they are detrimental to the common good of the receiving nation, are not authentic rights at all but rather *abuses*, and that recognition of these supposed "rights" is opposed both to national and international justice and to the common good of all. Pope Pius XII, asserting the right to emigrate, formulated it in this strong, conditional way:

> If a Country offers the possibility to host a great number of men, it will not have to forbid, for insufficient reasons and unjustified causes, the access to needy and honest foreigners, less than reasons of public utility are not opposed, to evaluate with the maximum scruple.[7]

This "public utility" is precisely the common good of the host country. The right to immigrate, therefore, is not absolute but limited by certain conditions. The first of these is the ability of the receiving nation to accept immigrants without serious consequences for the common welfare. Even the document, published by the Papal Commission Justitia et Pax, regarding the apostolic constitution, although favorable to immigration, admits this restrictive condition:

> It is naturally due to the public powers, that they are responsible of the common good, to establish which is the proportion of refugees or immigrants that their Country is in a position to receiving, taking into account of its possibilities of work and its perspectives of development. . . . The State must guarantee that situations of serious social imbalance are not created, accompanied from sociological phenomena

of refusal that can have place when the presence of a too much wide group of persons of another culture is perceived like a directed threat to the identity and the habits of the local community.[8]

Conclusion

Christian doctrine does not require that a civil people, in exercise of the virtue of social charity, must deny its cultural tradition and religious ethics, submit to invasion by foreigners, or to political, legal, and economic ruin. It does not teach that a society succumb to chaos, or commit suicide, in the illusory hope of saving an ill-fated people. The right and duty of legitimate defense belongs not only to individuals but also—above all—to society, especially if what is at stake is not just its peace, order, and security, but also its Christian identity, hard-won by centuries of sacrifice, conflict, and prayer.

Endnotes

[1] *Il Giornale*, Milan, November 29, 1998.

[2] Cfr. E. Gilson, *Le thomisme*, Vrin, Paris, 1972, pp. 227–236.

[3] A. Del Noce, *Rivoluzione, risorgimento, tradizione*, Giuffre, Milan, 1993, p. 270.

[4] Pius XII, *Summi pontificatus*, Encyclical of October 20, 1939.

[5] John Paul II, Apostolic letter for the International Year of Youth, 1985.

[6] M. Berger, *Immigration: approche chrétienne*, Action Familiale et Scolaire, Paris, 1985, p. 85.

[7] Pio XII, Exul familia, Apostolic constitution on migrants' aid, August 1, 1952.

[8] Papal Commission Justitia et Pax, The Church against racism, November 3, 1988, § 29.

14

DYSTOPIA UNLIMITED: OR, THE FLOWERS OF REGRESS (AND CATASTROPHE)

by Chilton Williamson, Jr.

Utopia Limited: Or, the Flowers of Progress is the title of one of the least known of W. S. Gilbert's and Sir Arthur Sullivan's Savoy Operas, which premiered in 1893 in the last years of the reign of Queen Victoria, Empress of India.

The plot of the opera has to do with the monarch of the South Sea Island of Utopia, King Paramount, a fervent admirer of English culture and institutions who rules over a lazy and rather backward people and has sent his daughter, Princess Zara, to college in England. On her return home, she brings with her six paragons — or "flowers" — of English culture, including a company promoter who proceeds to turn the country into a limited liability company. In result, everything in Utopia now runs so smoothly that sickness, crime, litigation, and so forth no longer exist, and the populace is starving to death for want of corrective employment. At this point, the princess realizes her error. She had neglected to include the great English institution of Government by Party in her plan of reform! Install Party in Utopia, she insists, and "No political measures will endure, because one Party will assuredly undo all that the other Party has done; and while grouse is to be shot, and foxes worried to death, the legislative action of the country will be at a standstill! Then there will be sickness in plenty, endless lawsuits, crowded jails, interminable confusion in the Army and Navy, and, in short, general and unexampled prosperity!"

King Paramount's plan to renovate the culture, customs, and institutions of his country by importing a foreign standard reminds me of the determination of our own government, over the past four decades, to reconstruct (some would say, deconstruct) the United States according to a pattern that differs radically from the original. Yet, by comparison with the plans our current rulers entertain, the king's agenda was modest. He might have invited the Flowers of Progress to bring with them their sisters and their cousins, whom they reckoned up by dozens, and their aunts! Better yet, he might have encouraged the Flowers to persuade the entire British populace to emigrate to Utopia. Even then, he would have needed to do more had he wished to match the revolutionary boldness of future American governments. It would have behooved him to become a Francophile, as well as an Anglophile; to import Jacobin ideas, and as many Frenchmen as wished to come to his country! And after that, there would still be Italy, Spain, North Africa, and the Indian and Asian subcontinents to absorb, culturally and demographically! Where would the process ever end? Only in the fanciful libretto of a satirical operetta, one might conclude—absent the concrete historical reality of the immigration policies that the United States government has pursued from the passage of the Immigration Act of 1965 down to the present time.

Whether *Utopia Limited* has a happy ending is a matter very much in the eye of the beholder. The principals all intermarry and go on to live affluent lives in a context of social and cultural chaos. That, too, reminds me of the aspirations our "leaders" have for our country today. Yet opinion polls and popular reaction to their transformational program suggest that there are many millions of people in this country for whom such a prospect amounts to a dystopia rather than a utopia, and who would consider this dystopia to be rather unlimited than limited in its nature.

There is a strange and unfortunate delusion abroad in the United States today. It is the notion that mass immigration of the nearly unregulated kind is—indeed, must be—an unqualified good for everyone concerned, immigrant and native-born alike: a universal benefit granting innumerable additional benefits entailing no offsetting costs to anybody.

Like most delusions, this one is utterly counterintuitive. Common sense, as well as historical experience, suggests that an influx of scores of millions of variegated aliens drawn from the world over will *not* make American society "stronger" that diversity is *not* our strength; that tens of millions of immigrant workers *must* take jobs from American workers, not create others for them to take; that hiring immigrants to do the "jobs Americans won't do" for lower pay and fewer, if any, benefits (some of these constitutionally mandated) than Americans would agree to accept *must* be destructive to the welfare of the American working class; that enrolling the wretched of the world in American welfare programs in return for ... what? ... *does* not, and could not possibly, add up to a positive economic exchange for the country; that porous borders *necessarily* compromise national security in an age of international terrorism and epidemic disease; and that the explosive population growth in our country, fueled chiefly by Third World immigration, *must* nullify the environmental legislation of the past hundred years, further threaten endangered species, deplete our natural resources—including fresh water supplies—constrict the future of American agriculture, and make the preservation of what wilderness still remains finally impossible.

Common sense and a knowledge of history, however, are precisely what our governing class presently lacks and has no interest in learning. We are said to have passed beyond what Francis Fukuyama calls "the end of history," as C. S. Lewis's Prince Caspian and his companions aboard the *Dawn Treader* passed—*almost!*—beyond the very end of their world:

> *Where the waves grow sweet,*
> *Doubt not, Reepicheep,*
> *There is the utter East.*

In the utter East, our masters assure us, the old rules and restrictions no longer apply. *The End of History! The End of Limits! The End of Reality as We Knew It!* That, again, of course, depends on what our understanding of reality is.

The Great Immigration Delusion—this assurance that mass immigration is a "win-win" proposition for all parties involved (which is everyone)—is not an especially widespread fantasy, and it does not run deep in American life, as the current upwelling of popular anti-immigration protest indicates. It does, however, run consistently in the right circles, where it has been accepted as dogma for a couple of generations now by the people who create what is called "mainstream opinion," as well as by those who translate mainstream opinion into statute law.

According to mainstream opinion, if immigration is arguably good for America and native Americans, then it stands to reason that it is inarguably good for the immigrants themselves. How could a humane and progressive country, the moral and political beacon to the world, possibly deny the huddled and oppressed of the world free and unquestioned entry into the Land of Dreams—what the Chinese call the Golden Country—when their presence confers no less than what the United States stands to gain by accepting them here? Immigration benefits the receiving country, and the immigrants received by it, about equally. Where mass immigration to the United States is concerned, there can be no losers. Why, therefore, should immigration be an issue at all, far less a problem?

So, at any rate, goes the official argument: The party line promoted by government (the federal government, especially), the U.S. Chamber of Commerce, industrial agriculture, organized labor, the Sierra Club, multicultural enthusiasts, immigration and ethnic advocates, the media. Unfortunately for all concerned, the party line, in this case, as in most others, is quite simply wrong—and dead wrong, at that.

A Disappointing Future

My general argument, conveniently abridged, is simply this: Everything that makes our country agreeable to us Americans, and attractive to foreigners who wish to come here, stands to be wrecked by mass immigration to the United States, making the place nearly uninhabitable for the native-born and a serious disappointment to the lately arrived foreign-born, their children, and their descendants.

Of course, we and they, natives and immigrants, will not be dismayed equally by the same transformations. Americans have traditionally valued, as their actual birthright, wilderness, wide open spaces, low population density, and free and easy contact with an unpolluted outdoors. Immigrants, who come, almost exclusively, from the urban slum areas of densely overpopulated countries, have no interest in these things, if they do not indeed find them alien, intimidating, and even abhorrent. However, they do certainly value those environmentally related benefits they never enjoyed at home—not least, for instance, an abundance of fresh and uncontaminated water.

A two-part series of investigative articles appearing in the *New York Times* in the fall of 2006 described the critical dearth of water in India, whose population is exploding in proportion to its burgeoning economy.[1] Owing to urbanization and the expanding requirements of agriculture, the subcontinent's water table is declining drastically. Farmers with healthy wells are selling their water at high prices to those in need; others are drilling boreholes to tap and pump groundwater faster than the monsoon rains can replenish them. The situation amounts to a critical threat to India's economic and political ambitions to become a major power, calling into question the country's ability to feed even her present-day population of well over a billion people. In the great cities, such as Mombay, middle-class women are compelled to devote the better part of their day to finding and hauling water for household needs as well as for drinking; much of it is hauled by train at enormous expense to the government. (Similarly, in the American West, the Ogallala Aquifer underlying the Western Plains states has been substantially drawn down over the past century by agriculture and urbanization, while the Colorado River draining the desert West is oversubscribed in respect of water rights to the point where politicians have seriously proposed that all farmers drawing water from the Colorado River be paid to cease crop cultivation *in perpetuo*.)

Other benefits much appreciated by immigrants include cheap food in plenty and a sufficiency of energy-related resources to heat and light their homes, power their appliances, and fuel their cars. All of these goods are dependent, of course, upon reliably vast supplies of oil, a commodity whose increasing scarcity and cost in the United States are among the main causes for President George W. Bush's disastrous war on Iraq. Ideological optimists insist that advanced computer-related technology promises an economy far less oil-driven than today's; yet the manufacture of computers, including the plastics of which they are substantially composed, requires a considerable amount of oil and petroleum products, just as computer chips must be washed in billions of gallons of water (plain H_2O that may well, in the not-too-distant future, become better known as "white gold.") Similarly, freedom from disease and epidemic, much of which is caused by overcrowding and pollution, is appreciated by immigrants as also by Americans, who learned long ago to take good health for granted. Yet the massive immigrant influx to this country over the past several decades has reintroduced into the United States many dangerous diseases, such as tuberculosis, that were long ago eradicated here, while introducing other, and equally dangerous, ones, such as West Nile virus and untreatable forms of TB, with dengue—which is rampant in Latin America, including Mexico—all too likely to follow soon.

Clearly, native- and foreign-born alike have a great deal at stake in the maintenance of the U.S. population at what environmentalists call sustainable levels. With that population estimated by some demographers as likely to reach 500 or 600 million people by the end of the 21st century—almost entirely as a result of mass immigration—it is clear that immigration at the present level of about a million a year (not counting the uncountable illegal immigrants) must produce adverse environmental and social effects that will be felt by all of us living here in America, no matter what our origins.

After crucial concerns for natural resources and the land, we have the future of constitutional government in America to consider: not George W. Bush's fascist democratism but our Anglo-American political institutions, including the rule of law and respect for order in government. Whoever is familiar with the history of the Mexican Revolution from 1910 to (effectively) 1928 should recognize the Mexican exodus to the United States for what it is: a version of *reconquista* that must inevitably entail, in time, the Mexicanization of the American political system—that is to say, its destruction and barbarization. Here again, Americans have the most to lose; but the Mexican-Americans themselves will have much as well. After all, the chief reason for their inability to make a comfortable living—and to live securely while doing so—in their home country is the thoroughgoing corruption and endemic violence of Mexican society.

Why undertake the rigors of illegal entry to start a new life in America, if you are to import the old life with you—on your back, so to speak? (This explains why a significant percentage of Hispanic Americans are in favor of immigration restriction and against an amnesty plan for illegal immigrants.) The eventual grafting of Third World politics onto the American system inevitably will institutionalize violence, corruption, and tyranny in our own country.

I know of no episode more representative of Mexican politics than the assassinations of President Francisco Madero, the gentle but ineffectual and rather unworldly revolutionary who improbably succeeded in overthrowing President Porfirio Díaz in 1911, and of his brother Guastavo. When the civil war had lasted already three years, General Victoriano Huerta, Madero's commander-in-chief, was determined to overthrow the president and set himself in his place. Huerta began by inviting Gustavo to lunch at Restaurante Gambrinus, one of Ciudad México's best eating establishments. Over the meal, he casually requested Gustavo's revolver, a request in which his guest trustingly acquiesced. Huerta instantly pointed the gun at the other man's chest and informed him he was under arrest. Huerta's co-conspirators thereupon removed Gustavo Madero to the Ciudadela, where a kangaroo court pronounced him guilty of treason. On his way from "court" to another part of the Cuidadela, rebel soldiers attacked him, and one of them stabbed the one-eyed Madero with a sword in his good eye. Now wholly blind and pouring blood, Gustavo staggered about, flailing helplessly with his fists, while a mob gathered to taunt and mock him uproariously. His torment, however atrocious, was short, as he was dispatched minutes later by a shot from a soldier's revolver, on his way to the firing squad. Three days later, his brother's turn came when the president was shoved into a car, driven to a street behind the penitentiary, and dispatched with a single shot to the neck as he stepped from the vehicle.[2]

An echo, however faint, of this scene can be discerned in another incident occurring 91 years later (July 22, 2004) and in another country, when a Colorado activist named Terry Graham attended a public forum in Denver. The forum, "Immigration: What Reform Will Bring to Our Nation," was sponsored by First Data/Western Union, a company that realizes a huge (and presumably growing) annual profit derived from the transfer of remittances sent by Mexican immigrants in the United States to their relatives south of the Rio Grande. (According to Joe Guzzardi, the California columnist, "First Data, through its various subsidiaries and foundations, has provided substantial funding for organizations that encourage massive illegal immigration.") Graham took a seat in the North High School auditorium and activated a tape recorder to capture the proceedings. Upon rising to remark publicly on the fact that every one of the speakers "happened" to be in favor of mass immigration and to demand that participants with opposing arguments be invited to speak, she was instantly assaulted by Julissa Molina-Soto, a 31-year-old Mexican immigrant of uncertain legal status. According to an eye-witness account, "[T]he woman suddenly launched herself from about four seats away at Ms. Graham and began beating on Ms. Graham's head with two closed fists. Every three or four blows, the woman would grab at Ms. Graham's hair and continue to hit Ms. Graham while pulling Ms. Graham's hair. She would then release her hair and resume beating Ms. Graham's head with closed fists."

The Molina-Soto female abated her attack on Miss Graham long enough to seize the recorder and tear the tape from the machine, after which she renewed her assault on her victim. Molina-Soto was arrested in due course by the police. Terry Graham received treatment by paramedics and afterward was led from the auditorium under a hail of verbal threats and abuse.[3]

The Mexican proclivity to violence, which has so far displayed itself mainly at the grassroots level of American politics, has been observable for years at sports events—for example, the violence and looting attendant on soccer matches in which a Mexican team is a participant—and neighborhood incidents in which Mexican immigrants have run the Mexican flag up the school flagpole in defiance of protesting American students. (In at least one instance that I have read of, the Americans were constrained from countermeasures by their own complacent, and effectively complicit, police officers.) So far, the Mexican immigrant population has shown little interest, beyond the notorious street protests on behalf of Bush's amnesty legislation in the spring of 2006, in involving itself in American politics—much to the dismay, one suspects, of Mexico City, whose extension of dual citizenship to Mexican-Americans is a clear-and-present challenge to the integrity of the American political system. But involvement is coming, urged not only by the Mexican government and by Mexican ethnic lobbies such as La Raza and MALDEF but also by the two American national parties, with the encouragement of the President of the United States himself! And as it comes, it will gradually extend the sort of street violence of which Terry Graham was a victim into the halls and institutions of American governance. This result is made all the more likely by the cocky self-assurance, frequently shading into aggression, on the part of the illegal population, which understands perfectly well that the sympathies of the American establishment, bent on deconstructing the United States and, as Bertoldt Brecht once put it, electing a new people to suit the existing government, are with them—politically, economically, culturally, and racially.

It is an interesting question whether the violence of Mexico's drug wars today imitates the violence of Mexican politics, or vice versa. Since the Mexican political structure and culture antecede the drug culture by centuries, it is likely that the first hypothesis is the correct one. Either way, the drug wars that contribute so greatly to the overall climate of violence in Mexico are likely to be a major contributory factor to the coming barbarization of society and politics in the United States that is the process of Mexicanization. Certainly, the barbarities committed by the Mexican drug lords and their henchmen are a direct reflection, and extension, of the atrocities perpetrated by Mexican politicians and their armies during the Mexican Civil War.

According to the *New York Times* (October 26, 2006), "An underworld war between drug rivals is raging in Mexico, medieval in its barbarity, its foot soldiers operating with little fear of interference from the police, its scope and brutality unprecedented, even in a country accustomed to high levels of drug violence."

In a single comprehensive sentence, the *Times* attempts to promote two staggering misconceptions regarding Mexico that cry out for correction. First, the barbarity here alluded to is not in the least medieval, but it is quintessentially Mexican in nature. Second, Mexico is not accustomed to drug violence only, but to social and political violence as well. As reported by James C. McKinley, Jr., a late-night party under way in a *tabernero* in Uruapan was interrupted by men in military uniform brandishing machine guns who, after ordering the patrons to freeze, proceeded to roll five bloody human heads from a plastic trash bag across the floor. "This is not something you see every day," the *tabernero* remarked to Mr. McKinley. "Very ugly." Ugly enough, and then some: The five victims, dealers of methamphetamines who were themselves addicted to the drug they were paid to peddle on the street, had been kidnapped the day before from their meth lab. The following evening, the kidnappers severed their heads from their still-living bodies with a bowie knife and transported them to the *Sol Y Sombra* for an effective display.[4]

In truth, atrocities of this sort are indeed something one sees — or hears of, anyway — in Mexico almost every day, while remaining virtually unknown, even among drug rings, in the United States. (The Saturday Night Massacre involving Al Capone's gang was, by comparison, a model of a humanitarian execution.) In the months preceding the Uruapan killings, drug-related killings included 24 beheadings; an attack on a police station by men armed with bazookas and grenades; the kidnapping (in full daylight) of several law officials; and the shooting or fatal torture of 123 other officials, including three prosecutors and two judges. In 2005, an estimated 1,800 people were murdered in the drug wars, a total investigators expect will be exceeded by the figures for 2006. The Mexican government argues that the escalating violence is a sign of its success in breaking up the major, family-dominated cartels, in result of which the lesser sharks are engaged in a vicious battle to pick off the spoils. In point of fact, there is hardly need of reason or explanation for such inhuman cruelty, atrocity being as Mexican as *sopapillas*. Surely it is only by great good fortune that the 2006 election, in which Felipe Calderón (of the Partido Actión Nacional) defeated Andrés Manuel López Obrador (of the Partido de la Revolución Democrática), and López, rather than concede, organized massive street protests lasting for weeks, did not develop into a sort of mini-civil war attended by the usual bloodshed. As I write, the takeover of the city of Oaxaca, which left-wing protesters have paralyzed for months, by the federal police sent in by President Fox in his last weeks in office seems headed for just such a conclusion.

While the importation of a tradition of self-indulgent violence, sadism, lawlessness, intemperance, intolerance, and irresponsibility is surely the greatest threat to the American political system posed by mass immigration from the South, it is hardly the only foreseeable result of the Mexicanization of the American polity. Tens and scores of added millions of desperately poor and uneducated proletarians (a large proportion of them without English) imply an inordinate boost in welfare costs, entailing a significant expansion of an already oppressive and intrusive bureaucracy at every level of government and of increased government regulation as a means of coping with perfervid population growth. Anglo-American freedoms, though they still mean much to us, appear to be of secondary importance at best to most immigrants, the majority of whom are drawn here by the lure of wealth, not by Western institutions beyond the economic ones. Yet, as the country is increasingly swamped by Third World peoples bringing with them their own institutions, or lack of such, it seems likely that the American standard of living must erode, in time, along with its public standards, to the point where an Asian-style bureaucracy will have less and less plunder to deliver to the mass of its importunate citizens. Here again, Americans have more to lose, but the immigrant population has much—in the long run, anyway—to forfeit as well.

Consider next the corrosive effect that mass immigration has had, and continues to have, on the traditional American core culture and America's unique civilization, tracing back a full four centuries now. Proponents of mass immigration and multiculturalism wax ecstatic on the subject of how previous generations of immigrants have enlightened, sophisticated, and further civilized what amounted historically to a narrow provincial offshoot of the British Isles and Northern Europe. But that is hardly the point. What matters is the imposition of numerous alien supplicant cultures upon the indigenous one, which, whatever its shortcomings, represented the cultural and intellectual flowering of a unique, interesting, and spectacularly successful people. Naturally, the displacement of the Old America and the Old Americans who made it means nothing to the immigrants, who are more likely to be reassured—even gratified—by their downward trajectory.

On the other hand, they, along with us, hardly stand to benefit in the end by an America that is perennially in a state of being, rather than of becoming—of adolescence, rather than of maturity—resulting in a cultural and philosophical confusion that does not permit an assurance of moral and metaphysical certainty, but only of chaos. Of crucial importance in this respect is the future of Christianity, whose further decline and diffusion through the mass immigration of non-Christians should be feared by anyone—native or immigrant—as the moral and religious traditions, restraints, and inhibitions that so far have kept mutually hostile and suspicious members of a "diverse" population from each other's throats continue to erode.

Likewise, in the violently contested sphere of economics (economics being, in modern times, queen among the sacred social sciences, as theology was formerly queen of all human knowledge), the American seeking to maintain his economic well-being and the immigrant seeking to attain it for himself have little to gain and everything to lose (if not in their own lifetimes, then surely in those of their descendants) from the economic consequences of mass immigration, which are already seen to include the steady proletarianization of the populace; lower wages for the working class and greater profits for globalist corporations; steeper and wider economic divisions between the classes; increased taxation; greater dependence on foreign resources; and continued economic centralization.

And take now the problem of present cultural fragmentation and eventual balkanization, hitherto experienced by Americans in mild form compared with the ferocity so many immigrants seek to escape by leaving home to come here. Racial, ethnic, and religious rivalry; civil war, civil strife, *reconquista*; increased security problems relating to terror; the erosion of personal liberties consequent upon these things; and the further centralization of power followed by the eventual rise of a police state: All of these evils are potentially a part of America's future, thanks to unrestrained and uninterrupted immigration over the past 40 years. *Cui bono?* The answer looks to be, those among the native-born whose sole concern is for the immediate present, and themselves in the present.

In conclusion, there is the prospect of racial and ethnic constituency politics carried over into foreign policy. This, of course, is a phenomenon with which Americans have been familiar for generations now, but which an increasingly diverse population ensures in aggravated form: an even more aggressively intrusive approach to international affairs than prevails today, fueled by self-destructive wars of aggression or distraction as Washington vainly seeks to accommodate the agenda of one group of colonizers here, on behalf of its home country, after another.

Water seeks its own level. The importation of the Third World to America must end in America's being added to the Third World. Once again—*cui bono?* When salt has lost its savor, what further use or value has it? Having opposed immigration in candid terms for more than two decades now, I am all too familiar with the arguments—or, rather, the nonarguments—of people who raise their voices in righteous anger, stop their ears, and cover their eyes at any mention of restriction. The immigrationists, who are really delusionists, seem to me comparable to passengers on a ship enveloped in a traveling pocket of impenetrable fog who, angered by the persistent blasts of a foghorn emanating from a lighthouse at the end of a rocky spit from where the keeper enjoys unimpeded visibility, yell out to him in chorus with angry demands that he cease and desist, by turning the foghorn off.

Act Local, Act Global

The foregoing is, in part, an attempt at touching upon, summarizing, drawing out, and contextualizing the earlier-appearing chapters in this book. Left unconsidered until now is Roger McGrath's chapter, "National Sovereignty Goes Local," in which the author surveys local responses in the United States to illegal immigration—that is, steps taken recently by town and city councils, county commissions, and state legislatures to protect their citizens from the millions of unlawful aliens present within their respective jurisdictions. There are not a great many people who argue from constitutional principle against state and local initiatives in what is, after all, a matter constitutionally entrusted to the federal government, although political liberals and members of minority groups have often made loud objection to them on the ground of purely emotional reactions. So far as I know, no one has yet worked up a reasoned argument criticizing local action on the illegal-immigrant front as intrinsically dangerous to the division of federal powers and the constitutionally fixed balance appertaining to responsibilities delegated to the states, the localities, and the federal government, respectively. Perhaps this has something to do with the fact of local response to illegal immigration having arisen almost overnight; in that case, more likely than not, someone is devising such an argument even as I write these lines.

Even so, nonfederal immigrationist office holders have challenged local action in opposition to illegal immigration on an *ad hoc* and superficial basis. For example, in April 2006, Governor Janet Napolitano vetoed an Arizona legislative bill expanding the state's trespass law to arrest illegal immigrants anywhere in the state, on grounds that immigration arrests should remain a federal responsibility (as to why, the governor seems not to have explained). Similarly, in August 2005, District Court Judge L. Phillips Runyon of New Hampshire ruled that immigration enforcement is the prerogative of Congress and that, therefore, the arrest of an illegal immigrant on a trespass charge by a local law-enforcement officer was unconstitutional. Confronted by such intransigence higher up, local office holders whose constituents have found themselves beleaguered by illegal immigration have often responded with a practical, commonsensical stoicism. Thus, the mayor of Costa Mesa, California, who would like to be able to mobilize his police force in a crackdown on illegal immigrants, says of what actions he is currently able to take, "It's what I am able to do right now." It is the prerogative of bigger political fish, like Governor Perry of Texas, to assert that "Texas cannot wait for Washington, DC, to act." Perry's boldness, resolve, and independence are surely admirable. And yet, is it conceivable that the mobilization of state and local governments to deal with as many as 20 million illegal aliens is fraught with the potential to produce yet another of those dangerous political deformations that mass immigration threatens to wreak on the American political system?

Here we may begin by considering whether illegal immigration should really be perceived as a local versus a national problem, rather than a national versus a global problem. Dr. McGrath works from the assumption that the crisis is progressively a local one, best addressed from the bottom up. On the other hand, the Sierra Club has been insisting for years that the immigration problem is a subset of the international migration problem, while migration is directly the result of the global population crisis, absent a solution for which subsidiary issues like migration and immigration can never be resolved. In other words, the Sierra Club, and people who think as its members do, insist that the immigration business must be tackled from the top down.

It all depends, in part, on how you experience, and therefore perceive, the problem. A Denver city councilman can scarcely be expected, in his role as city father of a town inundated by immigrants, to have much of a care for the global population issue. Similarly, the president of the Sierra Club, ensconced in his richly appointed office in the clouds above San Francisco, is unlikely to be as concerned about illegal aliens squeezing out the native-born in the local restaurant and hotel trades as he is in the unavailability of contraceptives in India; he is occupied with far grander things than the California labor market.

Is he right or wrong to take the global perspective on immigration, whether legal or illegal? Or the Minuteman, defending his acre of border turf? The answer seems to me to be, in the crisis, purely a matter of efficacy. It is all a question of how much can be best accomplished at what level of response in present circumstances.

The jurisdictional issue as it relates to the control of illegal immigration is hardly comparable to that in respect of the control of public education, a question deeply imprinted by strong social, cultural, political, and constitutional concerns. There is simply no justification of any sort, in what is supposed to be our system of government, for federal control of education, for which local and state governments were intended to have exclusive responsibility. Indeed, the federal government is entrusted under the Constitution with defending the nation against invasion, protecting the integrity of the states, controlling immigration and naturalization, and so forth. But not even the critics of a local response to illegal immigration argue that Washington cannot delegate the enforcement of its immigration laws to state and local authorities; while certainly no extralegal standards exist to discourage such a delegation of power.

"Local," in the end, is a relative term. And there are indeed areas of activity where action taken at a lower level of society is essentially more "pure"—that is, more proper to its nature—than action taken at a higher one. In the case of illegal immigration, it would be nice if the federal government would do its duty by the Constitution; so far, it has not. (There is no doubt in my mind that President Bush is liable to impeachment for his failure to secure the border and for his actual facilitation of illegal aliens coming across it.) But if the federals refuse to confront the national crisis of illegal immigration, then someone else must—and should.

Who should that someone be? Without doubt, the answers differ according to circumstance across what is, after all, a very large and—if you will pardon the expression—"diverse nation." And yet the various possible answers, whatever they are, will be found to sit above a common denominator: by whomever the job can be done most efficiently, and effectively. If this means at the lowest jurisdictional level at which anyone has the clear ability to do anything at all toward resolving the gravest present threat to the nation's future—one as fraught with peril as any war—then that implies no more than the exercise of one of the most venerable and respected implements in Anglo-American law: the Posse Comitatus, used so effectively by Joe Arpaio, sheriff of Maricopa County, Arizona, to organize a volunteer posse for the apprehension, incarceration, and repatriation of illegal immigrants. It is all he can do right now, after all—and therefore is doing, and should be doing, under our historic, if threatened, system of law.

I have written here a concluding chapter, *not* a conclusion, to *Immigration and the American Future*. Rather, the foregoing is an impressionistic summary of the preceding chapters, which, taken together, present a gigantic reality that, like the elephant, though it needs to be considered as a whole rather than in part, cannot for that reason be summarized, but only apprehended in awe. To use another simile, the immigration question, similarly with abortion, is one of those towering public policy issues of our day that, like a great English oak, when torn up by the roots brings every growing thing within the space of half an acre square along with it.

Unfortunately, the reality of mass immigration threatens to rend and destroy the fabric of the historic American nation as effectively as the abstract issue has been sabotaging and wrecking the substance of public discourse in America these past 40 years—and longer. It is in hopes that such destruction may be averted that The Rockford Institute offers this book to interested readers with a particular interest in the immigration crisis, and to the public in general.

Endnotes

[1] http://www.nytimes.com/2006/09/30/world/asia/30water2.html?ex=131/7268800&en=220b8ca559ef3a46&ei=5090&partner=rssuserland&emc=rss.

[2] See *Villa and Zapata: A History of the Mexican Revolution*. Frank McLynn, Carroll & Graf Publishers: New York, 2000; and "Pure Personality: The Meaning of Francisco 'Pancho' Villa." Chilton Williamson, Jr., *Chronicles: A Magazine of American Culture*, November 2006, pp. 18–20.

[3] http://www.vdare.com/guzzardi/050107_immigration.htm.

[4] "With Beheadings and Attacks, Drug Gangs Terrorize Mexico," *New York Times*, October 26, 2006; Late edition-Final, Section A, p. 1, cd. 2.

SELECT BIBLIOGRAPHY

Alba, Richard, and Victor Nee. "Rethinking Assimilation Theory for a New Era of Immigration." *International Migration Review*, Vol. 31, No. 4, Winter 1997, pp. 826-874.

Azuela, Mariano. *The Underdogs*. Trans. by E. Munguia, Jr. New York: Signet/Penguin, 1963.

Berger, Michel. *Immigration: approche chrétienne*. Paris: Action Familiale et Scolaire, 1985.

Biffi, Giacomo Cardinal. *Immigrazione*. Torino: L.D.C., 2000.

Bookman, Milica Zarkovic. *The Demographic Struggle for Power: The Political Economy of Demographic Engineering in the Modern World*. London and Portland, OR: Frank Cass, 1997.

Borjas, George J. *Heaven's Door: Immigration Policy and the U.S. Economy*. Princeton: Princeton University Press, 2001.

Bouvier, Leon F. *Peaceful Invasions: Immigration and Changing America*. Lanham, MD: University Press of America, 1992.

Brimelow, Peter. *Alien Nation: Common Sense About America's Immigration Disaster*. New York: Harper Perennial, 1996.

Buchanan, Patrick J. *State of Emergency: The Third World Invasion and Conquest of America*. New York: St. Martin's Press, 2006.

Carosa, Alberto and Guido Vignelli. *L'invasione silenziosa: L'immigrazionismo: risorsa o complotto?* Roma: Il Minotauro, 2002.

Castañeda, Jorge G. *The Mexican Shock: Its Meaning for the United States*. New York: The New Press, 1995.

Cornelius, Wayne A. et al., editors. *Controlling Immigration: A Global Perspective.* Stanford: Stanford University Press, 1994.

Cox, Caroline and John Marks. *West, Islam & Islamism: Is Ideological Islam Compatible With Liberal Democracy?* London: Institute for the Study of Civil Society, 2006.

Fallaci, Oriana. *La forza della ragione.* Bergamo: Rizzoli International, 2004.

Faye, Guillaume. *La colonisation de l'Europe: Discours sur l'immigration et l'Islam.* Paris: L'Aencre, 2000.

Fuentes, Carlos. *The Crystal Frontier.* Trans. by Alfred Mac Adam. New York: Farrar Straus & Giroux, 1997.

Fuentes, Carlos. *The Old Gringo.* Trans. by Margaret Sayers Peden and author. New York: Farrar Straus & Giroux, 1985.

Hanson, Victor Davis. *Mexifornia: A State of Becoming.* New York: Encounter Books, 2003.

Hao, Lingxin. "Remaking the American Mainstream: Assimilation and Contemporary Immigration." *Social Forces,* Vol. 84, No. 2, December 2005, pp. 1309-1311.

Horowitz, Donald L. *Ethnic Groups in Conflict.* Berkeley: University of California Press, 1985.

Huntington, Samuel P. *Who Are We? The Challenges to America's National Identity.* New York: Simon & Schuster, 2004.

Krass, Erich, and Alex Pacheco. *On the Line: Inside the U.S. Border Patrol.* New York: Citadel Press, 2006.

Krauze, Enrique. *Mexico: Biography of Power: A History of Modern Mexico, 1810-1996.* Trans. by Hank Heifetz. New York: HarperCollins, 1997.

Loret de Mola, Rafael. *Ciudad Juárez.* Mexico City: Oceano, 2005.

Malkin, Michelle. *Invasion.* Washington, D.C.: Regnery Publishing, 2002.

Melotti, Umberto, editor. *L'abbaglio multiculturale.* Roma: S.E.A.M., 2000.

National Research Council. *The New Americans: Economic, Demographic, and Fiscal Effects of Immigration.* Washington, D.C.: The National Academies Press, 1997.

Nitoglia, Stefano. *L'Islam com'è, un confronto con il Cristianesimo.* Roma: Il Minotauro, 2002.

Noriega, Chon A., et al., editors. *The Chicano Studies Reader: An Anthology of Aztlan, 1970-2000.* Los Angeles: UCLA Chicano Studies Center, 2001.

Officer, James. *Hispanic Arizona.* Tucson: University of Arizona Press, 1988.

Oppenheimer, Andres. *Bordering on Chaos: Guerrillas, Stockbrokers, Politicians, and Mexico's Road to Prosperity.* New York: Little, Brown, 1996.

Paz, Octavio. *El laberinto de la soledad y otras obras.* Revised edition. New York: Penguin, 1997.

Ratzinger, Joseph. *L'Europa di Benedetto nella crisi delle culture.* Roma-Siena: Libreria Editrice Vaticana e Edizioni Cantagalli, 2005.

Ratzinger, Joseph and Marcello Pera. *Senza radici-Europa, relativismo, Cristianesimo, Islam.* Milano: Mondadori, 2005.

Ruiz, Ramón Eduardo. *Triumphs and Tragedy: A History of the Mexican People.* New York: Norton, 1992.

Sartori, Giovanni. *Pluralismo, multiculturalismo ed estranei.* Milano: Rizzoli, 2000.

Scheuer, Michael. *Imperial Hubris: Why the West Is Losing the War on Terror.* Washington, DC: Brassey's, 2004.

Sheridan, Thomas. *Arizona: A History*. Tucson: University of Arizona Press, 1995.

Skerry, Peter. *Mexican Americans: The Ambivalent Minority*. Cambridge, MA: Harvard University Press, 1993.

Sperry, Paul. *Infiltration: How Muslim Spies and Subversives Have Penetrated Washington*. Nashville, TN: Thomas Nelson, 2005.

Suárez-Orozco, Carola, and Marcelo Suárez-Orozco. *Children of Immigration*. Cambridge, MA: Harvard University Press, 2001.

Teitelbaum, Michael S., and Jay Winter. *A Question of Numbers: High Migration, Low Fertility, and the Politics of National Identity*. New York: Hill and Wang, 1998.

Trifkovic, Srdja, *The Sword of the Prophet—Islam: History, Theology, Impact on the World*. Boston, MA: Regina Orthodox Press, 2002.

U.S. Commission on Immigration Reform. "U.S. Immigration Policy: Restoring Credibility," 1994 Report to Congress (the Jordan Report).

Williamson, Chilton Jr. *The Immigration Mystique: America's False Conscience*. New York: Basic Books, 1996.

ABOUT THE AUTHORS

Wayne Allensworth

Wayne Allensworth is a corresponding editor for Chronicles: A Magazine of American Culture and the author of *The Russian Question* (Rowman & Littlefield, 1998). From 1991 to 2001, Mr. Allensworth worked as a Russia analyst for the Foreign Broadcast Information Service, before returning to Texas, where he works as an independent research analyst. He has written extensively on border security and immigration control.

James Bernsen

James Bernsen is a journalist and researcher from Austin, Texas. He has worked as a press secretary to two U.S. senators and has served as a legislative aide in the Texas House of Representatives. For three years, Bernsen was a senior correspondent for the *Lone Star Report*, a highly respected public policy newsletter covering Texas politics.

James Bissett

Mr. Bissett is the former Canadian ambassador to Yugoslavia, where he served from 1990 to 1992. He was also ambassador to Bulgaria and Albania. He had diplomatic postings in the Balkans, London, and in the Caribbean, where he was Canadian high commissioner in Trinidad and Tobago from 1982 to 1985. He was an assistant undersecretary for social affairs at the Foreign Ministry. From 1985 to 1990 Mr. Bissett was the executive director of the Canadian Immigration Service. Mr. Bissett also was a member of the Intelligence Advisory Committee of the Canadian Privy Council Office. Upon retirement from the Foreign Ministry, he worked in Russia from 1992 to 1997 as the chief of mission for the International Organization for Migration. Since returning to Canada in 1997, he has acted as a policy consultant on immigration and refugee issues and writes regularly for Canadian newspapers.

Peter Brimelow

Peter Brimelow is the editor of *VDare.com*, a webzine devoted to immigration policy and the "National Question"—whether the United States can survive as the political expression of a particular people. A legal immigrant from Britain, he is the author of *Alien Nation: Common Sense About America's Immigration Disaster* (1995) and, as senior editor of *National Review*, was responsible for the magazine's brief period of opposition to Beltway immigration orthodoxy until purged in 1998. His writings on immigration policy have appeared widely, most recently in the Cambridge University symposium *Debating Immigration* (2007). He has an M.B.A. from Stanford University Graduate School of Business and has been a financial journalist for *Barron's*, *Fortune*, and *Forbes*. He is currently a columnist with Dow Jones' *MarketWatch* webzine.

Alberto Carosa

Alberto Carosa is a freelance journalist and writer with a special interest in cultural and religious issues. With Guido Vignelli, he has coauthored a book, *L'invasione silenziosa* (*The Silent Invasion*), showing that illegal and uncontrolled immigration is likely to change irrevocably the social fabric of E.U. member countries, playing into the hands of those intent on destroying national identity and sovereignty. He is a regular contributor to such magazines and journals as *Chronicles*, *Inside the Vatican*, *Catholic World Report*, and the *Wanderer*. His articles and interviews have appeared in dailies such as the *Wall Street Journal*, *International Herald Tribune* (Italy Daily supplement), and *L'Osservatore Romano*.

Thomas Fleming

Thomas Fleming is the president of The Rockford Institute and editor of *Chronicles: A Magazine of American Culture*. He holds a Ph.D. in Classics from the University of North Carolina, Chapel Hill, and has taught classics and humanities at Miami University of Ohio, Charleston College, and Chapel Hill. He is the author of *The Politics of Human Nature*, *Montenegro: The Divided Land*, *The Morality of Everyday Life*, and, with Paul Gottfried, *The Conservative Movement*, as well as articles, reviews, and editorials in the *Independent on Sunday* (London), *Washington Post*, *Chicago Tribune*, *Los Angeles Times*, the *Spectator* (London), *National Review*, *American Political Science Quarterly*, and *Quaderni Unbinati*. He has received the H.L. Mencken Award (1995) and the American Values Award (1988).

Steven Greenhut

Steven Greenhut is a senior editorial writer and columnist for the Orange County (CA) *Register* and writer for *Orange Punch*, the newspaper's blog. He joined the *Register*'s editorial-page staff in 1998, after serving as editorial-page editor of the *Lima News*, a daily newspaper in northwest Ohio. He is the author of the 2004 book *Abuse of Power: How the Government Misuses Eminent Domain*. His columns are often printed in newspapers across the country, and he is an occasional contributor to magazines, including the *Freeman* and *Chronicles*. Mr. Greenhut is a regular guest on KPCC public radio, as well as a frequent commentator on other radio and television shows, and he speaks to groups across the country about California politics and property rights.

David A. Hartman

David A. Hartman is the chairman of The Rockford Institute. With a B.S. from Case-Western Reserve University and an M.B.A. from the Harvard Graduate School of Business, he served as a business economist on a broad range of econometric studies before rising into big corporation management. After successful entrepreneurial ventures in manufacturing, transportation, and banking, he retired as the chairman of Hartland Bank group to resume economic studies, now focused upon public policy. Mr. Hartman's published studies have covered a broad range of federal and state government issues, including taxation, spending, education, and globalism. His particular focus has been on the effects of public policy on income distribution, demographics of the family, and general prospects for the well-being of Americans.

Roger D. McGrath

A Phi Beta Kappa and Magna Cum Laude graduate of UCLA, Roger D. McGrath, Ph.D., taught various courses in American history at several universities for more than 30 years. He is the recipient of the Panhellenic Council's "Outstanding Professor" award and the California Military History Medal, and was nominated for the Mortar Board Faculty Excellence Award. His writings include *Gunfighters, Highwaymen, & Vigilantes* (1984), chapters in *Violence in America* (1989) and *Taming the Elephant* (2003), several forewords, and well more than a hundred articles, columns, and book reviews in such diverse publications as *Chronicles*, the *Wall Street Journal*, the *American Conservative*,

Immigration and the American Future

the *New York Times*, the *New American*, and *Harper's*, among many others. He is a contributor to the *Encyclopedia of the America West*, the *World Book Encyclopedia*, the *Encyclopedia of the Irish in America*, and the *Encyclopedia of the Great Plains*. He is a featured commentator for the History Channel, appearing in such documentary series as *The Real West*, *Biography*, *Tales of the Gun*, *The Presidents*, *The Conquerors*, and *Wild West Tech*.

Gregory McNamee

Gregory McNamee has made his home in the Arizona borderlands since 1975. He has written extensively on the natural history of the Southwest, including the prizewinning book *Gila: The Life and Death of an American River* (1994) and forthcoming books on an endangered grassland in southern New Mexico and on Arizona's national parks and monuments. Mr. McNamee is a contributing editor for *Encyclopaedia Britannica*, for which he writes regularly on world geography, culture, science, technology, and other topics. He is also a regular contributor to many other publications. An editor, publishing and media consultant, and photographer, he is the author of 27 books, most recently *Moveable Feasts: The History, Science, and Lore of Food* (Praeger, 2006). His website is *www.gregorymcnamee.com*.

Edward S. Rubenstein

Edwin S. Rubenstein, the president of ESR Research, is an economist and public-policy expert with experience in business and journalism. Since 2003, he has written a weekly column on the economics of immigration for *VDare. com*. Immigration's impact on native wages, the distribution of income, government spending, crime, health-insurance coverage, and the environment are among the topics he has researched. Rubenstein was a contributing editor at *Forbes* and economics editor at *National Review*, where his "Right Data" column was featured for more than a decade. His TV appearances include *Firing Line*, *Bill Moyers*, the *McNeil-Lehrer News Hour*, and CNBC. From 1997 to 2002, Mr. Rubenstein was director of research at the Hudson Institute, a public-policy think tank headquartered in Indianapolis. Mr. Rubenstein earned a B.A. from Johns Hopkins University and an M.A. in public finance from Columbia University.

Guido Vignelli

Guido Vignelli is a scholar of ethics, political philosophy, and the social doctrine of the Church. He was one of the founders of the Lepanto Cultural Center (Rome), of which he is now vice president. Since 1995, he has led the SOS Children Project, which organizes information and protest campaigns concerning the damage wrought by the mass media on the psychological, moral, and religious formation of minors. From 2001 to 2006, he was a member of the Italian government's Commission of Study on Family, for which he wrote the programmatic document *La famiglia e lo Stato: inquadramento della politica familiare (Family and State: A Profile of the Politics of the Family)*. He is the author of *Il Sacro Cuore, salvezza delle famiglie e della società (The Sacred Heart, Safety of Families and Society*, 2004) and, with Alberto Carosa, *L'invasione silenziosa* (2002), about the dangers of mass immigration, as well as two other books.

Chilton Williamson, Jr.

Chilton Williamson, Jr., is the author of *The Immigration Mystique: America's False Conscience* (Basic Books, 1996) and numerous essays on the immigration crisis for *Chronicles: A Magazine of American Culture*, *National Review*, *VDare.com*, and other venues. He is the author of seven other published books, including works of fiction and narrative nonfiction, among them *The Hundredth Meridian: Seasons and Travels in the New Old West*, portions of which offer first-hand reportage of the situation on both sides of the U.S.-Mexican border. Mr. Williamson, formerly literary and senior editor at *National Review*, has served since 1989 as senior editor for books at *Chronicles* and the author of two columns, "The Hundredth Meridian" and "What's Wrong With the World."

www.ingramcontent.com/pod-product-compliance
Lightning Source LLC
Chambersburg PA
CBHW070735270326
41927CB00010B/1995